The Quality of Mercy

The Quality of Mercy

Women at War
Serbia 1915-18

Monica Krippner

DAVID & CHARLES
Newton Abbot   London

British Library Cataloguing in Publication Data

Krippner, Monica
   The quality of mercy
   1. European War, 1914–1918—Medical and sanitary
     affairs
   2. Medicine, Military—Great Britain
   3. European War, 1914–1918—Campaigns—Serbia
   4. European War, 1914–1918—Women's work
   I. Title
   940.4'7541   D629.G7

ISBN 0–7153–7886–4

Typeset by ABM Typographics Ltd., Hull
and printed in Great Britain by
Redwood Burn Ltd. Trowbridge & Esher
for David & Charles (Publishers) Limited
South Devon House Newton Abbot Devon

This book is dedicated to the memory of Mrs Lilian Vidaković who took such generous and constructive interest in its preparation, but who died, on 12 November 1979, while it was in the press.

CONTENTS

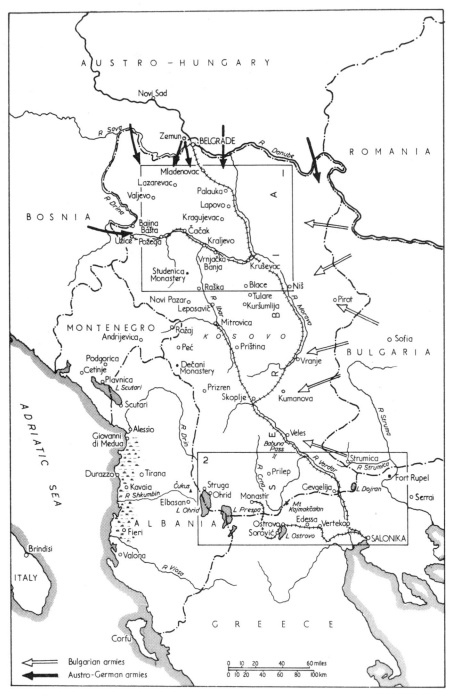

Map A   Invasion of Serbia by the Central Powers, autumn 1915
(*enlargements of insets on pages 57 and 194*)

PROLOGUE

Florence Nightingale, who had died only a few years before World War I broke out in 1914, had become a legend in her lifetime. Through her amazing hospital work at Scutari in 1854-6 during the Crimean War this dedicated woman had elevated the nursing service and its medical standards to the level of a highly respected profession. She had lived to see her valuable work acclaimed, honours had been bestowed upon her, excellent training facilities for nurses at leading hospitals had become firmly established, and Florence surpassed Victoria among the favoured names for girls. Fired by Florence Nightingale's example young women from diverse backgrounds found a rewarding and acceptable vocation open to them—nursing.

Yet, for some unaccountable reason the spectacular service during World War I of women doctors and surgeons, who did so much to alleviate suffering in front-line hospitals in various theatres of war, remains little known and barely acknowledged. In Serbia, Russia, France and elsewhere during the 1914-18 conflict these pioneer doctors, and their administrators, VADs and orderlies, did as much for their own sex in the medical profession as Florence Nightingale and her nurses had done sixty years earlier in the Crimea for the nursing service.

Women had only for a short time been admitted to Oxford and Cambridge and were still, however well they had qualified, barred from taking their degrees. Dublin and Edinburgh universities had been the first in Britain to admit women medical students, albeit reluctantly and often with offensive restrictions. But women in other professions—George Eliot the author; travellers like Mary Kingsley and Lady Hester Stanhope; the budding Arabist and archaeologist, Gertrude Bell; and *The Times* colonial correspondent, Flora Louise Shaw, later Lady Lugard—had, by their example, shown that it was possible to overcome the social restrictions and moral injustices of the waning Victorian and Edwardian periods. But it needed courage, determination and self-respect.

9

By the time war was declared on 4 August 1914 there were many nurses and a number of qualified medical women in Britain who, much as most of them deplored the war, regarding it as the tragic outcome of the policies of blundering statesmen, were devout patriots determined to participate to relieve suffering in any possible way. But none of them could have foreseen that within a few months many British medical women would be serving in field hospitals behind the front lines in Belgium, France and even in distant Serbia.

By autumn 1915 World War I was over a year old and had already cost more than a million lives. The French and British armies were entrenched opposite the Germans along the Western Front, the first Dardanelles campaign had been a disaster, and the Russians were in retreat along the Eastern Front. Serbia, the small Balkan country over which the dreadful holocaust had originally begun, was thrust aside by the events preoccupying the main Powers. Yet this was Serbia's hour of direst need.

From the south the Austro-German offensive against Serbia had begun in earnest. Belgrade the capital had fallen; overnight the Bulgarians had entered the war, invading Serbia from the east; the Serbian army was being relentlessly driven back, and vital northern towns like Valjevo, Kragujevac and Mladenovac in the rich Šumadija highlands, were about to be overrun by the enemy. About a hundred miles south of Belgrade, along an east-west line beside the Morava river, lie the provincial centres of Kruševac, Vrnjačka Banja and Kraljevo. These towns were now in a state of total disruption. The enemy was advancing rapidly and, as they panicked into flight, Serbian soldiers, ox-wagons full of wounded, and countless civilian refugees were jamming the roads and choking the towns and villages. Serbia was on the verge of collapse.

For a year British and Allied medical units had been working in Serbia, tending thousands of battle-wounded from the first phase of the war, and victims of the subsequent virulent typhus epidemic that had ravaged the country. A conspicuous feature of many British medical teams was the predominance of women surgeons, physicians and administrators. Prominent among these units were those of the Scottish Women's Hospitals (SWH), staffed entirely by women; and the Serbian Relief Fund (SRF), administered by

10

women. In addition, many enterprising individual women had come out as doctors, nurses or medical orderlies with, for example, the British Red Cross, or quite independently, joining the Serbian Red Cross and other local hospitals or relief organisations on arrival.

As the Austro-German divisions stormed the Šumadija highlands Dr Beatrice McGregor, the Chief Medical Officer (CMO) of a SWH unit at Mladenovac, and her administrator, Miss Pares, packed up their entire hospital within forty-eight hours and got all their equipment south to Kragujevac where, converging from various corners of Serbia, were many of their countrywomen, also making their escape before the enemy advance. From Valjevo, Dr Alice Hutchison and her staff had a terrible time evacuating their vast hospital over the Šumadija hills, negotiating streams where bridges had been destroyed, before they finally reached Vrnjačka Banja. Nearby they found a British Red Cross hospital where, among many others, Elsie Corbett and Kathleen Dillon were coping desperately with wards overflowing with wounded and dying soldiers and civilians.

Dr Inglis, founder of the Scottish Women's Hospitals, had come out to Serbia the previous May to assess the situation, and to help where she was most needed. When the evacuation order came she rallied all her staff and they did what they could, discharging all patients who could walk—even those who could barely totter—until, moved beyond measure by the misery and terror of the Serbian patients at being abandoned to await the enemy, Dr Inglis resolved to ignore the evacuation order since, 'if we are to help the Serbs now, we must stick to our posts.'

Also at Kragujevac was Mrs St Clair Stobart, administrator of the large, seventy-strong third Serbian Relief Fund unit. As the enemy advanced she split her unit in two, leaving the main part at Kragujevac under Dr Mabel King-May, while she herself took charge of a small detachment of doctors and nurses attached to the Serbian Army Medical Corps which became known as the 'Stobart flying column'. This column, with Mrs Stobart riding at its head, set off with a number of wagons and ambulances in search of the elusive front, so as to be on the spot should the Serbian army make a last-ditch stand.

Further south, in Skoplje, lying directly in the path of the Bulgarian advance, was the large hospital of the combined first and second Serbian Relief Fund units under Leila, Lady Paget, who had been in Serbia since the autumn of 1914. With the unanimous agreement of her staff, Lady Paget had elected to remain to stand by their hundreds of Serbian patients when the Bulgarians eventually, and inevitably, occupied the city.

Flora Sandes, a medical orderly returning to duty in Serbia after convalescence in England following a severe bout of typhus, had reached Monastir (now called Bitola or Bitolj), an important Serbian town near the Greek frontier, only to find herself cut off from any chance of reaching her hospital. Her drastic solution to this dilemma was to join a Serbian army ambulance unit, a step that would eventually lead to her extraordinary career as a combatant soldier in the Serbian army.

At this point the drama divides—enacted by those who chose to remain behind with their Serbian patients to await the enemy, and by those who elected to escape by participating in the gruelling winter retreat through Albania. For some, any choice came too late: Mrs Mabel Dearmer, Dr Elizabeth Ross, Sister Lorna Ferriss and others had already given their lives during their selfless work for the Serbs.

Many British medical women had sailed away from their own country, which had rejected their services, to work with Allied armies, mostly under appalling wartime conditions. Nowhere was their courageous and selfless service more evident than in the bitter Serbian campaigns between 1914 and 1918, where they proved themselves, under terrible stress, perfectly capable of the most exacting surgical and hospital work, of having the stamina to endure the hardships and privations of front-line field hospitals; and of possessing discipline, fortitude and devotion to duty in the face of all the uncertain and frightening hazards of war.

Kragujevac, Mladenovac, Kraljevo, Vrnjačka Banja, Kruševac, Valjevo, Skoplje, Gevgelija, Kajmakčalan—strange, outlandish, tongue-twisting place-names which, over sixty years ago, during the Serbian campaigns, were to become as familiar to the British household as Ypres, the Somme, Verdun and Gallipoli. They were mispronounced, and mistransliterated from the Cyrillic alphabet—Kraguyevaz, Krageovats, Kragoyevatz; Skoplje was just as often referred to by its Turkish name, Uskub, so they both became familiar; and Bitolj was Monastir in some newspapers and Bitola in others. To many British women working out there in the field hospitals these funny-sounding places were to become as much a part of their lives as Aberdeen, Warwick or Londonderry.

Probably no group of women have given so much of themselves under such tremendous odds, and emerged so magnificently—and so unsung in their own country. Modesty was de rigeur, publicity unheard of and, except for newspapers, the mass media did not exist. Barring some articles on Serbia and the units in national and provincial newspapers in the early part of the war, and some modest books, written later by some of the women, their deeds have never been recorded.

But, who were they? How did these women come to be serving as doctors, nurses, VADs and administrators in a distant Balkan country at war? Given the prevalent taboos against women in any kind of professional capacity, how had they, overnight it seems, managed to brush aside rigid conventions to the extent that they were successfully carrying out complicated surgery and running entire hospitals and ambulance columns in a devastated theatre of war? For the answers we must, as the King said to Alice, begin at the beginning.

1
1914: PEACE AND WAR

For the people of Britain and most other European countries, the year 1914 began like any other. In fact it ushered in peace. The Balkan Wars had ended, the Ottoman Empire had crumbled and the Turks were practically out of Europe which, it is true, had left a dangerous vacuum. But Britain and the other European powers had managed more or less to balance the power again with the Treaty of London. All seemed well in the world.

Unaware of the unusual destinies that awaited them, a number of women from all backgrounds were pursuing their various lives. Some were professional women—doctors, pharmacists, radiologists and nurses—but many were not. Some were married with children, others were single. Not one of them could have foreseen that they were soon to become transport drivers, chief surgeons, sanitation inspectors, quartermasters, first-aid workers, even capable administrators, frequently under the most appalling conditions, the sort of conditions that demand endurance, stamina, enterprise, initiative, leadership, the ability to take orders, and to give them—in short, all those aptitudes that women were not supposed to have. Women, ideally, were still meant to be fragile, helpless, preferably quiescent, and certainly never to aspire to positions of civic responsibility and decision. But change was in the wind, and most women were responding to it. Even among the most passive there was a tremor of excitement, of anticipation of better things to come, or at least of better attitudes. A few of these women play major roles in the drama that is about to unfold; others make brief appearances. This is not a chronicle of the activities of emancipationists and suffragettes. Rather it is about women who did not wait to be emancipated, but who seized a war-given opportunity to emancipate themselves, thus forming the spearhead for the more hesitant members of their own sex.

Flora Sandes was in her element as she drove the great motor-car full tilt down the country road, flying through the complicated gear changes, revelling in the power of her recent acquisition, a second-hand French sports model. Already she was scaring the wits out of the peaceful locals as she hurtled along Surrey's narrow country lanes around Thornton Heath. The neighbours shook their heads and, in time-honoured tradition, doubtless voiced their predictable reactions—that no good would come of all this dangerous racing around, and she the daughter of a clergyman; that she ought to be getting married; after all she was nearly thirty, but was still a good-looking young woman, tall and slim with fine brown eyes, and well-educated, too. To cap it all she worked in London at one of those new-fangled secretarial jobs, taking work away from a man when she should be staying at home with her father to help run the house, especially now that he was retired and widowed—her mother had died a few years previously. Flora, everyone would agree, was a very nice girl, but wild and headstrong, quick-tempered, too—that Irish streak! Comments along these lines reached Flora's ears but she did not care. She longed for excitement and meant to get the best out of life.

Flora Sandes had spent her early childhood in the Suffolk countryside and later in Thornton Heath where her father, a clergyman, had retired. It was a pleasant country childhood, shared with brothers and sisters, and kindly tolerant parents who spoiled her a little because she was the youngest. Though not rich they had enough for a good life without any frills, but with a cook and servants to take care of the menial tasks; and it was even possible to send Flora abroad to learn French and German, a linguistic training that would one day be far more useful than she could ever have imagined. Only one thing marred an otherwise happy existence—Flora's eternal chagrin at not being born a boy. It was not that she rejected her femininity, it was just that boys had all the fun. The world was wide open to them, challenging them to enjoy their freedom, to have adventures, to indulge in a myriad fascinating exploits. But, for girls . . .? Much later, when the reality of her adventurous life had exceeded the wildest dreams of her youth, she was to write: 'many years afterwards . . . I had long realised that if you have the misfortune to be born a woman it is better to make the best of a bad job, and not try to be a bad imitation of a man'.

Flora rode well and learned to shoot. Once she had done a course with the Women's First Aid Yeomanry Corps, founded by an enterprising army captain. Mrs St Clair Stobart, who had also once briefly joined this Corps, had been rather scathing, finding the whole thing a little absurd with women dressed in scarlet tunics, divided skirts and helmets, who 'brandished whips and were doubtless picturesque', and dashed around on horseback supposedly able to pluck wounded soldiers off the battlefield! Flora must have found it all great fun but probably did not take it too seriously. But of more value, she attended St John's Ambulance first-aid courses from time to time, and accumulated a number of impressive certificates.

And so time passed with the family hinting about marriage and settling down, and Flora steadfastly ignoring such signs of conventional concern, but exploiting every limited possiblity to inject her life with the excitement and zest that she so craved. Then, in the middle of that lovely 1914 summer, in Sarajevo a hitherto unknown Serb revolutionary murdered a not particularly popular Austrian archduke, the heir to the Habsburg throne of Austria. The drums rolled, statesmen hurried off to war councils, and armies were alerted. War was in the air. Flora followed it all with bated breath. Should war break out surely women would be needed—she could drive, she had her first-aid certificates; perhaps she could be a dispatch rider or an ambulance driver. She could even shoot. But it all seemed to simmer down and the swords were slipped back into their scabbards. People breathed again and turned back to the sunshine of their summer.

But, far from Britain, and behind the scenes, the pattern of war was being completed. The day on which the Austrian Crown Prince, Archduke Franz Ferdinand, had been assassinated was Vidovdan, 28 June, Serbia's sacred national day. On this day centuries before, in 1389, Miloš Obelić, one of Tsar Lazar's knights, entered Sultan Murad's tent and slew him, an act which precipitated the tragic Battle of Kosovo which crushed the Serbian nation, establishing Turkish hegemony over it for nearly five centuries. To the Serbs Kosovo and Vidovdan still represent the ultimate in everything—courage, suffering, betrayal, sacrifice and nobility. And this was the day inauspiciously chosen for Archduke Franz Ferdinand to pay an official visit to Sarajevo, the capital of Bosnia, which Austria had annexed in 1908. In 1878, the Treaty of Berlin had entrusted Austria-Hungary with a military mandate over Bosnia-Herzegovina after the Turks had

17

been driven out. Since this was to be ostensibly a preparatory phase leading to eventual autonomy, the annexation of 1908 had aroused particular fury towards the Austro-Hungarian monarchy. Vienna claimed that this action had been taken because of the danger of a resurgence of Turkish power in the region, instigated by Kemal Ataturk and his fanatical 'Young Turks', who had virtually taken over in Turkey.

The nationalist sentiments that the annexation unleashed were supported by neighbouring Serbia which, historically, ethnically and linguistically, was the same Slav nation—indeed, a union of the two countries was an expressed goal on both sides of the border. Only in religion did they differ—during the centuries of Turkish rule over 70 per cent of the Bosnians had become Moslems. Thus, for the archduke's visit to be arranged on Vidovdan—a day almost as important to the Bosnians as to the Serbs—was perhaps the final provocation for an immature young Serb nationalist and revolutionary, Gabriel Princip, who assassinated the archduke and his wife as they entered the city centre, thus igniting the fuse which was soon to lead to the explosion of World War I.

For a short time after the assassination Austria threatened Serbia with dire retribution while the Serbs protested their innocence at being party to any underground movement hostile to the monarchy. The tumult seemed to abate. But in the shadows irrevocable forces had been set in motion. Germany regarded the tension resulting from the assassination as advantageous for manipulating the situation to her own ends. For a long time she had made no secret of her desire to become a power in the Middle East, the *Drang nach Osten*, or what the newspapers of the day called the 'Berlin-Baghdad axis', referring the Germany's desire to complete the railway line from Berlin to Baghdad, to establish German settlements, to build factories and harbours and to seek raw materials in the Middle Eastern countries, and thus very efficiently fill the vacuum left by the collapse of the Ottoman Empire. One obstacle to this colonial ambition was the growing independence of various Balkan states, not the least being the newly independent nation of Serbia, proud but poor, but backed by distant powerful allies—Britain, France and Russia—and lying right on the path to Baghdad.

To add to the general unease, Austria was very apprehensive about Serbia. For some time the foundations of the monarchy had been shaken by several factors, above all by various nationalist movements elsewhere within its territories that were becoming manifestly more vociferous and more violent. Suddenly centuries of corrupt and sterile Turkish domination had collapsed, giving way to a number of aggressively independent countries—Serbia, Bulgaria, Greece, Romania—which had found their nationhood in recent decades in the wake of wars, insurrectionist movements and civic violence. These nationalist successes had been very encouraging to the hopes and dreams of similar movements in those countries fretting within the territorial bounds of the moribund Austrian monarchy. In fact matters were getting out of hand and the Court and its various ministries in Vienna seemed to be paralysed before the relentless tide of nationalism that threatened from all sides.

It was February 1914 and for the second time within the past twelve months Mrs Mabel St Clair Stobart was on her way to British Columbia, this time for the wedding of her younger son who managed a large ranch in the foothills of the Rocky Mountains. Accompanying her were her eldest son, on leave from Nigeria, and her second husband, John Greenhalgh, a former judge in Burma who had, astonishingly enough for any period, quite meekly consented to his wife's wish to retain her former married name.

The daughter of Sir Samuel Boulton of Copped Hall, Fotherbridge, Hertfordshire, Mrs Stobart had already packed a phenomenal variety of experiences into her fifty years. She was a strange, brilliant controversial person towards whom nobody could be indifferent—she generally aroused intense antipathy or total devotion. Though she had no formal education she was widely read, a very talented writer, and something of a mystic with a remarkable intellectual discipline that was later to make her a scholar on spiritualist questions and something of an authority on the Apocrypha. Like many people with an incisive, abstract mind she tended to be introverted and distant. In addition, she was egocentric, autocratic and a law unto herself. Yet her lively intellect, her extraordinary will-power, physical courage and stamina, and her self-assured ability—some called it arrogance— to sail magnificently through all officialdom, ensured her many admirers as well as some detractors in everything she undertook.

19

Her childhood had been conventional enough for one born into a wealthy county family. There had been governesses and servants, garden parties, dances and private concerts, for she loved music and was a competent pianist. Famous people were sometimes guests; Oscar Wilde came once, but she took an instant dislike to him. From when she was very young she had always sought to excel, and made something of a fetish about overcoming fear. She was an excellent horsewoman and was once county tennis champion; she played a very good game of golf, even writing a small book about the game; and she loved fly-fishing. With her first husband, Colonel St Clair Stobart, who came from an old Dorset family, she made fishing expeditions to unusual places—salmon fishing in Finland and northern Sweden, and trout fishing in Corsica. It was not so much the catch that was important, she once claimed, but the beautiful surroundings of trout and salmon waters that attracted her and gave her peace.

She had been a twofold pioneer. First, and most important, she had founded the Women's Sick and Wounded Convoy Corps, a medical unit staffed by women including doctors, and in 1912 she had led it to Bulgaria where, under atrocious conditions, they had established and run a complete surgical hospital at Kirk-Kilisse near the front line during the Balkan War with Turkey. This was the first time ever, during wartime, that women doctors and surgeons had served at a front-line hospital tending terrible battle injuries and doing complicated emergency operations, proving themselves to be every bit as skilful as their male colleagues.

Earlier Mrs Stobart had, in the popular sense, been a pioneer with her first husband when they had tried their fortunes on a vast farm in a lonely distant corner of the South African veldt. In the tradition of the time they had trekked over the Karoo with their ox-wagons, horses, tents and supplies. And on the farm, not content with being a pioneer's wife and all that it entailed, she had opened a Kaffir store, trading basic foodstuffs, simple textiles, tobacco and tools with local tribesmen and rare white neighbours or missionaries. After several years the Stobarts returned to England and, shortly afterwards, on the boat back to South Africa, Colonel St Clair Stobart died, putting a sad end to the South African pioneering venture.

That 1914 spring and early summer, after her son's wedding,

Mrs Stobart stayed on a while in British Columbia revelling in the ranch life, as she always did, rounding up wild horses, camping and fishing in the wilds. It was all so magnificent and so remote from the horrors of the war she had so recently experienced in the Balkans. And in those majestic surroundings she was putting the finishing touches to her book, *War and Women*, about the work of the medical women in her Convoy Corps at Kirk-Kilisse. She had come to hate the dreadful futility of war. During the truces she had visited the front-line trenches to find 'enemies' chatting with each other, sharing cigarettes; in the wards of her field hospital she had watched prisoner-of-war orderlies tend wounded enemy patients with the care and kindness they would have given a brother.

Someone once described her at this time as a 'petite, frail-looking lady with an abundance of beautiful hair'. Contemporary photographs show her to be fine-featured, almost sharp-boned, with strange remote eyes that seem to look beyond one into a further distance. In her writings there is a glimpse of something else, of a woman who knew that if she had been a man, or at least had had the equal educational opportunities of a man, she would have done even more extraordinary things and would have been acclaimed. She seems to have been driven by a deep inner restlessness, as if it were impossible for her to fulfil all her potentialities. Certainly she did not wish to be a man; in the conventional sense she was far too successful as a woman, since men were drawn to her and she did not get on very well with women nor they with her. But the restrictions she endured as a woman of that era impelled her towards contemporary movements concerned with emancipation and suffrage. She wanted men's opportunities to be available to women but, since they were not, she quite simply created such opportunities to prove that she and other women could be essentially feminine and yet have all the intellectual, moral and even physical attributes necessary to cope with the hazards of war. This she had proved beyond dispute by the work of her Convoy Corps in Bulgaria. But the message had to be hammered home to prove that the Bulgarian episode had not just been a freak success.

Thus on her return to England that summer she began to participate in some of the women's suffrage meetings and rallies and, in fact, an important meeting was due to be held at London's

21

Kingsway Hall on 4 August. And since it was not in her nature to be an onlooker nor indeed just a participant but to be a leader, she was soon looking around for something and someone to lead.

Further north, in Scotland, an equally determined but totally different kind of woman was engaged in a very full professional and political life. In 1865 Dr Elsie Inglis was born in India where her father had been chief commissioner at Lucknow. Later the family moved to Tasmania, Australia, where Elsie went to school until they all returned to Scotland when she was about sixteen years old.

To study medicine was still extremely rare for women. In fact Elsie Inglis made her preliminary medical studies at the Edinburgh School of Medicine for Women, founded in 1886 by Dr Sophia Jex-Blake, the courageous medical pioneer who had done so much to enable women to study medicine, founding Britain's first medical college for women in London, followed shortly afterwards by the one in Edinburgh. Dr Jex-Blake was still in charge of this school when Elsie Inglis enrolled. Later, Elsie Inglis continued her clinical studies in Glasgow and passed her examination in 1892; then she went as a house surgeon to the new Hospital for Women in Euston Road, London, where she worked with another famous medical pioneer, the first woman to qualify in Britain, Dr Elizabeth Garrett Anderson, and her daughter, Dr Louisa Garrett Anderson. A year later Elsie Inglis did a further short course at the famous Rotunda in Dublin. When the University of Edinburgh at last admitted women to examinations for degrees Elsie Inglis graduated MB CM in 1899.

Dr Inglis came from a close-knit family to whom she was deeply attached, especially her father whom she loved dearly. They were a very religious family and, up to her death, Elsie Inglis never wavered in her devout belief in God and a life in the hereafter.

Her father supported her completely in her desire to study medicine, and she drew continual strength from his interest, his deep understanding and unfailing wisdom. Because he was a good and just man he was a sincere supporter of women's emancipation, a subject that his daughter, in her growing awareness, discussed at length with him by letter during her student days. Once she wrote to him, 'I wonder when married women will learn they have any other duty in the world than to obey their husbands . . . you don't know what trouble we have with the husbands. They come in the day before an operation . . . and worry them [their wives] with all sorts of outside things and want them home when they are half dying.' These women, she added, 'don't seem to think they have any right to any individual experience'. Such daily occurrences in the hospital wards only served to commit her more deeply to the cause of women's emancipation. In her book, Lady Balfour quotes a friend of Elsie Inglis: 'She was in no sense a manhater; to her the world was composed of men and women, and she thought it a mistake to exalt the one unduly over the other.'

By 1914 Elsie had been the honorary secretary of the Federation of Scottish Suffrage Societies, and vice-president of the Edinburgh Women's Liberal Association for many years, but just before the war she left the latter because she felt that she could serve the cause of women better by not being a member of any political party.

Once she had made up her mind about some course of action she displayed a serene and smiling stubbornness that totally disarmed her opponents. Her contemporary admirers tend to excel in their eulogies, almost to sanctify her to a degree that becomes suspect. But it does emerge that, in all her medical undertakings, she was indeed something of a paragon. Her subordinates found her kind and encouraging though firm and quite a disciplinarian; her patients adored and trusted her; and the Serbs were almost to canonize her. Yet she could be outraged, and show it; and she could be coldly intimidating if she imagined a principle she upheld had been violated in any way. She was particularly harsh with the militants in the suffragette movement, claiming that their 'anarchy'—she detested any form of anarchy, of civic disobedience—could only retard the ultimate triumph of a cause rooted in all that was just and righteous. Her puritanism and dedication to duty were fortunately balanced by a very lively sense of humour, and an unexpected tolerance towards opposing views, even on religious issues, sometimes expressed by her colleagues and friends.

Though not a beauty in the salon sense—she was rather short and tended towards plumpness—she loved to dress well, was attractive, with blue-grey eyes and soft brown hair, could be very charming and radiated a transparent sincerity and simplicity. By several accounts she seems to have had a curious and somewhat disconcerting capacity for switching off, for suddenly moving onto

23

another plane as if in touch with forces beyond the reach of those around her. She tended to be absent-minded and a little forgetful and was not the best organiser in the practical sense; she was a visionary, and a brilliant, persuasive speaker, often witty, and very determined once embarked upon some course of action. But the practical side was better left to others.

In 1914 Dr Inglis was fully involved in a very satisfying life and work. Further studies had taken her to Vienna and to America, and now she was in private practice in Edinburgh with a friend, Dr Jessie MacGregor. They shared a large and pleasant house, which was open to a constant stream of lively and interesting friends from all walks of life. In addition, Dr Inglis lectured in gynaecology at the Medical School for Women and devoted much time to her Maternity Hospice, which she had founded as a nursing home and maternity centre staffed by medical women; and what spare time still remained was given up to her political and suffrage activities. On top of everything, concerned by the persistent rumblings of war, she decided to form a VAD unit. Edinburgh's worthy civic fathers were rather contemptuous in their puritan disdain for this female detachment but, unperturbed, Elsie Inglis went ahead and in July 1914 she became commandant of the Sixth Edinburgh VAD.

During that hot mid-summer, while Dr Inglis was preoccupied in Edinburgh with her numerous medical activities and her VAD, and Mrs St Clair Stobart was attending rallies in London, another meeting was in progress in distant Potsdam. Here, on 5 July, Germany pledged her support for any retaliatory measures Austria might inflict on Serbia. This opposing block—the so-called Central Powers—was steadily consolidating its forces and strategy. Russia, aware of the dangers and alarmed at the possible international implications of the assassination at Sarajevo, warned Vienna that any unreasonable demands on Serbia would not be tolerated. But, despite this warning and the fact that the official Austrian investigator could find no evidence of the Serbian government's complicity in any plot, Austria presented a drastic ultimatum to the Serbs on 23 July. Given the overheated atmosphere and explosive nature of the situation, some of the demands contained in the ultimatum could be considered reasonable—for example that the Serbian government suppress notorious anti-Austrian elements, that apologies be made for hostile statements uttered against the monarchy by public figures in Belgrade, that Gabriel Princip and his accomplices who were already under arrest be tried for murder. But two demands no sovereign state could accept—that Austro-Hungarian representatives be admitted into Serbia and given carte-blanche to assist in the suppression of nationalist anti-Austrian societies, and to help conduct the trial of persons suspected of complicity in the assassination.

On the advice of Russia, Serbia agreed to all the demands save the last two, which clearly violated her sovereignty, and suggested that these two points be referred to the Hague tribunal. Austria-Hungary, with the tacit approval of Germany, immediately informed the Serbs that the answer was unsatisfactory and proceeded to amass the Imperial armies and move towards Belgrade on what was to be a 'punitive expedition', but which was soon to lead inexorably to the world war that few foresaw and nobody wanted.

'The murder of an Archduke meant no more to me than some tale of an imaginary kingdom [sic] in Zenda', was the reaction of Mrs Mabel Dearmer on hearing of the Sarajevo assassination. Mrs Dearmer, a beautiful and elegant woman, was a talented Edwardian writer, illustrator, playwright and theatrical producer, whose career had begun with poetry and story-writing for young people. When poster-painting came into vogue she tried her hand at it very successfully, and this led to her illustrating books, including *The Seven Young Goslings* by her friend, Laurence Housman. Finally, however, she found her true vocation when she turned to producing plays.

Mabel Dearmer had been an imaginative, precocious child, turbulent and emotional, and always dreaming of a stage career. As a young girl she had been ambitious for fame and all that it could bring—acclaim, luxury and wealth. At 18 she had gone to an art school, at 20 she married a young curate, and by 22 she was the mother of two sons, which could have been the end of her youthful dreams of fame. In fact it marked the beginning of their realisation. Percy Dearmer had a living at Primrose Hill with a fine vicarage in a beautiful garden, but a slender income. Therefore he was glad to encourage his lovely and gifted wife to seek an outlet for her creative energies, and thereby perhaps a means of fulfilling her dreams. Her immediate considerable success with children's tales and illustrations and the resulting additional income for the household were satisfying beginnings. From then on, despite occasional disappointments and failures, she went from strength to strength, until she eventually switched over completely to producing plays. She was particularly successful at theatre for young people, and excelled in staging morality plays.

By Easter 1914 Mabel Dearmer's latest production at the Little Theatre had been a resounding success. But the season had taken its toll and she felt in need of a long rest, a period of renewal, far from her theatre world. A friend lent her a dream cottage in the Cotswolds—thatched, with mullioned windows, and a lovely garden with pink roses, jasmine, clematis, a yew hedge, and an orchard nearby. There, in this sequestered retreat, Mabel Dearmer settled at the end of June. Friends came and went; her husband stayed when his parish duties allowed it; she forgot about the theatre and concentrated on preserving fruit from the garden, cooking for her visitors, and getting to know the villagers who responded to her warm and lively personality. The weather was glorious and she sank happily into the country life. No newspapers came to the cottage, and so immersed was she in her idyllic life that nothing of the outside world touched her. Thus was the murdered archduke as remote from her as the 'kingdom in Zenda'.

Meanwhile the war clouds gathered over Serbia already exhausted from the recent Balkan Wars. Her economy was shattered, agriculture devastated by war and neglect, and the people at the end of their resources. Serbia had gone to the limit to appease the Austrians for these and other reasons—threats from neighbouring Romania, which was under a Hohenzollern king and largely pro-German; from Bulgaria, eagerly awaiting revenge for the outcome of the Treaty of Bucharest by which Serbia had acquired most of Macedonia; and from the Albanians, whose national status was not yet settled and who were paranoically suspicious of their neighbours. Their feudal chieftains had been bribed by the Austrians and they were eager to establish Albanian claims on some of the southern regions of Serbia.

One month after the assassination, on 29 July, Austria began the bombardment of Belgrade; the seat of the Serbian government, accompanied by the diplomatic corps, was moved from Belgrade further south to Niš; and Russia moved her troops towards the Austro-Hungarian frontiers. Britain ordered the concentration of her fleet in home and Mediterranean waters; war seemed imminent between Germany and France since, fearing France's alliance with Russia, Germany wished to eliminate France from the arena as quickly as possible. On 1 August Britain announced that she could not ignore any threat to Belgian neutrality; on 2 August Germany committed her first act of war by crossing into the Duchy of Luxembourg and seizing the railway system. On the same day France was assured of British support should the German fleet attack the French seaboard. Germany's ultimatum to Belgium requesting transit for her armies across Belgian territory was courageously rejected, so Germany declared war on France. On 4 August the Germans invaded Belgium and, at midnight that same day Britain declared war on Germany, five weeks after Vidovdan.

On that fatal day in August Mabel Dearmer received a telegram from a friend in the House of Commons: 'There is a war and we are in it.' She was so shocked that she turned her back on this stark reality and sought refuge with her flowers and her gardening. War and killing were anathema to her, a professed socialist and pacifist, more from her deep religious convictions than from any political doctrine. For a while she refused to face the awful truth that had struck her world, and retreated into religious contemplation until, one dreadful day, a second telegram came, this time from her younger son, Christopher, then studying languages in France: 'I am coming home to enlist.' Then her friends began to disappear; her husband was preoccupied with the extra demands of his anxious parishioners; her eldest son, Geoffrey, enlisted. Suddenly she was aware that the summer idyll was gone forever. She was alone in her despair and in her total inability to rouse any hatred for the enemy.

2
WAR FEVER

That 4 August declaration of war released a shock-wave throughout Britain which, for the weeks leading up to that shattering
announcement, had been in a state of uneasy suspended anima-
tion. Now people were seized by a frenzied reaction. Recruiting
offices sprang into existence overnight and men, some mere boys,
queued enthusiastically to enlist; voluntary organisations and
auxiliary units mushroomed everywhere, often with very odd
names and objectives—many quietly to fade away while others
survived to render valuable service throughout the war. All over
the country women were in a flurry of apprehension and in-
decision, not sure what to do at first but certain that the hour had
come for them to serve their country other than by 'keeping the
home fires burning', a popular catch-phrase in slogan and song
that jarred the sensibilities of all women, not only the emancipationists—'your place is in the home', it clearly said.

Already the day before, when war seemed imminent as Germany
invaded France, Mrs Fawcett, President of the National Union of
Women's Suffrage Societies (NUWSS), announced that the
executive committee had decided to suspend political activities
and open a 'Women's Service' bureau in London to direct the
efforts of non-professional women eager to do useful work. Before
the end of the year over 1,300 volunteers were placed, many doing
VAD courses or working in auxiliary hospitals.

As Mrs St Clair Stobart left her meeting in the Kingsway
Hall, where speaker after speaker had deplored the war, Lady
Muir McKenzie stopped her: 'Mrs Stobart, what are we going to
do? Don't you agree that women should take an active part in the
defence of the country, at least by serving in relief or ambulance
units?' Mrs Stobart most certainly did—in fact, without further
ado she took over some rooms in St James's Square and immediately began to organise a women's medical corps, along the
lines of the Convoy Corps she had led to the Bulgarian front two
years earlier. Within a month her new corps, the Women's

Imperial Service Hospital, was behind the lines at Antwerp. Naturally she was the administrator while her patient, self-effacing husband, John Greenhalgh, was again treasurer, a role he had filled during the Bulgarian campaign since, explained Mrs Stobart, 'as had been understood between us', he always accepted a subordinate position in her units.

As swift off the mark was another experienced relief worker, Lord Abinger's daughter, the 47-year-old Hon Mrs Evelina Haverfield who, by 6 August, had helped launch the Women's Emergency Corps, and then became commandant of an off-shoot of this corps, the Women's Volunteer Reserve, ostensibly 'a trained and disciplined body of women' who did military drill, wore khaki uniforms and saluted their officers, much to the delight of the press, which had a field day with sallies and cartoons. Mrs Haverfield would later join forces with Dr Elsie Inglis, but in late 1914 she served briefly as commander-in-chief of the Women's Reserve Ambulance (the Green Cross Corps), which was one of the founding units of the future WAAC.

War had hardly been declared when Dr Elsie Inglis went into top gear. She immediately mobilised her VAD members and worked hard at their training, then sought a way to offer this unit and other trained women for war service. With a daring, patriotic and very practical idea, she went straight to the Scottish suffragette offices: 'What about launching a collection to equip a field hospital staffed entirely by women, and offer it to the War Office for service in any theatre of war with the British army?' This was an imaginative, double-edged offer: as well as being a worthy contribution to the war effort it would promote the cause of professional women, especially doctors. One of the minutes of the 12 August committee meeting of the Federated Suffrage Societies of Scotland records Dr Inglis's proposal 'to equip a hospital . . . staffed entirely by women—if not required at home, to be sent abroad'. And so the scheme was born. It began modestly enough with the goal of £1,000 to launch one hospital and was to end, before the war was over, with voluntary contributions totalling nearly £½ million, and fourteen fully equipped field hospitals which served in Belgium, France, Serbia, Romania, Russia and elsewhere—alongside almost every Allied army or Red Cross except the British. For the sad fact was that Dr Inglis's imaginative and generous offer was turned down flat by the British War Office:

29

'My good lady, go home and sit still', was her abrupt dismissal by some harassed official totally unable to deal with this quiet and obviously well-bred woman doctor with her eccentric proposal to send an entire field hospital staffed by *women physicians and surgeons* on active service!

Undaunted, on 20 August Dr Inglis sent letters to the ambassadors of Belgium, France and Russia, asking whether their governments would be interested in a hospital 'for use at the seat of war'. Unencumbered by the inhibitions of the British War Office, these governments accepted gratefully and with alacrity. From that moment the Scottish suffrage offices in Edinburgh became the headquarters of the Scottish Women's Hospitals for Foreign Service, to give these voluntary field hospitals their full title. Elsie Inglis, who became the honorary secretary, was a little dubious about the 'Scottish' in the title, and wrote at length on the matter to Mrs Fawcett saying that she would like a 'non-committal' name for the units, and preferred 'British' instead of 'Scottish', but she added that, since the idea had originated with the Scottish suffrage movement, 'one understood the desire to call it "Scottish" '. Later, in letters to the press, and in circulars seeking contributions, Dr Inglis generally carefully explained the 'Scottish' —'as the scheme began in Scotland'. Eventually, not only did Scots, English, Irish and Welsh women serve in the units, but many came from further afield—Australia, New Zealand, India and elsewhere.

From the moment war was declared Flora Sandes, proclaiming her availability on a go-anywhere, do-anything basis, was frantically trying to join something and was not having much luck. At one end of the scale she was not a trained nurse, and at the other she was certainly no cook, and her first-aid certificates were not impressing anyone very much. Nevertheless, she left her address at every Red Cross and volunteer service office in the county, just in case something turned up. Suddenly, one day, the local Red Cross called her: 'Miss Sandes, would you be prepared to leave for Serbia immediately with a small party of first-aid workers and nurses?'

Though she had only a vague idea of where Serbia was, Flora accepted without question. Madame Mabel Grujić, the American wife of the Serbian secretary of state for foreign affairs, had come to England on an urgent mercy mission, appealing for desperately needed medical supplies, doctors and nurses for her beleaguered country.

And so, a little more than a week after the outbreak of war, Flora Sandes, with a three-month contract in her pocket and hardly believing her luck, found herself with a party of eight including Emily Simmonds, an English theatre sister who had trained and now lived in America, and Mabel Grujić herself, crossing the channel on the start of the long journey to Serbia—a journey which, under wartime conditions with the concomitant delays and discomforts, took three weeks. Since the small group was meagrely financed, and every penny was being saved for more urgent needs, they travelled third class by rail most of the way across France and Italy, and finished up in a cattle boat from Piraeus to Salonika, then by slow train through the wild and lovely Vardar valley north via Niš, Serbia's provisional capital, and so to Kragujevac.

At Kragujevac, near the First Reserve Hospital, the little band were quartered in a small spartan room where they slept on straw palliasses. Fortunately they had had the good sense to bring some practical English camping equipment—portable canvas wash basins, sleeping bags, insect powder and hot-water bottles—so they did not fare too badly. Flora Sandes even brought her violin which remained with her throughout the worst of the campaigns. From the moment of their arrival they were all plunged into work, Flora and Emily being assigned to the First Reserve Hospital to work under Serbian surgeons.

The situation was appalling, with an extreme scarcity of even the most basic medical supplies such as bandages, instruments, beds and bedding, drugs and anaesthetics, and very few doctors and nurses. Serbia had not only lost a large part of her medical force during the Balkan Wars, for many doctors and nurses had died during the fighting or in one of the various epidemics, but there had been no time to replace them through normal peace-time studies. There had been no real peace for so long. In Valjevo, an average provincial town of about 25,000 inhabitants—among the 5,000 sick and wounded in the hospitals there was a mortality of 70 per cent—150 deaths a day. The main hospitals had not been re-equipped and no adequate supplies of any kind existed for all the temporary auxiliary hospitals. Every reasonable, usable building in the towns and countryside had been commandeered—

schools, convents, factories, warehouses, monasteries, barracks, even farm buildings and churches—for use as hospitals and casualty stations.

The more fortunate ill and wounded, who had managed to be admitted to a hospital of some sort, lay two to a bed, or were packed along the corridors on straw mattresses, or even on the bare stone floors. Dressings, if they were done at all, were unchanged for days on end, and the often makeshift operating theatres resembled medieval dissecting chambers as operations—mostly amputations because of gangrene and frostbite, or severe head injuries due to shrapnel—were hastily and roughly done, often without anaesthetics and mostly by lamplight. Outside in the courtyards and muddy grounds, ox-wagons of wounded men awaited even minimum attention of at least a little food, mostly bread and water, sometimes a few beans. All around flickered countless campfires where the sick and weary soldiers huddled seeking some warmth and comfort through the cold, lonely nights.

Flora and Emily worked like demons. At first Flora had been extremely squeamish and nauseated and felt deeply ashamed as, repelled by the stinking, putrefying misery around her, she had retched in a corner. But sheer pressure of work, the exhausted state of the hospital personnel, the extent of the suffering, and the courage of the men and their pathetic gratitude for any attention, enabled her to overcome her initial revulsion and to acquire a certain detachment from the horror of piles of amputated limbs, and the swollen, suppurating bodies of these suffering, uncomplaining men. Soon Emily, a highly experienced surgical nurse, was more than assisting the few exhausted surgeons; she was also operating, with Flora assisting her. And the day was not far off when Flora, trained by Emily, would be successfully carrying out the more straightforward operations herself, assisted by a prisoner-of-war orderly.

When their three-month contracts were up in December, Flora and Emily hurried back to England where they both engaged in a concerted campaign on behalf of Serbia. Flora wrote appeals for contributions to a relief fund and gave lectures. For the first time the British public was confronted with eye-witness accounts by one of their own countrywomen of the conditions in Serbia. The plight of this small country, battling against the might of the Austro-Hungarian monarchy—David confronting Goliath—caught the imagination and pity of the public. Serbia became news. An avalanche of articles, interviews, first-hand accounts and pictures landed via the newspapers on the breakfast tables of Britain.

Through the courtesy of the *Daily Mail*, which printed her moving appeal, Flora collected £2,000 in three weeks. The British Red Cross made a valuable contribution by giving her free freight and packing and by vouching for her to the passport authorities since she could now be officially regarded as a *bona fide* free-lance with the Serbian Red Cross. This enabled Flora and Emily to return to Serbia in January 1915 with more than 110 tons of vital medical supplies and hospital equipment, which they personally delivered to Valjevo which by then was paralysed by a full-scale typhus epidemic.

Meanwhile, press reports and the tireless campaign of Mabel Grujić had resulted in the formation of the Serbian Relief Fund (SRF), with its headquarters in London's Cromwell Road. Partly sponsored by the Scottish Women's Hospitals, the early Serbian Relief Fund units were staffed by both men and women, though mostly the latter, but they always had a woman administrator. By mid-November 1914 the first SRF unit, commanded by Leila, Lady Paget, reached Serbia to establish a fine 600-bed hospital on a hill outside Skoplje in the southern part of the country. Lady Paget, whose husband, Sir Ralph Paget, was later made British Commissioner for the British relief units in Serbia, was an ideal choice. Not only had she already gained considerable experience through working in Serbian hospitals during the Balkan Wars but she was to display a rare gift for command. A tireless worker and expert organiser, who earned the respect and devotion of the Serbs and of those who served under her, she had astonished her family's social circle who remembered her as a conventional and delicate young woman, whose main travels before her marriage had been in the company of her mother seeking cures at Europe's various fashionable watering-places.

Up to this point the Scottish Women's Hospitals had been mainly involved with events in France and Belgium, where their units were serving magnificently with the French and Belgian forces. In France they had been an instant success, indeed a sensation. With forthright Gallic curiosity, French journalists had asked it it were really true that these charming women surgeons actually operated? Could one of them witness such an operation being performed? In the interests of entente a journalist was admitted to the operating theatre and a while later, looking slightly green, he was seen rushing out of the hospital yelling to his colleagues, 'C'est vrai! Elle coupe! Elle coupe!'

But now the plight of the Serbs found a champion in Dr Inglis. First she approached the Serbian embassy with the offer of a SWH unit and then, to reinforce this action, she wrote to the celebrated historian, Robert W. Seton-Watson, who was renowned and respected throughout the Balkans, especially in Serbia, asking him to approach the Serbian authorities at a high level. Seton-Watson telegraphed an immediate reply: 'Serbian Government gratefully accepts expedition: Writing details.'

Despite the overwhelming odds, when Austria's punitive expedition crossed the frontiers on 12 August 1914, Serbia met it with such fierce resistance that it became a rout and a military debacle for the Austrians, who beat an undignified but temporary retreat. In September the Austrian armies again entered the country and advanced slowly without meeting much resistance. They even reached Belgrade where they confidently began their victory celebrations. But too soon; their triumph was short-lived. The Serbs had not been beaten, they had run out of ammunition and were awaiting fresh supplies promised by the French. These arrived just in time and the Serbs rallied magnificently, surging forward against the Austrians who, over-confident, were caught off-guard. For the second time within four months the Serbs drove the enemy off their territory. By 14 December the only Austrians in Serbia were 70,000 prisoners. As Vojovda Putnik, the Serbian Chief of Staff, aptly put it: 'there is not an Austrian soldier at liberty on Serbian soil . . .' But the enemy armies had left behind a deadly ally—typhus.

Serbia's medical organisation, as Flora Sandes and her party had soon found out, was totally inadequate to cope with the wounded from this first phase of the war, let alone a typhus epidemic that was to sweep the country assailing alike soldiers, civilians, relief workers and prisoners of war. To make matters far worse the typhus coincided with a particularly severe winter, in a country noted for its bitter winters. With very little food and fuel, no means of distribution, totally inadequate medical and clothing supplies, few medical personnel, hospitals bulging with ill and wounded soldiers, the prospects looked terribly bleak.

'Send us where we are most needed', Dr Inglis had insisted. She was taken at her word and when Serbia's position seemed quite hopeless the first Scottish Women's Hospital unit for Serbia, with Dr Eleanor Soltau in charge, sailed from Southampton in December and reached its destination, Kragujevac, in January 1915. To be completely self-sufficient Dr Soltau had insisted on taking all the necessary equipment, even basic food supplies, medicines, beds and bedding—enough for one hundred patients. But on arrival they had to admit 250 patients immediately and this was just the beginning; by early spring the unit was responsible for 650 beds in Kragujevac.

Within a few weeks of the unit's arrival Dr Soltau, overwhelmed by the magnitude of the disaster, the stream of wounded and now the spread of typhus, wired frantically to headquarters: 'Dire necessity for fever nurses.' The 'dire' was very calculated. For some reason the Serbian authorities tried to suppress news of the typhus epidemic, in fact the military censors even rejected telegrams or letters referring to typhus. So Dr Soltau gambled on 'dire' being too obscure a word to be understood by the censor and that it would therefore remain unchanged. It did, and Dr Elsie Inglis got the message.

Dr Soltau planned to open a special typhus hospital at Kragujevac, an action that won the warm approval of Dr Inglis who wrote back that ten fever nurses were en route to the unit. But by then it was quite evident that far more was needed to help Dr Soltau's overtaxed unit, and to bring relief to other provincial centres, which had no medical assistance at all, such as Valjevo where the situation was worsening daily with typhus spreading, wounded unattended to and no relief teams.

In England volunteers were lining up and contributions pouring in to aid the Serbs. Additional units—SWH, SRF and others—were formed and equipped and alerted to stand by ready for immediate departure for Serbia once their transport could be arranged. Among these was the large Anglo-Serbian hospital, later known in Serbia as the 'Berry unit', under the joint command of James Berry FRCS and his physician wife, both from the Royal Free Hospital, London. This unit would eventually be one of the best equipped to arrive in Serbia.

3
'THE NOBLE BAND OF WOMEN'

It was March, 1915, and in St Martin's-in-the-Fields a special farewell service, arranged and conducted by Dr Percy Dearmer for the Third Serbian Relief Fund Unit, had just come to a close. To please a friend who had joined the unit, Mrs Mabel Dearmer had come to the service; as it ended, to her shocked dismay she heard her husband announce from the pulpit: 'This is only au revoir. Since I have been appointed chaplain to the British units in Serbia, I will be travelling out with you.'

Though, just before the service began, he had mumbled something to her about his going to Serbia, Mabel Dearmer had not really registered the import of what he was saying. Now, as she sat and tightly fought her tears her world seemed to crumble—first her two sons, then most of her friends, and now her husband. Everyone seemed committed except herself. As she struggled for composure, through her tears she saw, standing nearby in the aisle, Mrs St Clair Stobart who had been appointed unit administrator and whom she knew quite well. Suddenly, without any preliminaries, she went up to Mrs Stobart and put her question:

'Can you take me to Serbia?'

'What can you do? What are you trained for?'

'Nothing. But I am an ordinary sensible woman and can learn quickly.'

With intense, appraising eyes Mrs Stobart regarded Mrs Dearmer, taking in the elegant dress, the long earrings, finally touching her beautiful fur coat:

'You must leave this at home.'

'Of course.'

'You must accept discipline.'

'Naturally.'

'Very well. You can come as an hospital orderly. Call at the office for a list of clothes wanted and be ready to leave in three days.'

Excitedly, Mabel Dearmer rushed off in search of her husband. Milling around were many women in their grey uniforms with various coloured collar-tabs—red or blue for the doctors, purple for the nurses—and pushing through the crowd came Percy Dearmer. His wife seized him by the arm:

'Percy, I'm coming to Serbia. I'm an hospital orderly!'

'What fun!' was his reaction, surprised at nothing where his wife was concerned.

Mrs Stobart had narrowly escaped being shot as a spy by the Germans when they had overrun Antwerp, but she had been released and repatriated in time to take charge of the Anglo-French Hospital unit near Cherbourg. It was there that she heard of Serbia's plight and the appeals for volunteers to serve in the relief teams. 'Clearly Serbia was my destiny', she stated, and resolved immediately to lead a unit there as 'my experience in the first Balkan War in Bulgaria had stood me in good stead.' Of this there was no doubt. Few women had her wartime experience, and the renown of her Convoy Corps on the Bulgarian Front made her a natural choice to lead a relief unit to Serbia.

Thus, Mrs Stobart relinquished her command of the Cherbourg unit and headed straight for London and the Serbian Relief Fund committee. She was warmly welcomed and put in charge of the large, superbly equipped third SRF unit with a staff of fifty including seven women doctors; her husband, John Greenhalgh, in his established role of honorary treasurer; and now Mrs Dearmer as a last-minute recruit.

No time was wasted and, with Dr Mabel King-May as chief medical officer, the unit sailed from England on 1 April 1915 for Salonika, eventually reaching their destination, Kragujevac in Serbia, towards the end of the month.

By February the whole relief campaign for Serbia had gathered momentum. Accounts were coming in of the magnificent work done by Dr Soltau's and Lady Paget's units. On 30 January the *Evening Standard* reported an appeal for more fully trained women to be sent to Kragujevac and published the text of a telegram from the Serbian government requesting 'more women physicians to be sent' at its own expense. Already, Dr Inglis's faith in women medical teams for war service was more than vindicated. And in February, Queen Mary consented to become patroness of the

Serbian Relief Fund, whose committee included some of the top people of the day, or of the future, from every exalted walk of life: Lord Curzon, Winston Churchill, Lloyd George, Bonar Law, Cardinal Bourne, G. M. Trevelyan, Lord Haversham, Sir Arthur Evans, Lady Boyle, Mrs Carrington-Wilde and many others.

Everyone was now launching appeals. The good work initiated by Mabel Grujić, energetically backed by Flora Sandes, had become almost self-generating. Miss Annie Christitch,* a young Oxford-educated journalist from one of Serbia's leading families, had thrown all her considerable talents into the appeals drive, writing articles and lecturing on the culture and history of her country; later she and her mother ran a relief organisation in Valjevo—the 'Christitch Mission'. Princess Alexis of Serbia organised sales of war relics to help the Serbian Relief Fund. Then there were special theatre matinees, concerts, bazaars, and lectures such as that given by Gustave Antoine, the Serbian Consul at Antwerp, and reported in full in the *Daily Telegraph*. London's Lord Mayor held a public meeting at Mansion House to call attention to the situation in Serbia. On 24 March the *Manchester Guardian* published a long article by Sir Thomas Lipton on his recent travels in that war-torn country, and another quoting excerpts from the letters of relief workers already in Serbia, describing their experiences while nursing the wounded and the typhus victims.

But the undisputed queen of all fund raisers was Miss Kathleen Burke. Dr Inglis had 'discovered' this enchanting young woman when she became secretary of the London committee. On a hunch, Dr Inglis one day suggested to Kathleen Burke that she go to Oxford in her stead to address a meeting on behalf of the Scottish Women's Hospitals. With considerable misgivings Kathleen Burke had done so. It was a triumph—she emerged as a remarkable and compelling speaker and from that moment never looked back. She became a sensation, a tireless ambassadress for the Scottish Women's Hospitals and the Serbian Relief Fund, and an indefatigable fund raiser for all the relief organisations in all the spheres of war, particularly France. Her first resounding success after Oxford was in France where, after a tour of the military hospitals to see what was needed in the way of supplies and

* Miss Christitch spent most of her life in England—she died in 1972—and always wrote her name thus. Naturally I have kept this spelling.

personnel, a dinner in her honour was given by General Pétain. Then she undertook two journeys to America where she soon became known as 'our beloved girl'. She spoke in the Carnegie Hall and was the first woman ever to address the New York Stock Exchange, whose members immediately parted with half a million dollars! Altogether, during her trips to and around America she collected the extraordinary sums of £63,000 for the Scottish Women's Hospitals and £290,000 for French hospitals.

Rapidly, the women's medical units for Serbia became headline news. Throughout Britain the press trumpeted panegyrics extolling the qualities of the 'noble band of women', those administering angels who were risking their lives rescuing the Serbs from disease or death, striding into danger with heads held high, keeping stiff British upper lips, braving the horrors of war far from home in some alien Balkan corner, and so forth. Ladled on thick and sweet, it made the 'noble women' squirm, and they responded with irony and jest: 'early this morning we arrived at Salonique. Proud hotels of that historic city. "The noble women" distributed in your chambers must shed new glamour on your thresholds'—was the entry in one journal.

Transporting these units to their destination was no easy task. Occasionally they sailed from Bristol, Liverpool or Cardiff, but mostly it was by channel steamer to France, then by train via Paris to Marseilles. Sometimes they even enjoyed, quite literally, a Cooks tour in Paris en route. Given the proximity of the Western Front, it was a rather uncomfortable paradox to find Paris still so gay and fashionable. When they could, the French naval authorities and the British Admiralty were most co-operative, finding places for the women on troop and hospital ships from Marseilles.

Once Elsie Inglis ended an appeal for funds and supplies by asking her audience, partly in jest; 'I suppose nobody here could lend me a yacht?' To her astonishment someone was indeed lending his yacht all the time. For most of the war, braving submarines and torpedoes, Sir Thomas Lipton and his luxury motor yacht, *Erin*, plied ceaselessly between Marseilles and Salonika, transporting supplies and personnel, including most of the British Red Cross units who served in Serbia and Salonika. A self-made multi-millionaire, who owned tea and coffee plantations in Ceylon and was one of England's tea kings, Sir Thomas was a fanatical yachtsman who dreamed all his life of winning The Americas Cup—he made his last attempt in 1930—and an enormously generous rough-diamond humanitarian who, among his numerous charitable exploits, founded the Alexandra Trust to provide the poor with cheap and wholesome meals.

It was on the *Erin* that Elsie Corbett and Kathleen Dillon met as they travelled with a British Red Cross unit to Serbia in May 1915. This meeting was the beginning of a valuable partnership of two very capable and dedicated VADs who served together throughout the war in Serbia, first with the Red Cross then with the Scottish Women's Hospitals, and a close friendship that lasted the remainder of their lives.

The Hon Elsie Corbett, daughter of Lord Rowallan, had just turned twenty-one when war broke out. In the fashion of the day she had been to a finishing school abroad, had 'done' several London seasons, had been presented at Court, had attended the usual rash of balls, and had had an orgy of theatre and ballet parties. In short, she had been a typical pre-war debutante, though to some extent a reluctant one because, being basically shy and withdrawn, the whole ritual was often a considerable ordeal. In her family there was a proud medical tradition and one of liberal civic service; thus it was perfectly natural that she should also have attended first-aid and home-nursing courses and should have obtained her certificates, which had enabled her to start working regularly at the Kilmarnock Infirmary.

One day the family doctor asked her why, since she was interested in nursing, she did not volunteer for Serbia where typhus was raging and nurses were needed desperately. Warmly encouraged by her father and in the face of the acute disapproval of many relatives and friends, Elsie Corbett applied immediately and was accepted as a VAD by a British Red Cross unit preparing to leave for the Balkans. Early in May, destined for a Red Cross hospital at Vrnjačka Banja, Elsie Corbett, with twenty others, set out for Marseilles, 'where we boarded Sir Thomas Lipton's large steam yacht, *Erin*, and embarked on a luxury cruise of the Mediterranean'. Soon after the *Erin* weighed anchor, she met Kathleen Dillon, who came from a distinguished Oxfordshire family, was a cultivated young woman, an excellent horsewoman and a highly qualified VAD. Sir Thomas entertained them and their companions royally. He loved good-humoured practical jokes such as

(above) The Scottish Women's Hospitals America Unit at Ostrovo were very proud of their bugler; (below) Dr. Kathcrine Macphail dances the kola, the Serbian national dance, with a Serbian colonel and his men

(above) A Scottish Women's Hospital mobile dressing station behind the front lines during the Serbian army's northwards advance in 1918 *(AMB)*

(below) The spartan mobility of a SWH field dressing station at Vertekop in 1917 is demonstrated by the tent and the folding bed and table *(AMB)*

(below) The funeral in Salonika of Mrs. Harley, chief of the SWH Transport Column attached to the Serbian army in 1916 She was killed by shrapnel at Monastir in 1917 and was buried in the Allied War Cemetery, the only woman among thousands of fallen soldiers (AMB)

(*above*) Lady Paget and her Serbian Relief Fund unit in Skoplje stayed behind to become prisoners-of-war when the Bulgarians overran the city in October 1915. Here she is shown six months later, being escorted by Bulgarian officers in the first stage of her unit's repatriation

(*below left*) Dr. Elsie Inglis, founder of the Scottish Women's Hospitals, in formal uniform – designed by herself – of commander of the SWH. The photograph was taken early in 1915. Dr. Inglis was decorated by the Serbs with the Order of the White Eagle (the first time ever awarded to a woman), the Order of St Sava, and the Order of the White Eagle with Swords

(*below right*) Mrs. St Clair Stobart, administrator of the Third Serbian Relief Fund unit, in her field uniform, and the characteristic floppy-brimmed hat which she always wore

faking telegrams recalling the unit back to England; but he was essentially a warm-hearted, emotional man and tears would course unchecked down his cheeks as he read them copies of letters of condolence he had personally written to the families of those unit members who had given their lives—mostly through typhus— during their service in Serbia.

By the spring of 1915, therefore, the third SRF unit was on its way. The second Serbian Relief Fund Unit, the Wimborne unit— so-named because Lady Cornelia Wimborne had raised the funds for it—had already gone out to Skoplje to combine with Lady Paget's unit whose work had been severely hindered by typhus. Sixteen nurses and doctors had succumbed to the disease, in- cluding Lady Paget herself. Fortunately all recovered and Lady Paget was back on duty two months later.

When matters appeared so extremely bleak in Serbia, and she was ill with diphtheria, Dr Soltau had wired to Dr Inglis, begging her to come to Kragujevac. Thus, early in May, Dr Inglis arrived there to become the general supervisor of all the Scottish Women's Hospitals in Serbia. Though she was chiefly based in Kragujevac, where Dr Soltau's unit was responsible for three hospitals—one each for surgery, typhus, and relapsing fever —with over 600 beds, Dr Inglis maintained close contact with all the SWH and SRF units, and the Serbian Red Cross and Army Medical Corps.

It was love at first sight between Dr Inglis and the Serbs. They were a people near to her heart—courageous, simple, tough, honest, natural and uncomplaining—'nature's gentlemen' she called them. She adored them and they in turn revered and loved her. Not only were they deeply grateful to this gentle, dedicated Scottish doctor and her units, who had come from so far to help them in their hour of despair, but they succumbed to her simple charm and courtesy and the serenity and goodness that shone from her radiant personality. Later in Serbia they used to say: 'In Scotland they made her a doctor, in Serbia we would have made her a saint.'

As funds flooded in, more units had been raised and were ready to embark for Serbia. Dr Inglis had been overjoyed to enlist the redoubtable Dr Alice Hutchison as chief medical officer of one of them. The latter was with the French forces in France where she had gone with the first SWH unit to serve abroad; before that she had travelled as an emissary of the Scottish Women's Hospitals to Calais and Paris to see what the French most needed and where the units could be best used. Diminutive and pretty with flaming red-gold hair, always gaily and fashionably dressed, she was the daughter of a medical missionary in India, a man renowned as a fearless traveller and devoted doctor throughout the western Himalayan region. 'Anyone who knew him could have no trouble in tracing the source of the intrepid courage, and unfailing resourcefulness, and the devotion to work found in the daughter', wrote Eva Shaw McLaren, Elsie Inglis's sister.

Alice Hutchison was an excellent, experienced doctor with a profound understanding of the mental as well as the physical state of her patients. At the outbreak of war she was the physician in charge of the dispensary at Canongate, run by the Sisters of St Vincent de Paul. Before that she had endured her baptism of fire at Kirk-Kilisse in the Balkan War with Mrs Stobart's Convoy Corps. Apart from being a capable doctor she was unconventional, witty and charming. During rare moments of relaxation she and her unit members enjoyed many lively hours together. But, on occasions, Dr Hutchison could be a fiery little tigress, fighting for the welfare of her patients, or the rights of her staff. Later, when she was taken prisoner, even the enemy learned to respect her sobriquet, the 'little general'.

Therefore, it was understandable that Dr Inglis wanted her for Serbia, more especially to take a unit to Valjevo. Dr Soltau once reported: 'I could not get to Valjevo, so Valjevo came down to me', referring to the lines of ox-wagons full of men suffering from gangrenous wounds that one day appeared outside Dr Soltau's hospital. These neglected peasant soldiers had heard of miracles worked by the women doctors so they had endured the ordeal of the ox-wagon transport over the hills to Kragujevac. Flora Sandes and Emily Simmonds, working under appalling conditions at a hospital in Valjevo, were among the very few foreign relief workers who had found their way to the stricken town, one of the first to be hit by the typhus epidemic.

Late in April Dr Hutchison's unit set forth from Cardiff in the ss *Ceramic* with what was claimed to be the best field hospital ever to be placed under canvas. At the port the dock workers and crowds of 'tommies' gave them a rousing send-off, with jests and good-humoured banter and, as the ship slowly slipped out to sea, the entire Welsh dockside joined in a touching and harmonious rendering of the 'Song of Farewell'.

From the beginning, the unit's laundry orderly decided to run a unit diary, or journal, which she called *Serbian Outpost* or, to give its Serbian title, *Predstraža Srpski*. On that day of departure her first entry refers to the purser 'tearing his hair over the problem of placing cooks and washerwomen in the particular social niche to which they should belong. Eventually', she adds with some wit, 'the menial found herself the cheerful possessor of a cabin to herself. She was heard to declare her determination to sit firmly on the very lowest rung of the social ladder in future'.

Until Malta the voyage was uneventful 'though in the danger zone some of us are said to have slept dressed with an eye to immediate shipwreck and with their hoard of gold upon their persons. The opportunity for heroism was however denied the "noble women".'

At the end of April the unit disembarked at Malta where Dr Hutchison was asked by the Governor, Lord Methuen, to interrupt her voyage to Salonika so that her unit could help nurse the numerous British wounded about to arrive from the Dardanelles and the Gallipoli landings. The unit was stationed at the fifteenth-century hospital of the Knights of Malta, then just called the Valetta Military Hospital, and quartered at the Cameretta Barracks. Dr Hutchison was deeply conscious of being assigned to such a historic building with its ancient medical tradition, and describes it at length in her letters. At one point she remarks, 'where formerly Knights of St John, in their flowing white robes, tended their sick folk, may now be seen, moving among the beds, four painfully modern women doctors in their painfully modern ward coats!'

A few days after the unit had settled in, the first batch of wounded arrived—dirty, gaunt, unkempt, with blood-stained dressings, many of which had not been touched since first-aid had been given at Gallipoli ten days earlier. Mostly these were Australian and New Zealand soldiers, who had borne the brunt of the disastrous Gallipoli landings. From the beginning they got along famously with the unit members, who were delighted to find the soldiers jeering at the 'sentimental effusion of the *Malta Chronicle* over our "wounded heroes"'. The 'noble band of women' and the 'wounded heroes' understood each other perfectly.

47

Two weeks later, after sincere expressions of gratitude and appreciation from Lord Methuen, and some moving and hilarious farewells from their patients, Alice Hutchison and her unit sailed for Salonika, and then entrained to Valjevo which, after numerous Balkan delays and mis-routings, they reached at the beginning of June. Though they were all completely captivated by Valjevo's surroundings of rolling wooded hills and valleys and longed to explore this enticing countryside, the staff immediately buckled down to erecting their hospital tents. Alice Hutchison was full of excited anticipation: 'I am longing to see the lines of white tents, and the flags waving, and patients tucked into nice clean beds with pretty red coverlets.'

Within two weeks the vast hospital encampment was erected, comprising—all under canvas—various offices for the CMO and the administrator, a large mess tent, cook-houses, sleeping quarters, six large ward marquees, a surgery, laundry, patients' kitchen, reception tents, bath tents and various smaller tents for fuel, stores and so forth. As she watched the enormous complex of tents go up, Dr Hutchison felt they were 'an emblem of hope and wonder'.

Into what unknown regions were they all embarked, she wondered, and to what end?

4
TYPHUS — WINTER

Dr Frances Wakefield felt weightless, disembodied, floating up from nowhere into realms of momentary consciousness. Hallucinating images drifted before her: she was home in Kendal, then on the lake with her brother and his seaplane, reed huts of the Nigerian mission station floated by, and English voices far away. The images faded as she slowly emerged from the darkness of her fever to glimpse the reality of the dirty rafters above, and the straw on which she lay in the squalid peasant barn—Serbia. It all flashed back—the war, the typhus; then English voices again: 'She's conscious.' Yes, she could hear, but it was difficult to speak. So she had come through. What about the others? Many unit members had caught typhus during that terrible epidemic. Then, bending over her was the familiar, gentle face of the senior physician, whom she had last seen fighting the end phase of typhus with a temperature of 106°F—the dreaded sudden soaring to fever heights from deceptive signs of recovery.

'Dr Wakefield, you are all right now.'

'And the others?' she managed to whisper.

'Most have recovered.'

'But not all?'

'No, not all. Now you must sleep. Drink this.'

She swallowed the bitter medicine and slept. And so Dr Frances Wakefield, a young physician in Dr Soltau's unit, recovered, slowly and painfully because she had been very ill. Some weeks later she was back on duty.

Before her own illness, Dr Wakefield had personally treated Dr Elizabeth Ross from Tain in Scotland, who had previously worked extensively in Persia. This gallant doctor had come out alone and was attached to a Serbian fever hospital in Kragujevac where she worked under grim conditions with two Greek doctors, a few orderlies and no trained nurses. Dr Soltau's SWH unit had arrived there in December 1914, just before Christmas, and Dr Ross soon made herself known to her fellow countrywomen, who learned to

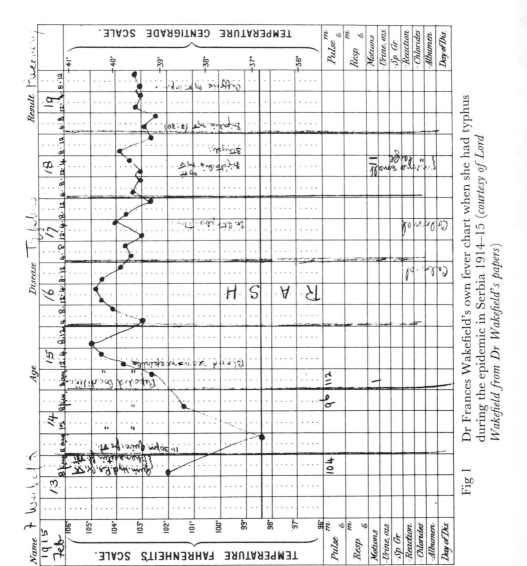

Fig 1　Dr Frances Wakefield's own fever chart when she had typhus during the epidemic in Serbia 1914–15 (courtesy of Lord Wakefield from Dr Wakefield's papers)

admire her skill and gentle manners, her knowledge of fever medicine, and the adoration of her patients. But they were appalled at the conditions in her hospital—the shocking dirt, the unwashed patients two to a bed; dysentery, typhus and recurrent fever cases lying side by side; little wood for heating, unreliable water supplies and insufficient food. Dr Ross went through the worst of the epidemic, tending night and day without respite her desperately ill patients in the overcrowded, insanitary wards. This took its toll. When struck down herself she was too weakened by exhaustion and the privations she had endured to combat the fever. Despite the care given her by Dr Soltau's staff, and by Dr Wakefield in particular, she died in February 1915. In the weeks that followed three members of Dr Soltau's unit died from typhus: Sisters Louisa Jordan and Minishull and Miss Madge Neill-Fraser.

It was only a few years earlier, in 1909, that a French medical team, led by Charles Nicolle, had discovered that lice transmitted typhus. This virulent disease is most frequent in wartime among refugees, troops and prisoners of war since it thrives on bad sanitation, dirt, neglect, overcrowding and extreme cold because cold, hungry homeless people seek refuge in warm, often insanitary, overcrowded shelters. Typhus, in the conditions that prevailed in Serbia, often had the additional secondary complications of severe pneumonia and, especially with the wounded, gangrene. Serious frostbite was very common, and then the outlook was particularly grim because neglected frostbite inevitably leads to gangrene. The amputation of limbs was one of the most common operations in the Serbian hospitals during the war and the sadly familiar sight of ex-soldiers minus one, often both, legs in Serbian towns and villages after the armistice was grim testimony to that drastic wartime surgery.

But, even in those days, if a typhus patient was basically healthy and well cared for from the onset of the illness, the chances of recovery were high, as was evident from the numerous instances when unit members contracted the fever. Though a few did die the great majority recovered, most returning to duty after a short convalescence. Of the foreign relief teams, only in an American-staffed hospital was the death toll high—four out of eight American doctors died. Later, Dr Isabel Emslie commented that the Americans seemed very prone to certain epidemic illnesses.

51

After typhus began its relentless spread throughout Serbia during that winter, the relief doctors soon found that the lice tended to settle in body hair where they laid their microscopic eggs. Thereafter, any patient admitted to the unit hospitals was first scrubbed and washed, then completely shaved—head, legs, arms, chest, facial and pubic hair—in fact, shaved to the skin.

For their part the typhus doctors and nurses, with hair cropped short, wore a strange white monk-like garb in the shape of a long one-piece calico garment with Turkish-type trousers tucked into high rubber boots or socks and bound at the wrists and ankles with bandages soaked in naphthalene, a tight skull cap with nurse's veil over their cropped hair and a face mask. In any case, for overall hygiene reasons, and for convenience, most unit administrators insisted that their staff cut their hair short. Many might bewail the shearing of their locks, but discipline and duty prevailed. No doubt the uniforms and the short hair—the 'Eton' crops —contributed to the sour myth that many of these unit women were tough, even mannish. Perhaps a few were, but the generalisation was far from true.

Dr Soltau was near despair. On reaching Kragujevac with their spendid equipment her staff were appalled at their inadequacy in the face of the suffering and misery that awaited them. The slender energetic surgeon and her skilled medical teams had come prepared for surgery, for wounded soldiers from the front, but were not equipped for the onslaught of typhus. Nor were they prepared for the multitudes of ill and wounded men turning the towns into open-air lazarets, where ox-wagons laden with battle-wounded with fractured limbs, horrible head injuries, abdominal wounds, gangrene and frostbite waited for hours, even days, exposed to the bitter rain and cold. Inside the local hospitals Eleanor Soltau found the situation even worse. In squalor and misery the wounded and sick lay crowded together, generally on the filthy floors, the lucky ones on straw, but most on bare stone or boards. Men with recently amputated limbs lay alongside men delirious with fevers. Dressings, suppurating and vile, were days old; some men were already dead and many were dying of sheer neglect in the stinking, unventilated atmosphere of those terrible wards. It was not the fault of the unfortunate Serbs. What medical teams still remained did what they could, but they were a mere handful of exhausted doctors, nurses and orderlies working day and night, with no medicines, few instruments, no anaesthetics, and thousands of patients. The casualty rate among the Serb medical teams was appalling. Thirty per cent died of typhus or the cholera which also appeared in certain areas, and 60 per cent went down with typhus—a measure of the hopelessness of their situation and of their devotion to their work.

Eleanor Soltau and her nurses and doctors, inured to all manner of suffering, were shaken to the marrow by the magnitude of the disaster confronting them. But she refused to submit to despair, and ordered her staff to begin work immediately. A hospital in Kragujevac was put at their disposal. First the wards were emptied then cleaned, disinfected and whitewashed. Equipment and medicines were unpacked and installed, the patients were washed, their wounds dressed, then they were put into fresh clean beds. The gratitude of the men was boundless. Dr Soltau had come with a hundred beds; by the time her hospital was ready she had triple that number of patients and queues awaiting admission, and this before the advent of the typhus epidemic. But she coped by requisitioning nearby buildings—houses, sheds, stables, anything —getting her staff skilled in making straw palliasses, and enlisting some Austrian prisoners of war as orderlies to handle the rough work.

Like many women doctors who had done at least some of their studies in Zurich, Germany or Vienna, Eleanor Soltau spoke German well. This was a godsend in coping with the considerable language problems arising from the polyglot hospital population— Serb, Austrian, Hungarian, Czech, and now English. 'An interview', she wrote, 'involves four people. The Matron speaks English, the laundress Serbian, I come in with German, and the kitchen-maid with German and Serbian.'

Towards the end of January typhus struck in earnest. From an occasional endemic disease it became a raging epidemic. Various theories were expounded on why it was suddenly released in such a deadly manner. Some, as in always the case in wartime, blamed the enemy; the Austrians, they said, left typhus behind with their 70,000 prisoners of war after their first abortive invasion. But far more likely it was the inevitable outcome of the prevailing conditions: the total disruption in the whole country, the unchecked movement hither and thither of uprooted refugees and soldiers, the cold, hunger, general privations and the total breakdown of routine medical services. There were no checks, no controls, no sanitary inspectors, and a total absence of any dispensaries for the civilian population. Lady Paget, in a report from Skoplje, exonerated the Austrians for the spread of typhus: 'the disease being endemic in the country it therefore only needed the conditions of overcrowding and dirt consequent on a state of war to bring about a devastating epidemic'. Dr Berry of the Berry unit was, by implication, harder on the Serbian authorities than on the Austrians:

> . . . the disease has been introduced and disseminated by patients, who were sent into the towns in batches at short notice and without any information as to what was the matter with them. Sometimes 100 or 150 were just dumped down in the middle of the night . . . They had to be squeezed in anyhow, often two to a bed. Many of these brought typhus, either declared or in the incubation stage. Patients and hospitals swarmed with lice, and the disease spread rapidly.

Dr Frances Wakefield, whose typhus attack was mentioned at the start of this chapter, was a member of the well known Wakefield family of Kendal in the Lake District. One of her brothers had invented a seaplane and, when a medical student, she would go with him on the lake to act as his mechanic when he made his trial flights. Another brother, also a doctor, was to become the medical officer with Mallory's ill-fated Everest expedition of 1924. When war was declared Frances had immediately resigned from her post as a medical missionary in Nigeria and sailed home to volunteer and had joined Dr Soltau's unit. Over thirty years later, with a lifetime of experience and accomplishments behind her in a dozen different lands, Dr Wakefield still recalled that Serbian typhus epidemic with the vividness of a trauma:

> With so much misery about we could not expect special attention and comforts when we fell ill. We did what we could for each other, but our primary duty lay with the Serbs. Each doctor or nurse less meant double work for the others. We gambled on our good health to pull us through and it mostly did. Once, I remember, a senior sister went down with a high fever—it wasn't typhus, probably a severe 'flu—and after a

couple of days, still with a high temperature, she suddenly got out of bed saying, 'Enough of this mollycoddling, there's work to be done and it will do me good.' She went back on duty, at full pressure, and recovered completely. Reaction to one's illness often reflects a state of mind—forget about oneself, especially when others around are far more ill, then one often gets well without even noticing it. At one time or another most of us did this during that awful winter in Serbia.

Dr Wakefield remembered her chief medical officer with warmth:

Eleanor Soltau was a fine doctor, skilled and experienced, and a warm, endearing personality—a little reserved perhaps, but not intimidating. She drove herself and we followed. Even when she was desperately ill with diphtheria she wouldn't let up. We had to force her into bed. Because of this her illness was particularly acute, and led to her being invalided back to England in spring.

They all admired the Serbs:

They are a phenomenal people—hardy, tough and enduring and, when ill, trusting and uncomplaining. They are ideal patients. Our only bone of contention was fresh air. For some odd reason these peasant soldiers from the countryside loathed, even feared, fresh air and ventilation. It was a constant battle to keep the windows open to prevent the dreadful stuffiness they all loved. But they are a brave people—they know how to live and they know how to die. We really loved them.

And to the question as to whether the Serbs minded being treated by women doctors, Dr Wakefield answered:

Quite the contrary. First, these simple peasant lads respect women, especially the mother figure, which, of course, given the special circumstances, we were. Second, they preferred us to the army doctors—they claimed that women surgeons were more gentle, never rough, and generally more tender and patient. After all, most women are, aren't they?

Mrs St Clair Stobart's comments about the Serbs' attitude to women doctors tally with those of Dr Wakefield. She wrote: ' I was a little surprised at the matter-of-fact way in which the men all accepted women doctors and surgical operations by women. Indeed they highly approved because women were, they said, more gentle and yet as effective as men doctors.'

At Valjevo, the town that had so worried Dr Soltau, Flora Sandes and Emily Simmonds, who had returned in February from their campaign in England on behalf of the Serbs, were in the thick of the typhus epidemic. The president of the Serbian Red Cross had sent them there with most of the 110 tons of precious medical supplies they had brought out with them. To their dismay they found that, with the exception of the director of their hospital, all the doctors in the town were ill. As a result they were put in charge of the operating theatre in the large local hospital. An American doctor they met outside Valjevo gloomily prophesied: 'I'll give you two young ladies a month to live if you go to Valjevo. The mortality rate is 70 per cent.'

He nearly proved correct.

As at Kragujevac, when they had first come out during the autumn, Emily and Flora found themselves undertaking most of the operations, especially amputations. Besides this, they made the rounds of the wards a couple of times a day, did what they could for the worst cases, and even opened a sort of amateur dispensary. Flora told the familiar story:

> The conditions were indescribable—hardly any beds, filthy bedding, the whole place swarming with vermin. The town was practically quarantined; anyway no one in his right mind would willingly enter the place. No trains arrived or left; rations were very short; and for two months sugar, tobacco, milk and butter were totally unobtainable, and meat very scarce. What there was was sold at famine prices.

Soon Emily, the theatre sister, was as skilled as any surgeon, and Flora, the VAD, long past the squeamish stage, proved an able assistant, even operating herself on occasions. Alarming as this might sound for the unfortunate patient, there was no other way; better to risk these skilled but amateur surgeons than the alternative, certain death. As it turned out Emily and Flora had an extremely high recovery level among their patients. With only two Serb orderlies to help them they often operated for sixteen hours a day *and* did the dressings. 'There was no time for much actual nursing', Flora wrote. She could have added that they had no nurses!

In April, Flora and Emily, within a week of each other, both went down with typhus, Flora very badly. But within six weeks they had more or less recovered and, with no real convalescence, went back to work. Twenty-one doctors died in Valjevo that spring.

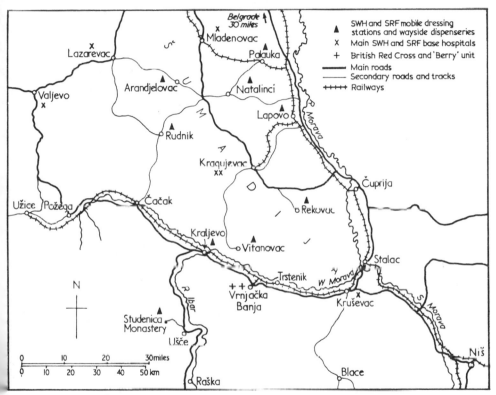

Map B   Šumadija and the Morava valley regions of northern Serbia
(*upper inset of general map on page 8*)

'How often have I wished for you since my arrival here . . . You are an angel', wrote Madame Grujić to Lady Paget in September 1914 on hearing that she was bringing a relief unit to Serbia. The two women, the one the American wife of the Serbian secretary for foreign affairs, and the other the wife of the former British minister to Serbia, had already become friends in adversity when

57

they had worked together in a Belgrade army hospital during the 1912 Balkan War.

Mabel Grujić was one of many admirers of Lady Paget, who endeared herself to all those who knew her well. She was beautiful in a refined and elegant way, and was a person of enormous integrity, very just and humane, with a deep sense of service to mankind. Later, as the administrator of a large unit of the Serbian Relief Fund, she took a sincere personal interest in all her staff; and no duties were too arduous or unpleasant for her to undertake. She would never ask anyone to do what she would not do herself. This fastidious society woman and former ambassadress had the best attributes of a leader, the rarest being the devotion and respect she attracted from every one of her mixed staff of men and women. She never sought acclaim, and even invited disapprobation in some circles in London and elsewhere by her fair attitude towards the enemy at a time when emotions and war hysteria tended to cloud reason and objectivity. Paget is the family name of the Marquess of Anglesey with whom she was connected; she was born a Paget and had married a Paget, her cousin Sir Ralph, a career diplomat.

In mid-November 1914 Lady Paget's First Serbian Relief Fund Unit reached Skoplje in southern Serbia (today Macedonia), which was the main military and administrative centre of the region. Numerous hospitals overflowed with wounded men crowded into dirty, insanitary wards. After scrupulously cleaning and disinfecting the buildings allocated to the unit, Lady Paget found streams of wounded men, most of them stretcher cases, 'in a fearfully neglected and dirty condition and some were much exhausted. Many had not had their clothes off for months, and their wounds had not been dressed from nine to thirty days. Septic compound fractures had been encased in plaster or starch casings in the field and had not been touched since, with the result that the limbs were tensely swollen with pus . . . Nearly all cases suffering from frostbitten feet in some degree, and many had one or both feet gangrenous.'

The conditions were much the same as those in Kragujevac and Valjevo, and Lady Paget and her devoted staff had as grim a time as anyone throughout that bitter winter. In addition to the wounded they had cases of typhoid, dysentery, relapsing fever, tetanus and typhus. Despite all their efforts many of the men were beyond human aid and at first the death rate was very high. In this unit most of the surgeons were men, the chief medical officer being Professor J. T. J. Morrison, Professor of Forensic Medicine at the University of Birmingham. Between them the surgeons performed nearly 400 operations between December and February.

Since they had the only X-ray apparatus in working order in the country many patients were sent to them from other hospitals, an additional heavy burden in their overworked and exhausted state. As if this were not enough they had to organise an outpatients department to treat the numerous ailing civilians since no civic medical facilities existed in the town.

Because of this overwork and the constant exposure to infection an excessive amount of sickness occurred among the staff. Between November and February rarely more than 50 per cent were on duty at any given time. This dismal record reached its apex when typhus struck many down, including Lady Paget and Professor Morrison; then 90 per cent of the staff were out of action! This high rate of sickness was ascribed by Lady Paget to the presence of so much gangrene and sepsis in the wards. Mostly the staff suffered from serious septic throats. It was a septic throat, combined with Graves's disease, that caused the first death in the unit, that of the orderly, Miss Clarke, who died on Christmas Day 1914.,

Occurrences of typhus were sporadic until January 1915 when it began to assume alarming proportions; by the beginning of February there were over 400 cases in Skoplje. At that stage no precautions existed for isolating the cases; consequently it spread like wildfire through the barracks and hospitals and became an epidemic. The Serbs, accustomed to typhus in its endemic form, did not seem to realise the gravity of the situation, so Lady Paget saw that the British units at least must take the matter in hand if the epidemic was to be contained. With two of her doctors she met with three medical officers from a British Red Cross hospital in Skoplje and together they drew up a list of measures essential to combat the disease. One of the doctors was delegated to go to Niš to obtain authority from the Serbian government to set up a joint committee of Serbian and British representatives for the sanitary control of Skoplje. In principle every recommendation was agreed to but, said Lady Paget, 'The difficulty of getting things to move has been the greatest obstacle we have had to contend with all the winter.' She had come up against the immovable wall of Balkan bureaucracy. However, at least she managed to set up two isolation blocks on a hill about a mile outside the city, and this became known as the Typhus Colony.

At about this time Lady Paget had a severe shock when she inspected the stables where the Austrian prisoners were quartered. The conditions were appalling:

> At the entrance we had to step through pools of filthy water which collected in the holes of the mud floor, and all along the sides and down the middle wretched figures in foul old uniforms were huddled together on dirty straw. Many were lying hidden under greatcoats, some shuddering, some quite still. As we lifted the coats to look under we found six dead bodies in a single building and no one to carry them away. All the living were in a painful state of emaciation, those who had no real illness being faint with hunger, for in the demoralization wrought by the outbreak of typhus there was no one responsible for their regular feeding.

To man her typhus colony Lady Paget recruited those of the fitter Austrian prisoners who had already become immune by having had typhus. They worked well and efficiently. The unit could not have managed without them. Lady Paget always made a point of treating her Austrian orderlies with kindness and courtesy, though insisting on strict discipline, and paid warm tribute to their loyalty and diligence. Their inner misery and uncertainty moved her deeply, especially their agony of homesickness and the despair they suffered at having no contact with their families. At the same time she does not forget to pay tribute to the Serbs for their generosity regarding their wounded prisoners—no objection was ever raised against them being treated alongside their own wounded in the hospitals.

As Dr Berry had done, Lady Paget inveighed against the lack of notice about the arrival of patients. Repeatedly she begged the authorities to let them have twenty-four hours notice of the arrival of batches of more than 20 patients, especially typhus cases. Equally repeatedly this request was ignored. This perfectly legitimate requirement stemmed from the enormous work involved in preparing for admissions, especially in carrying out all the necessary disinfecting procedures. Once 60 cases arrived with three hours' notice; on another occasion 95 were suddenly dumped on them; and the most flagrant instance was when, with no previous notice whatsoever, 120 cases arrived one night.

One of their worst nightmares was maintaining the water supply. Often it was cut off without warning, sometimes for a few hours, sometimes for up to two days. This was a torture to both staff and patients; the patients became parched with the thirst of high fevers, and the staff were utterly dependent on water for cleaning, disinfecting and cooking. Lady Paget recalled those waterless days: 'Never shall I forget going round the wards from bed to bed, seeing the flushed, fevered faces and the dry, parched mouths, and hearing the incessant cry of "Water, sister! water!" from every corner of the room. It was heartrending, and enough to drive me mad, when we knew we had not a drop of water to give them.'

Lady Paget would then send the ambulance, laden with small vessels, to scour the town for water from somewhere; and they would buy oranges and lemons at outrageous prices, to cut them into quarters to give to the men to suck.

March 1915 was a disaster month for the unit. Between the 6th and the 24th sixteen of the staff went down with typhus including Lady Paget. When she fell ill, on the 8th, only two nurses were on their feet—Sisters Isherwood and Scott—and, on the 17th, Sister Isherwood began typhus. For forty-eight hours, with a temperature of 104°F, she treated herself as best she could since Sister Flora Scott was alone in charge of 300 patients. By then Lady Paget and Dr Knobel were unconscious. Flora Scott could have wept with relief when, on the 24th, four nurses of the Wimborne unit arrived to help them. However, despite all the danger and misery, not a single member of Lady Paget's unit died from typhus.

Sister Flora Scott, who had left her own private nursing home to come to Serbia, had arrived at the end of January at the height of the typhus epidemic. To everyone's relief she brought with her a couple of her own nurses. They were very welcome indeed to Lady Paget's ill and overworked staff. 'I'll never forget our arrival in Serbia'. Flora Scott said, 'it all seemed so strange. Wild and magnificent country, but the people seemed so poor and so ill-clad against the bitter cold. We reached Skoplje in the afternoon and Lady Paget was there to meet us. She looked very drawn and tired, but was most charming and kind, and obviously very relieved to see us. But when she took us to our quarters we had our first real shock—we were all to share one room whose furniture consisted of packing cases although there was an old-fashioned stove in the corner and heaps of wood.'

That first night was extremely uncomfortable. At one stage Flora got up to examine her bed which, superficially, looked perfectly normal, only to find planks instead of springs, straw instead of kapok in the thin mattress. But they soon learned to rough it, and to accept the situation, especially when they saw the desperate state of the patients and the dedication of Lady Paget, who went out of her way to help the newcomers settle in. Soon the initial discomforts were forgotten in the volume of work. They were so exhausted by the end of each day that they collapsed into deep sleep on their spartan beds, and were well cared for by Austrian batmen detailed to bring wood and hot water and to light their old tile stove.

But Flora Scott never forgot that time when she was quite alone, except for one Austrian orderly, in the typhus wards. With considerable trepidation, and much courage, she had volunteered together with Sister Isherwood to work with the typhus patients when most of the unit members were ill, some of them with typhus. Now Sister Isherwood had fallen ill and Flora Scott was quite alone: 'The suffering was past description. It was dreadful in the wards—naked men wandering about in various stages of delirium, and very hard to get them back into bed. It was a mad rush from the time one went on duty until one went off, too tired to think of one's own feelings.'

One of her perpetual anxieties was that someone would be taken to the mortuary before he was really dead. This fear was by no means unfounded. The coma state of typhus in weakened exhausted patients can resemble death, and the mortality rate being anyway so high, the hazard existed, and did happen, of people being buried alive. Flora Scott relates the following terrifying incident:

I knew a man who had been in a Serbian hospital in the town. He was so ill that they said he was dying. At 8 o'clock one night he was put into a coffin and taken to a shed. He recovered consciousness and managed to crawl out of the coffin, even

62

back to the ward. This was not an unknown occurrence in Serbia in those terrible days. To make sure it never happened in our hospital I arranged that the head orderly, an Austrian, go to the mortuary at 8 o'clock each morning to examine our dead, just to be sure.

'Our typhus colony', she wrote, 'was situated in one of the loveliest places on earth but I honestly could not conceive of any place more sad or sorrowful, and the only one comfort and happiness was the gratitude of those poor sufferers.'

Despite the grimness and tragedy around them they did have lighter moments. Food was always a source of anxiety. It was very basic and never enough, just bread, a little soup and rice; but Flora Scott tells of an enterprising means of supplementing the rations:

One poor soul, with gangrene feet and quite unable to move from his bed, handed me a warm new-laid egg each morning. We couldn't imagine where he got it from. One day the doctor came to examine the poor fellow, and when his bed clothes were turned back there lay a hen! His source of new-laid eggs! No-one seemed to find it particularly odd or terrible to have eggs laid in bed!

Language problems once caused a hilarious and embarrassing misunderstanding. One day a struggling patient was brought in, gesticulating and articulating wildly and obviously fiercely resisting admission. He was an extreme case but nevertheless the staff handled him kindly but firmly for, by now they were quite accustomed to handling newly arrived patients delirious, even violent, with pain and fever. At this particular moment the interpreter was absent so the nurses concluded that this excitable and babbling Serb must be suffering from extreme shell-shock, and was perhaps even mildly unhinged so, despite his obvious reluctance, they got him undressed and bathed. However, since he was behaving so oddly, Flora Scott put a close watch on him. Finally the interpreter arrived and, amid much shocked amusement on all sides, elicited from the spluttering, furious man that he was in fact a king's messenger who, in his haste to get an urgent dispatch to the general in command of the area, had come to the wrong building!

Though the foul conditions in Valjevo, Kragujevac and Skoplje were the rule, there was an exception—Vrnjačka Banja, the baše for several British relief missions including the British Red Cross and the already mentioned Berry unit, sometimes known as the 'Berry mission'. Its official name, hardly ever used, was the Anglo-Serbian Hospital. This unit had been aboard the transport ss *Dilwara*, on which Flora Scott and her nurses had sailed from England and, consisting of 26 members, including 5 doctors and 10 nurses, was jointly commanded by James Berry FRCS and his wife, Dr May Dickinson Berry, both from London's Royal Free Hospital.

Since the Berrys had known both Serbia and Madame Grujić before the war they promptly responded to her public appeal for medical aid. With the considerable help and blessings of the Royal Free Hospital they formed a medical unit. Generous voluntary contributions, £1,000 from the Serbian Relief Fund Committee, and ample material assistance from the British Red Cross enabled the unit to be equipped with all the necessary medical and hospital supplies. In mid-January 1915 they set forth.

On arrival in Serbia the Berrys paid a visit to Lady Paget in Skoplje, then travelled north to their destination, Vrnjačka Banja, midway between Kragujevac and Niš, then Serbia's provisional capital. From the beginning the unit was fortunate. Vrnjačka Banja, situated amid rugged highlands, is to Serbia what Vichy is to France, the country's fashionable spa. Even in those days the town was full of rest homes, sanatoria, pavilions, pump-rooms, cure clinics and large villas—all the utilities of a health resort.

By comparison with Kragujevac and Valjevo the town not only had many, well-equipped buildings suitable for conversion into hospitals and isolation wards but, above all, it had abundant water supplies, not the least being the hot mineral springs which proved invaluable for the extensive disinfecting procedures. When one recalls the chaotic water problems endured by Lady Paget's staff, and by other units elsewhere in Serbia, the relief teams in Vrnjačka Banja were truly blessed.

On the outskirts of the town the Berrys took over a large abandoned casino and pump-room, known as the 'Terapia', for their main hospital. It had a vast dining hall, several large rooms and balconies suitable for conversion into wards, and numerous smaller rooms, storage areas, bathrooms, and a limitless water supply. It even had a steam laundry, an electric light plant and, luxury of luxuries, central heating and modern toilets. '. . . it was as good a hospital building as could be found in Serbia, outside Belgrade itself.'

To cap it all two Austrian prisoners were efficiently supervising all this technical splendour: Adolf, a hydro-engineer from the famous Marienbad spa in Bohemia, and Stefan, a Hungarian, who was an electrician from Carlsbad. According to local legend, Vrnjačka Banja's Serbian engineer had joined the army and gone to the front with the express object of capturing two engineers for his spa; he went on capturing Austrians and asking if they were engineers until at last he caught Adolf and Stefan and brought them back for the Terapia's machine rooms!

When the typhus patients started pouring in, Dr Berry and his staff were well prepared. Near the Terapia he had had erected a large barn-like timber building, known locally as a 'baraque', which could house fifty patients. This was the isolation ward. A strict admission regime was enforced for washing, shaving and disinfecting the patients. From the beginning it was stressed that the elimination of the louse meant the elimination of typhus; thus, elaborate precautions were taken for both staff and patients. So thoroughly was this regime implemented that not one member of the Berry unit caught typhus, nor did the disease ever spread among the patients in the main hospital—a remarkable achievement.

Dr Berry later wrote: 'To the loyal co-operation of all our members—doctors, nurses, orderlies and Austrians, who worked energetically in performance of the same object—elimination of the louse—must be attributed the absence of any spread of the epidemic within our hospital.'

5

SPRING

Mrs St Clair Stobart arrived in Serbia with considerable panache. She and her unit, the Third Serbian Relief Fund Unit, docked at Salonika on 17 April 1915 and, without delay, entrained for Kragujevac. En route Mrs Stobart called on Lady Paget's unit at Skoplje, and was clearly impressed by what she saw. Lady Paget, still weak and tired, having only just recovered from typhus, makes a passing reference to this visit.

Before reaching Kragujevac Mrs Stobart stopped again, this time at Niš where, abandoning her unit at the station, she and her husband, the unit treasurer, were received in appropriate state by senior government officials, among them Madame Grujić's husband, the Under-Secretary for Foreign Affairs in Serbia, and Dr Subotić, President of the Serbian Red Cross. Mrs Stobart's stately progress through Serbia may have been regarded with mixed feelings by her staff, but it had the desired effect on the Serbian officials who received her as a visiting dignitary and acceded to her every request.

Finally the unit reached Kragujevac in lovely weather, warm with early spring sunshine; the beautiful countryside resounded with an endless chorus of bird-song—nightingales, larks, and the eternal cuckoos—which together served to make the war a remote and ugly paradox. Just outside the town, on a large open area that was formerly the racecourse, a site was chosen for the unit's extensive canvas hospital. Whether this site was the best choice was later disputed. The ground was flat and rather soggy, not sloping and well-drained, and it eventually transpired that the area had been the camping ground of countless refugees, many ill with various fevers, and their numerous livestock consisting of oxen, pigs, geese and chickens. For her vast hospital Mrs Stobart needed considerable uncluttered space and she was extremely experienced in those features important for a good site. The racecourse seemed ideal and the Serbs would hardly have bothered to inform her, even if they had been aware of the significance, of its former role as a crowded refugee encampment.

With the advent of warmer weather typhus was being contained, but the epidemic was not yet over, let alone its aftermath. Until controls were tightly imposed there always loomed the danger of a fresh outbreak. One of the few things Mrs Stobart feared was typhus, and she took extreme precautions to safeguard her unit and its patients from the disease. It was to help offset the risks that she had insisted on taking out a hospital under canvas. Within days of their arrival, a small town of over sixty tents mushroomed into being: one 'street' of tents for the staff, a wide avenue of ward marquees, and a connecting line of tents for offices, kitchens, X-ray and dispensary. Throughout, every assistance was given the unit by Colonel Dr Lazar Genčić, head of the Serbian Army Medical Service.

The safe transport and eventual unpacking of the unit's extensive equipment were feats of organisation. Apart from the tents there were 300 beds, with all the bedding and blankets; bales of clothes for the wounded and refugees; quantities of kitchen utensils including four fuel stoves and ovens; several portable boilers for hot water; large tanks for cold water; laundry materials; £300 worth of foodstuffs; comprehensive medical stores; all sanitary necessities including disinfectors, portable baths and latrines; and several motor ambulances.

Dr Mabel King-May, the Chief Medical Officer, had under her with this first contingent 6 doctors, 18 nurses and 16 orderlies. Apart from the women there were 8 men including John Greenhalgh, Mrs Stobart's husband, Percy Dearmer, the chaplain, a couple of interpreters and several drivers or orderlies. Later, when Mrs Stobart established her roadside dispensaries, another 41 women including 7 more doctors, would swell the unit to over 70, making it one of the largest relief units to serve in Serbia.

Everyone was delighted with the tents. They were lined, which made them warm in bad weather and pleasant in the heat when the flaps could be folded back to let in the breeze. A military regime was immediately implemented: breakfast at 6 am, lunch at 11.30 am, tea at 4 pm, supper at 6.30 pm, and lights out at 9 pm. There was a rota system for night duty for the nurses, doctors and orderlies, and a 24-hour watch. Miss Monica Stanley supervised the kitchens, Miss Winnie Wolseley the dispensary, the laundry came under Miss Lorna Johnson; Dr Isobel Tate took charge of the X-ray unit; the secretary was Miss Anne McGlade; and Mrs Mabel Dearmer looked after the linen. Mrs Stobart wondered whether she would regret her hasty, last-minute recruitment of Mrs Dearmer. How, she wondered, would this fashionable artistic woman cope with the discomforts and rigours of tent life under wartime conditions? She need not have worried. Mrs Dearmer carried out her assigned tasks impeccably. 'She never asserted herself as Mrs Dearmer but kept scrupulously to her new part—in a word she played the game.' Her husband, Dr Percy Dearmer, though formally attached to this unit was, in fact, the chaplain for all the Scottish Women's Hospitals and Serbian Relief Fund units in Serbia.

Finally, to inaugurate their arrival and installation, Crown Prince Alexander of Serbia called on the unit and wrote his generous praise in the visitors' book.

No sooner had they settled in than they were welcomed by the traditional *guslar*. The *guslar* is the wandering bard of Serbia. Accompanying himself on an archaic fiddle, or *gusle*, he is to be found at weddings and *Slavas*, or saints' days, singing the epic songs of Serbia's heroic past, improvising songs about current events, not forgetting the scandals and gossip of the day, and composing tributes to the guest of honour. By tradition he is blind and is led on his itinerant journeys by a small boy. His primitive instrument, mostly made from maple, with one string of horsehair and a short arched bow, produces a weird plaintive sound, eminently suitable as an accompaniment for the recitative nature of Serbian narrative ballads. During the centuries under the Turks, when the educated classes had been crushed or banished and very little literacy existed in the land, the *guslari* played an important role for keeping alive the traditions and history of their people and informing them of current events. It is not for nothing that they have been termed the oral newspapers and archives of the nation. Though today, with the advent of modern communications, especially the radio, the *guslari* have all but vanished, they still occasionally appear in remoter country districts for the local festivals.

In 1915 the *guslari* were still a common feature of Serbian provincial life, more especially since this was a time of great national crisis when there was much to report, much to sing about, and so much to remember: the Battle of Kosovo; Vidovdan; the

The retreat: *(above)* a column struggling across the flooded plains of Kosovo; *(below)* with an endless stream of ox-wagons the Serbs push on through the winter snows over the mountains towards the Adriatic

(above) The Third Serbian Relief Fund unit – the 'Stobart unit', 1915.
Left to right:
Front row: Miss Florence Maw (VAD), Miss Lorna Johnson (laundry), Miss Beatrice Kerr (Sanitary Inspector), Mr. John Greenhalgh (Hon. Treasurer), Miss Monica Stanley (chief cook), Miss Cissy Benjamin (chief orderly), Miss Anne McGlade (secretary);
second row: Dr. Mabel King-May (CMO), Dr. Catherine Payne, Dr. Edith Marsden, Mrs. St Clair Stobart (Administrator), Dr. King-May Atkinson, Dr. Isobel Tate, Dr. Beatrice Coxon;
third row: Mr. Vooitch (interpreter), Mrs. McGregor, Sister Lorna Ferris, Sister Dorothy Newhall, Sister Ellen Collins, Sister Ada Read, Miss Dorothy Brindley (cook), Sister E. V. Bury, Miss Minnie Wolseley (dispenser), Miss Hill (orderly), Mr. Beck (refugee clothing);
fourth row: Sister M. MacLaverty, Sister Jessie Kennedy, Sister Mary McGrow, Sister Alice Browne, Sister Katherine Lawless, Miss A. K. Burton, Miss D. M. Acton (cook), Miss Anna Beach;
back row: Mr. Agar (X-rays), Miss Fairy Warren, Miss E. M. Cargin, Sister Alice Leveson, Sister Jessie de Waasgindt, Sister Constance Willis, Sister Isabella Thompson, Miss Phyllis Shakespeare (cook), Miss Laura Bradshaw, Mr. Korobenikoff (dresser)

deeds of the Hajduks, the daring bands who roamed the countryside leading a guerilla war against the Turks; Kraljević Marko,
who slept in the hills, but would awake and leap on to his horse,
Šarac, to lead his people to safety at a time of great danger; and
other epic events in the country's stormy history. Also, it was
natural for a *guslar* to pay tribute to these strangers who had come
in friendship to Serbia in her hour of need. To the uninitiated the
guslar's renderings sound more like a long plaintive monotone
than singing, and the greater the tribute the longer the song.
Obviously the proud *guslar* meant to pay worthy tribute to these
exalted women by giving the entire account of his country's
sufferings and the song went on and on. Mrs Stobart grew restive
and slightly desperate: 'I thought he would never stop. I saw with
despair that he meant to carry his country safely into freedom
from Turkish tyranny and that meant another 500 years!' To her
dismay some Serb soldiers decided to make their contributions:
'One soldier after another chanted or sang in mournful monotone
the old poetic legends by which the tragic history of their country
has been transmitted from one generation to another.'

This lengthy recital was then followed by the requisite improvised songs in honour of the guests and a poem of gratitude to
the Stobart hospital. As always on these occasions it was beholden
upon the guests to make a gesture in return. Much to the delight
of the *guslari* and the Serbs, and to the embarrassment of Mrs
Stobart, the unit made a gallant effort. 'By contrast the song sung
by the unit as an interlude seemed commonplace.' It was
'Tipperary'!

From the outset very strict measures were enforced to keep
typhus at bay. On admission every patient was placed in a
mackintosh sheet, then stripped, his clothes labelled and put in the
disinfector. Then he was bathed, shaved, rubbed with paraffin,
wrapped in blankets and sent to the ward-tent where clean sheets
and pyjamas awaited him. The doctors and nurses who attended
suspect typhus patients were dressed in the regulation typhus
uniforms'.

These precautions paid dividends and the epidemic never
spread in the wards of Mrs Stobart's hospital. Another fear
was typhoid, which was also prevalent, and which Mrs Stobart
feared almost as much as typhus. She insisted on every possible
sanitary precaution; outside latrines were dug and kept disinfected

and drains kept clear, and water was always boiled before use. Mabel Dearmer was very impressed by her adminstrator's hygiene measures: 'The enormous precautions that are being taken lessen the risk considerably . . . Mrs Stobart is frightfully keen on coming out of this without losing one of us—she works day and night at her precautions. If the unit comes back whole it will be the first to do so. It would be *mean* to go and die and spoil its chance of winning such a reputation—wouldn't it?'

Meanwhile Dr Eleanor Soltau's plea from Kragujevac for fever nurses, and her concern for Valjevo, had not gone unheard. In May, soon after Mrs Stobart's unit had settled in, Dr Elsie Inglis and Mrs Evelina Haverfield, whom she had managed to lure from her ambulance corps in France, arrived in Kragujevac with an additional unit including fever nurses to relieve Dr Soltau's exhausted staff. By then spring had brought warm weather and with it respite from the worst of the privations. Dr Inglis was moved and impressed to see first-hand the gallant efforts of the first SWH unit under Dr Soltau. They had established three hospitals—one for surgical cases, one for typhus, and a third for relapsing fever, typhoid and other endemic diseases.

After Dr Inglis' arrival, the surgical hospital was put under Dr Lilian Chesney, a brilliant surgeon, a considerable martinet, and a most unconventional personality. Her astonished Serb patients stared agape at the tall doctor as she went on her rounds followed by her current pets, two geese and a small pig, which trailed in her wake wherever she went. She fed them on chocolate and red wine! Fortunately, by then food supplies were adequate, anyway most of the patients were too ill to be hungry, otherwise her menagerie might well have landed in the pot. Some of her subordinates occasionally hoped they would. But the Serbs loved it all. Dr Chesney was not the best chief since she tended to have her favourites, and made no secret of her dislike for what she called the 'socialites'—a rather unkind generalisation directed towards all those volunteers from the upper social strata, who had come out as VADs or orderlies. High on her black list was the Hon Mrs Evelina Haverfield, much to the dismay of Dr Inglis, who admired them both, being acutely aware of the valuable individual qualities both women possessed: Dr Chesney was the able and unconventional medical woman; Mrs Haverfield was courageous, gallant and totally selfless. Dr Inglis, continuously acting as mediator between the two, despaired of them ever allowing for each other's differences.

One of Dr Chesney's medical assistants, Elinor Rendel, wrote to her mother: 'Dr Chesney is a great character. She is extremely kind to people she likes and very rude to people she dislikes. Lucky for me she is very friendly to me!' On another occasion Elinor Rendel wrote: 'Dr Chesney is the one bright star in this company. She is very clever and amusing and kind but she has the devil of a temper and can be quite ruthless on occasions.' Dr Chesney used to startle the more staid members of her unit by donning a modish wig over her compulsorily cropped hair, for more dressy occasions.

Evelina Haverfield was impulsive, humane and very warm-hearted, always devastated by suffering, human or animal, and always in quest of a cause. Not only was she extremely sincere, but she had already established a reputation as a courageous fighter against any manner of injustice or cruelty towards man or beast. Her suffragette activities had landed her in prison and, during the Boer War, she had gone out to South Africa to rescue abandoned, injured cavalry horses from the battlefields and nursed them back to health. One of her five sisters was Dr Ella Scarlett Synge, who had caused a furore in England when, at the invitation of the International Red Cross, she had visited POW camps in Germany and reported that, contrary to popular image, they were quite adequate and conditions were reasonable.

Mrs Haverfield's private life was unhappy—her first marriage, to Major Haverfield, had been dissolved, and her second, to Colonel Blaguy, seemed to be no more successful. Mrs Carrington Wilde, a leading member of the London SWH Committee, in a letter about Mrs Haverfield, writes: 'Mrs Haverfield was impulsive, generous to a fault, not a great reader of character so an unfair advantage was often taken of her generosity. She was all fire and spirit and overtaxed her strength in every possible way. She denied herself the commonest necessities and did the hardest manual work in Serbia in order to save a few shillings for her work.' And Dr Isabel Emslie (later Lady Hutton) said of her: 'We all fell under the spell of her charm and radiant smile, and admired her beautiful face with its clear-cut small features, her slim figure and her spun-gold hair.'

So, together with Dr Inglis, these two very opposite personalities, Mrs Haverfield and Dr Chesney, had taken over the Kragujevac hospitals set up by Dr Soltau. Apart from Dr Chesney in the surgical hospital, Drs Janet McVea, Janet Laird and Catherine Corbett, an Australian, were in the typhus hospital; and the relapsing fever wards were under Dr Elizabeth Brooke.

Because of the herculean efforts of the pioneer units and relief workers during the winter in coping with the awful state of the hospitals, the neglected wounded and then typhus, those units which arrived from April onwards found the situation more or less under control. Typhus was being gradually eradicated, and some routine had been established with regard to the general hospital work of tending the wounded, and those patients suffering from any of a myriad illnesses. Most of the hospitals were now clean and sterilised and, though still overcrowded, they were now manageable. More equipment and medical supplies had eased the lot of the surgeons and nurses and, since there was so far no real resumption of hostilities apart from sporadic skirmishes, ox-wagons of wounded no longer streamed day and night into the hospitals. Even so, the wards were still over-full, and the variety of illnesses and injuries taxed the knowledge, ingenuity and medical skills of doctors and nurses alike. Apart from the numerous surgical cases, the wards were full of patients with dysentery, typhoid, tuberculosis, every imaginable lung complaint, tumours and skin diseases, and every fever in the book.

Apart from the Serbs many Austrian prisoners were patients. One of Dr Edith Hollway's pet patients, a mere boy, was blind, diagnosed as due to 'shell-shock', that term so widely used during World War I when it was genuinely believed that the excessive shock symptoms were due to the physical concussion of shell explosions and incessant bombardment at close quarters. Only much later did it emerge that they were the severe psychological symptoms of extreme stress and battle fatigue of men facing death every minute of the day and night for weeks, even months, on end. This Austrian boy, with kindness and attention, especially on the part of one of the nurses who spoke German, eventually recovered his sight.

The eradication of typhus that spring was due largely to the efforts of a team of RAMC doctors. At the beginning of April, in Niš, Sir Ralph Paget chaired a conference of the British units on typhus. Among those present was Captain Bennett from the British Red Cross in Vrnjačka Banja, Dr Barry from Lady Paget's

74

unit in Skoplje; Dr Helen Hanson, Dr Lilian Chesney and Dr Eleanor Soltau from the Scottish Women's Hospitals units; and a Colonel Hunter from the Royal Army Medical Corps. The latter, together with Lieutenant-Colonel Stammers and thirty doctors of the RAMC, had been sent out by Great Britain to the Serbian government who then entrusted them with the express job of combating typhus. As a result of this blanket order and the meeting in Niš, Colonel Hunter and Lieutenant-Colonel Stammers went to work vigorously and effectively.

First they made two recommendations, namely that the lines of infection between the troops and the rest of the country be broken, and that quarantine stations be established behind the lines. These were accepted by the Serbian authorities and, to help implement these measures, all army leave was cancelled and all railway communications stopped for two weeks. This precious interlude was used for a massive disinfecting programme.

Lacking any other containers, Lieutenant-Colonel Stammers ingeniously set up, at strategic points, wine barrels as disinfectors where clothes and blankets were treated. Any person suspected of being infected was received in special isolation centres and held there for fifteen days; notification of the disease, or any suspicion of it, was enforced at the risk of severe penalties for neglecting to do so.

Colonel Hunter and his staff applied draconian measures to the railways. Only wooden-seated third-class carriages were permitted; from the more luxurious first- and second-class carriages every shred of fabric and upholstery was ripped out and the bare wooden interiors scrubbed and disinfected *every day* for the fifteen days in order to exterminate the deadly lice. In all towns every restaurant, hotel or place of public entertainment was compelled to close for many hours each day so that the floors, furniture and walls could be scrubbed. Thus, typhus was brought under control so that by the end of spring the worst was over, and by the end of June no new typhus cases were to be found in the hospitals. Most important, the machinery had been set up should another epidemic break out in the wake of the next phase of the war which, everyone knew, was only a matter of time.

Inspired by Colonel Hunter's measures, and warmly encouraged by the Serbian medical authorities, Mrs Stobart proposed a chain of roadside dispensaries to help the country civilian population,

75

who were not only suffering terribly as a result of neglect and the winter privations, but were potential carriers of infection as they drifted into the towns from their remote hamlets and villages seeking medical help or begging medicines for their bedridden families at home.

Within a couple of weeks of the unit's arrival the first two roadside dispensaries were set up not far from Kragujevac. The response was immediate and overwhelming. People poured in with dysentery, diphtheria, typhoid, scarlet fever, tuberculosis, ulcers, cancer, gangrene and terrible skin infections. One girl walked twenty miles to get medicine for her entire family of five, all down with typhus. The word spread and more people came each day. Mrs Stobart sent Dr King-May to England to ask the SRF Committee for additional staff and funds to establish a ring of roadside dispensaries at 25-mile intervals.

Mrs Dearmer, most enthusiastic about this scheme, wrote: 'Dr May . . . is going to London to get funds and to explain the scheme. We have had more than 100 patients a day at the wayside dispensary—ill with typhus, scarlet fever, intermittent fever, and diphtheria. We are going to have six of these dispensaries, between here and Belgrade . . .'

Dr King-May's mission was a success and soon led to the arrival in Kragujevac of a further forty doctors and nurses to supplement the unit's staff and to man the dispensaries. In addition to the two earlier ones, Mrs Stobart eventually had dispensaries, each staffed by a doctor, a couple of nurses and an orderly, at Vitanovac, Očersa, Rekovac, Natalinci and Rudnik. These were invaluable to the country people. Each dispensary handled an average of nearly a hundred people a day, and often the doctors and nurses, using their ox-wagon ambulances, went to humble peasant homes to attend the bedridden as best they could. This humane and imaginative medical aid to the neglected village people, initiated by Mrs Stobart, was her most valuable contribution to the Serbian nation.

The London committee's response to Dr Soltau's concern over stricken Valjevo, which had borne the brunt of the typhus epidemic, had been to send out a unit under Dr Alice Hutchison. As we have seen, she had arrived in Valjevo in June 1915 to set up another fine hospital under canvas. By then Valjevo had emerged from its terrible ordeal; in fact one hospital in the town was able to cope with the residue of typhus cases. Soon Alice Hutchison met the gallant Flora Sandes and Emily Simmonds, both exhausted after their harrowing winter in Valjevo, and weakened by their own illnesses from typhus. Since the fierce pressure had eased, and there was still no sign of the expected enemy offensive, Dr Hutchison urged the two girls to leave Serbia for a couple of months' well-earned rest and recuperation in England.

Valjevo may have got through its typhus epidemic, but it had done so at great cost to the Serbian medical staff of whom many had died, and to the civilian population who had been completely neglected. Again there was the familiar backlog of illness and suffering awaiting urgent attention, one being the prevalence of scurvy because of the winter malnutrition. Dr Hutchison's splendid hospital was a boon to the town as the doctors and nurses turned their expert attention to the ailing, malnourished townspeople.

Alice Hutchison sparkled with fun and knew that a happy unit was an efficient one. 'We have started a camp journal, and a bugle, and I intend to organise fortnightly entertainments whenever the work allows it. It's a grand thing to keep people happy, and I should like the thing to be a success.' Of this there was little doubt. Alice Hutchison was an excellent CMO, liked and respected by everyone. She was incapable of pomposity, of standing on her dignity, and had the wit to laugh at herself.

On the morning after their first night under canvas a small unidentified army 'plane caused a stir' and Alice Hutchison wittily describes the undignified collapse of their sangfroid: 'As it was wheeling and curving over our heads I tried to continue a conversation with the carpenter, till the carpenter began to move downhill, and finally followed by the chief medical officer, the cook with a kitchen ladle in her hand, the sanitary inspector with her broom, and all the other members of the unit. John Gilpin's flight was mild compared to ours.'

One of Dr Hutchison's constant delights was the friendship between one of her few male orderlies, McAllan a Scot, and a Hungarian prisoner, one speaking 'broad Scottish', the other 'an incomprehensible muddle of German', and both understanding each other perfectly. 'McAllan is really a treat and has become absolutely indispensible to me. His favourite axiom is that broad Scotch is the best means of making oneself understood in Serbia!'

Further south, Kathleen Dillon and Elsie Corbett had reached their destination after their 'luxury' cruise from England to Salonika in Sir Thomas Lipton's yacht *Erin*. Their good fortune had continued when they were detailed to join the British Red Cross unit stationed near the Berrys' hospital, the Terapia, at the relatively luxurious Vrnjačka Banja (sometimes called Vrnce, or Vrntse, for short). They arrived on 24 May 1915. After Sir Thomas's harrowing tales of the winter experiences of the earlier units, Kathleen and Elsie were agreeably surprised to find a charming spa in beautiful surroundings, reasonable living quarters where the two girls shared a room with a balcony in a pleasant villa, the Šumadija, a colourful peasant market, and even a few shops. Opposite their villa stood the hospital, the Slatibor, in a lovely garden. It was well equipped with seventy beds and a fine operating theatre.

Though very few typhus cases remained, many patients were suffering from post-typhus complications. But Kathleen and Elsie were mostly detailed to look after women and children with diphtheria, typhoid, scarlet fever and various forms of tuberculosis. They were immediately plunged into work, much of it sad and grim, especially tracheotomies on children suffering from diphtheria. But the two VADs, each an assistant to a nursing sister, gritted their teeth and worked furiously and devotedly. Once a small boy was brought in covered with blood and surrounded by the whole family shrieking with despair. Apparently he had accidentally shot himself in the leg – 'a not unusual occurrence', Elsie commented, 'in a country where everybody seemed to carry a firearm.' In this instance the boy was not badly wounded and soon recovered.

Terrible injuries to children were commonplace, caused by their playing with dangerous war toys such as discarded unexploded hand-grenades, 'dud' shells that suddenly came alive, clips of ammunition found in the grass, in deserted trenches, or by the wayside. The high incidence of children with their hands or feet blown off led both Dr Inglis and Elsie Corbett to comment that the wartime atrocity stories from Belgium and Serbia, alleging that the enemy had deliberately maimed children, arose because of war hysteria and over-emotional conclusions drawn from the distressing sight of children with dreadful hand or leg injuries. In reality these unfortunate youngsters were the victims of their unwitting games with the deadly refuse of war.

Elsie and Kathleen were fortunate in their matron, Miss Cal-well, well past middle-age, but a lively independent personality. Not only was she a fully qualified and experienced nurse, she was also a most cultivated woman who had travelled widely and spoke several languages, including German. Yeats and Lady Gregory had been friends of hers, and in London she had moved constantly in the leading literary circles. To relax, she loved to read German poetry aloud in her beautiful voice 'even though German was not the most popular language at the time'. One of her idiosyncracies was her steadfast refusal to believe in the existence of germs. But it did not seem to matter greatly since, Elsie claimed, 'under her compelling eye the most daring microbes fled, and nobody caught anything.'

Occasionally the three of them, Elsie, Kathleen and Matron, managed to escape a while into the lovely Šumadija countryside. In the valleys and up the hillsides they would explore the beech woods and pick magnificent wild strawberries and armfuls of wild flowers to relieve the sad monotony of the hospital wards. Once they went to a musical party given by their neighbours, the Berry unit, in the Terapia. To their utter delight they found English tea, cakes, even scones. Jan Gordon, an artist-engineer with the Berrys and his wife Cora, played and sang to the banjo; one of the nursing sisters turned out to be a very competent violinist; and a Serbian officer sang national folk songs.

By July, typhus had vanished and very few wounded were coming in. For the first time since their arrival the various units could find a little spare time, respite to breathe, and to look around and absorb something of the beautiful country they had all entered so precipitately with no immediate aim in mind but that of alleviating suffering. In that idyllic countryside war seemed so unreal that some began to be lulled into the belief that the Central Powers would not attack again. But the Serbs knew that their moment of truth would come—they just prayed that it would not be a winter war.

As spring faded into summer disaster struck the Stobart unit. Despite every possible precaution and the scrupulous boiling of milk and water, a typhoid epidemic broke out among the staff. Seventeen unit members, including Mrs Stobart, went down with it. Repeatedly the camp had been pronounced a model of outdoor sanitation by the local authorities, the British Red Cross and

RAMC experts, and medical visitors, but now some recalled their silent doubts about the choice of the racecourse and its previous role as a refugee camp.

Soon after Mrs Stobart fell ill Mrs Dearmer wrote to a friend about the sickness in the unit, which at first was feared to be typhus: 'If I get it, will you always remember that I am *very* strong with a terrific constitution, and most tremendously alive and well from my life in the open, so there is every chance of my pulling through.'

Suddenly, on 4 July, the unit was shocked to learn that one of the most popular nurses, Sister Lorna Ferris, had died. 'Why, only yesterday I passed by her tent and she gave me a cheery wave', said one of the VADs in shocked disbelief. Lorna Ferris, a healthy, strong 25-year-old, and an excellent linguist who had already mastered the rudiments of Serbian, was to have returned home to be married in September. But that night during a ferocious storm she had a relapse, haemorrhaged and died despite all the devoted efforts of her medical colleagues. 'Fortunately', wrote Dr Helen Hanson, 'she came with full parental approval, her mother believing girls should do as much for the nation as boys.'

Lorna Ferris was accorded a full military funeral, led by a Serb officer carrying a large cross on which her name was inscribed. The hearse, drawn by a pair of bay horses, was stacked with magnificent wreaths. Finally, in the Serbian Orthodox Church an Anglican service was held by special permission of the Archbishop of Belgrade.

Exactly one week later, on 11 July, the unit was shattered by a second death in their midst, that of Mabel Dearmer. Some weeks earlier she had gone down with typhoid but had seemed to combat her illness fairly well. And, since she had been inoculated at Malta against typhoid, no one worried, least of all Mrs Dearmer herself. But by 9 July she became desperately ill with a combination of typhoid and double pneumonia. Five of the unit doctors tended her and every twenty minutes she was given oxygen. 'It would be terrible if anything happened to her', Monica Stanley wrote that night in her diary, 'she is so nice and we are all so fond of her.'

But at dawn on 11 July Mabel Dearmer's strength gave out and her heart failed. That same day she was buried next to Lorna Ferris, with full honours and all the pomp and circumstance of a funeral stage-managed by the Serbian Orthodox Church. The

Serbian government sent magnificent wreaths, and the silver-coloured coffin was draped with the Union Jack. Government officials, French, Serbian and British officers, many people from other units, and even a representative from the royal household, all joined in a moving and memorable farewell to Mabel Dearmer, the beautiful author and children's dramatist who had given it all up to serve as a simple orderly with a relief unit in Serbia. A military band led the cortège and Serbo-Orthodox priests in their splendid Byzantine raiments conducted an impressive service in the cathedral. A French officer paid tribute to her from the cathedral steps: 'Elle était un soldat sans peur et sans reproche, qui est tombé avec la noblesse d'un soldat.'

After the funeral Dr Marsden and Dr Atkinson took the bereaved Percy Dearmer away from Kragujevac to help him prepare for his immediate return to England. He left Serbia two days later on 13 July. Three months later, on 6 October, his younger son Christopher fell at Sulva Bay in Gallipoli.

6

THE LONG, QUIET SUMMER

By mid-summer of 1915 pressure had eased sufficiently for some of the unit members to go home on well-earned leave after the gruelling winter, while others left for good. Dr Frances Wakefield, for instance, still weakened by her serious bout of typhus, decided not to renew her contract for further work in Serbia, but went to Egypt where, once she had recuperated, she was to pursue her wartime career.

Replacements came out and the hospitals were operating normally. Many army patients had been transferred to Serbian military hospitals and convalescent centres, and civilian patients now filled the vacated beds or sought medical care at the out-patients' and the roadside dispensaries. It was now possible for the staff to take fairly regular time off, even to go away for the occasional weekend. Recreation and conventional entertainment possibilities were few, but these enterprising women were quite able to amuse themselves. They called on their friends in the other units in the various centres, they explored the countryside, went walking, even riding sometimes, and did occasional shopping. 'The shops are quite nice and the shoes and clothes quaint. Singer's sewing machines are seen everywhere; also Sunlight soap, Colman's mustard, Peak Frean's biscuits, Peter's milk chocolate. These things remind me of home.'

It is somewhat astonishing to learn that, in the provinces of war-torn, fever-ridden Serbia, a nurse could find Sunlight soap and Peak Frean's biscuits!

Despite these unexpected finds in the shops of Kragujevac, ordinary shopping was not a very rewarding pastime. Goods were scarce and prices high. But picturesque markets, with gypsies and peasants in their colourful costumes, were—and still are—the traditional centres of all Serbian provincial towns and villages. Here one finds all the usual country produce: vegetables, fruit, eggs, cheese (including *kajmak*, a delicious creamy local cheese like slightly sour Devonshire cream), materials, handicrafts and all manner of livestock. 'Today I bought one sheep, some beef, five ducks, six kilos of sausages, 200 eggs, some carrots and peas. The sheep I gave 20 dinars for, and as 35 dinars go to the £1 it is not much. Ducks vary from 1½ to 3 dinars. Eggs were 9 dinars a hundred and very good.' Thus, Monica Stanley, the chief cook of the Stobart unit, reported on one of her marketing expeditions. The fact that farm produce was again reasonably plentiful was due to the good weather that undisturbed summer and, above all, to those who were left in the villages—the women, children and men too old to be in the army, who had gone on with the sacred ritual of tilling their soil and growing their produce as they had done through all the crises of their country's history.

Oxen are the main beasts of burden in Serbia, especially as draft animals. Mrs Stobart had two—'Derry' and 'Toms', so named because the London store had donated the unit two farm carts which had been brought out from England. But Dr Inglis nearly ran into legal difficulties with her yoke of oxen. One of her unit christened them 'Huz' and 'Buz', only to find they had contravened the law. 'Such a funny thing,' Dr Inglis later recalled, 'we had to sign a special Act to have them called Huz and Buz! It seems their Serbian names were something else, and you cannot alter an ox's name without an Act. I laughed till I cried.' Dr Chesney did her best to explain to some bewildered Serbs that the names came from Biblical characters and were very respectable. Later when the government lent the unit another yoke of oxen and Dr Chesney promptly called them 'Gog' and 'Magog', Dr Inglis protested fervently: 'those must be strictly pet names, for I am not going to sign Acts for altering the names of Government oxen.'

Lilian Chesney had decided that it was time to provide light relief from the gloom of the hospital wards and to organise an international get-together for convalescent patients, unit staff and visitors. She put on a gymkhana. There wasn't a horse in sight, but there was everything else from the playgrounds of Britain: egg-and-spoon races, sack races, obstacle races and musical chairs. It was a riotous success from the word go. Everyone enjoyed themselves hugely, above all the Serbs. Needless to say Lilian Chesney's lively compering did much to contribute to the general enjoyment. One of her more original events was a stretcher race for the Austrian orderlies, but rather reluctantly she had to concede to Dr Inglis' insistence that it was 'distinctly safer to have a well man in the stretcher.' Very successful, and good for morale, was a crutch race. There were many participants. And everyone hooted and cheered as the nurses competed in a needle-threading race—it is extremely difficult to thread a needle while weeping with laughter and being egged on by a crowd of lively, noisy Serbs. British, Turks, Hungarians, Austrians and Serbs all played together, roaring with laughter, and delighted with their simple prizes, mostly tobacco and cigarettes. Everyone won something.

It was a happy day. Later someone asked why they had not thought to invite the crown prince. 'Of course we never thought of soaring so high', said Dr Inglis. But she regretted this oversight: 'I wish I had thought of it for then the Crown Prince would have noticed the awful smell in our yard, and perhaps something would have been done.'

The Sunday following the gymkhana Dr Inglis, Dr Chesney and other unit members went over to the Stobart unit for a church service. Just as they arrived a violent storm struck the camp. Chaos reigned. Seventeen tents collapsed. At one corner all the patients were found sitting on the tent fly, which saved the tent; elsewhere a man on crutches was hurled out of his tent, got entangled with his crutches and the guy ropes, and sat down in a heap; yet the cooks cooked on in unperturbed control—the fire was still alight and the evening meal was being prepared even though all the tents and storeroom had collapsed or were flooded. Mrs Stobart took this disaster in good part and joined in the laughter once it was clear that no one was hurt.

The most popular place for the odd free day or weekend was clearly Vrnjačka Banja, with its comparative luxury. Both the Berry unit and the British Red Cross hospital were kindly hosts to members of other units, and the Berrys would often put on a modest concert, their star-turn being the Gordon couple, Jan and Cora, with their considerable repertoire of folk songs in all languages. Sometimes loftier cultural heights were attempted when, for example, the Niš symphony orchestra came to give a concert, or when the local playhouse put on a theatrical performance; but the latter were a little much for the non-Serbian speakers and it was noticed once that the unit chief, Dr Berry, was obviously 'struggling with sleep rather than improving his knowledge of the Serbian tongue'. But the prompter fascinated the British audience; he sat in a box in front of the stage, repeating every word of every part in a very loud voice.

For their part the Berrys often enjoyed the hospitality of the other units, often going to visit Mrs Stobart, and were full of praise for her fine camp—'the sanitary arrangements of this camp are especially worthy of mention'; and several times they stayed with Dr Inglis at her hospital in Kragujevac.

But walking and country picnics remained the most popular recreations or, for some, riding, when they could get horses from the nearby cavalry remount. Dr Berry often rode, but he got rather fed up with wayside strangers stopping him and insisting on his immediate diagnosis for their real or imaginary complaints. Barring his way they would 'reduce themselves to an embarrassing state of nudity by the wayside' before they were persuaded that they should come to the Terapia for consultation.

For Kathleen Dillon, a keen huntswoman at home, and Elsie Corbett, it was a special event when they sometimes managed to borrow horses and ride off into the lovely hills behind Vrnjačka Banja, with a simple picnic which they would enjoy in peace by the side of one of the many small clear streams.

Picnic forays sometimes took the women to the beautiful coronation church and monastery of Žiča just outside Kraljevo, the town of the kings, where they would admire the superb frescoes recalling the glories of mediaeval Serbian kings Stefan Nemanja and Dušan; or they went to Ljubostina monastery, hidden away in a narrow valley north of Trstenik. This monastery, founded in 1387 by Milica, the wife of Tsar Lazar who fell at the Battle of Kosovo, was for women. In their quiet retreat they wove lovely carpets on their looms, produced superb wines, farmed their rich lands and tended their forests. An immediate bond was established between the serene nuns of Ljubostina and the women of the units. In the main, the women used the ox-wagons for their more ambitious excursions: 'You would be surprised how comfortable one can make them by stuffing the hard corners with blankets and straw. And one could do a steady twelve miles a day, but we seldom went half that distance.'

Not to be overshadowed by Dr Chesney's imaginative efforts, Dr Hutchison's unit staged a costume ball, and invited the chief of the French mission to judge the costumes. *Serbian Outpost* reported at length on this event: 'Gone were the demure white-capped

85

ministering angels . . . In their place paraded the bold figure of Britannia, glittering in scarlet and gold; Italy, France and Belgium in their national dress, nuns, queens, suffragettes, peasants and clowns.' They played their roles; someone produced some musical instruments and the ball got into full swing. Later, to the strains of a military band borrowed from the obliging Serbs, the Allies— British, Serb, French and Russian—'sealed the Entente with dance and song.' How did the staff make their costumes? Nobody was sure, only mildly suspicious. 'Is it possible', asks *Serbian Outpost*'s editor, 'that the store-room key is not in quite such safe-keeping as some of us hoped? Some secrets are best left unresolved.'

After this success Alice Hutchison instituted the custom of having regular evening 'At homes' which were very popular. Each one was different. For example, on one occasion the Sisters, using an amateur stage and a makeshift but functioning curtain, put on a series of tableaux, depicting various scenes—serious, satirical and comic—from hospital life, the frailties and foibles of the staff and from Britain herself. One of the most effective in colour and grouping was that of Great Britain and her colonies. Once again amazement was expressed at the gorgeous raiment displayed and at the ingenuity by which a king's robes were evolved from bedcovers, and a queen's garments from a hearth-rug. These events frequently ended with the Serbian national dance, the *kola*, 'to the melancholy music of a gipsy violin under the light of the moon.'

The unit was also very proud of its bugle and the nurse who had mastered it. She had bought it in Malta and learned to blow it there: 'Rumour—scurrilous hag—attributes that proficiency to hours stealthily spent with khaki-clad instructors in the catacombs of Malta.'

That flirtations and even discreet affairs took place between the Serbs, or the British and French officers when they had the chance, and unit members was obvious and natural. Passing hints refer to them, but loyalty to one another and discretion were sacrosanct; discipline, though by no means authoritarian, was strict, and the sense of duty deep. Their work came first. Many were lively, attractive young women, and the Serbs were often fascinated by them. A number of the women did eventually marry Serbs, return-ing to Serbia after the war to live full and happy lives, adapting easily to the country they had grown to love during their wartime service.

(above) Am ambulance driver from the transport column attached to the SWH
America Unit at Ostrovo changes a tyre, helped by a British soldier

(below) An Australian nurse from the SWH America Unit at Ostrovo labels her
water can appropriately!

(*above*) Serbian soldiers carrying a wounded comrade in an improvised litter down to the field dressing station; (*below*) RAMC mule 'travoy' for carrying the wounded in Macedonia

A much sought-after excursion was that to Belgrade. Though earlier it had been extremely difficult to obtain the necessary authorisation, by mid-summer it was easier. Many of the women visited the Serbian capital to see for themselves the enemy lines across the river. Built on hills rising out of the plains, and above the two great rivers, the Danube and the Sava, Belgrade commands an imposing position—excellent for the days of medieval defence, walled up behind the formidable Kalemegdan fortress, but vulnerable in modern warfare, especially to aerial bombardment. The doctors and nurses were appalled at the damage done by even sporadic bombing and shelling. Though they found Belgrade an attractive city, and were glad to greet their friends in the British Fever Hospital, they were pleased to return to the familiar surroundings of the Šumadija highlands, even though they, too, were now subject to sudden air attacks, especially at Kragujevac. Bombs were dropped several times, and once the Stobart unit was hit. Though no one was killed, a number of patients who could not be moved to safety in time were injured, and the entire marmalade stocks were wiped out! As the summer wore on the attacks grew more frequent, and the French pilots would often go up to intercept the Austrians, once shooting a 'plane down practically on top of the Berrys' Terapia at Vrnjačka Banja. It crashed on their stores and did considerable damage.

Belgrade, only about fifty miles north of Kragujevac, seemed another world, with the Austro-Hungarian frontier of that time just across the rivers. In charge of the city's defence was a small International Force that included a British contingent of ninety men, all under the command of Vice-Admiral Troubridge. The British share of the force had four 2-gun batteries, manned by Serbian artillerymen, under Lieutenant-Commander Kerr RN, who was also the proud possessor of a tiny boat, not much bigger than a small river tug, rigged up with a home-made torpedo tube and a machine-gun. The first time they fired their torpedo the recoil capsized the boat! Fortunately everyone survived this misadventure, but they were more careful next time to place their torpedo in such a way that the mishap was not repeated. This ferocious little vessel, aptly called the *Terror of the Danube*, or simply *The Terror*, was responsible for sinking two much larger Austrian patrol boats and for keeping the main enemy river fleet penned up behind Zemun, a small Austrian port at the confluence of the

Danube and Sava rivers. While the British were in charge of these river operations, the French contingent took to the skies. They had a small group of daring aviators, including the famous air ace of the day, Paulhan, who before the war had won the coveted *Daily Mail* air trophy, and had already shot down three Austrian 'planes. These few fliers soon established their air superiority, often covering Lieutenant-Commander Kerr in his dashing operations with *The Terror*. One of the express objects of the International Force was to make it as difficult as possible for the enemy to cross the river, a task it carried out most efficiently though it was obviously in no position to withstand a massed enemy invasion.

The British Fever Hospital in Belgrade also came under Vice-Admiral Troubridge. Beautifully equipped, this fine hospital was generous in aiding the various British relief units, especially in admitting those staff members seriously ill with typhus. Two other British relief units were in Belgrade: the Young Farmers', so named because Britain's farming community had raised the funds; and the Wounded Allies unit. Both were sponsored by the Serbian Relief Fund Committee.

Bursting with energy and enthusiasm, and taking advantage of the lovely weather, Dr Elsie Inglis dashed around Serbia visiting the various Scottish Women's Hospitals medical centres, consulting with the other unit doctors and administrators, planning further field hospitals, conferring with the Serbian authorities, writing reports and lively letters back to London and Edinburgh which were frequently punctuated with 'please remember the Censor has not seen this', thus begging discretion from her recipients. She was enjoying every fulfilling minute of the lovely summer.

Mindful of the perpetual threat of epidemics, especially typhus, typhoid and dysentery, Elsie Inglis never lost an opportunity to prod the local authorities gently regarding the importance of civic hygiene, especially uncontaminated water supplies. She had been appalled at the open drains and inadequate and unprotected domestic water sources in the provincial towns. Because of her innate courtesy and warmth the Serbs loved her, and were far too wise to resent her gentle insistence on basic precautions regarding hygiene and drinking water. There just had been no time during the past disrupted years to look after these basic civil services.

After consultations with the Serb medical authorities and with Colonel Hunter of the RAMC, Dr Inglis persuaded the London committee to equip two more SWH units. One was stationed at Mladenovac, with a field hospital of 300 beds under Dr Beatrice McGregor, who soon had patients coming in at an average of twenty a day with pneumonia, typhoid and dysentery. The other unit, under Dr Edith Hollway, was sent to Lazarevac. Meanwhile, at a meeting with the heads of the various British units and General Subić, of the Serbian Red Cross and the head of the Army Medical Services, Colonel Genčić categorically dispelled any uncertainties about sending out more personnel and supplies: 'Your people must not be misled by the temporary suspension of hostilities, this phase is merely the lull before the storm.' He then went on to request that no one leave and that additional and supplementary personnel should come out to Serbia at once. This meeting dispelled any doubts that some may have had about the value of staying on.

With the four SWH field hospitals at Kragujevac, Valjevo, Lazarevac and Mladenovac; the two large SRF units at Kragujevac and Skoplje; the Berry unit and the British Red Cross hospital at Vrnjačka Banja; the second British Red Cross hospital at Skoplje; the large British Fever Hospital, chiefly for allied military personnel, in Belgrade; and several smaller units; over 600 British women doctors, nurses, VADs and orderlies were in Serbia that summer. And this does not include numerous independent medical women and relief workers, who came out on their own initiative and were attached to Serbian hospitals and relief organisations, such as Madame Christitch's unit at Valjevo. At one time fifty British women doctors were working in the country. Mrs Stobart's SRF unit alone had fourteen.

Apart from the British units there was a large Russian hospital at Kragujevac, a couple of American ones, and a large French medical mission. Much consultation took place between all the foreign hospital personnel who often helped each other in times of crisis. For example Dr Hutchison had lent the French mission hospital one of her surgeons and a couple of nurses; Dr Inglis once sent some medical staff down to Skoplje to help Lady Paget; and Dr Helen Hanson, when most of her colleagues from Dr Soltau's first unit in Serbia returned to England, stayed on to join Mrs Stobart when she was setting up her roadside dispensaries.

As the 1915 summer drew to its close the inhabitants of Mladenovac paid an extraordinary tribute to Dr Inglis and her SWH units. The townspeople had taken to heart her persistent propaganda for safe drinking-water facilities and had built a beautiful fountain, dedicating it to her and the SWH. The inscription, first in English, then in Serbian, reads:

IN MEMORY

of

THE SCOTTISH WOMEN'S HOSPITALS

IN SERBIA

AND THEIR FOUNDER DR. ELSIE INGLIS

1915

The dedication ceremony took place early in September. Everybody was present, all British units being represented by as many people as could be spared from their duties, including Mrs Evelina Haverfield, Dr Hutchison and the Berrys, and Serbian officials including Colonel Genčić who had come up from Kragujevac. The 1st British Field Ambulance Corps came, as did about twenty Serbian officers representing the cavalry, infantry and artillery, and all the local Mladenovac dignitaries—the mayor, the architect who designed the fountain and the engineers who built it. Five Serbo-Orthodox priests conducted the dedication ceremony at a table covered with a white cloth on which were a silver crucifix, a bowl of water, a tall lighted candle and two bunches of basil, one fresh and one dried. The British contingent were lined up on the right, the Serbs on the left.

After an impressive and moving little ceremony, speeches were made extolling the virtues of the SWH in general and of Dr Inglis in particular. All the British units were the recipients of generous praise and thanks. The Mladenovac mayor ended by saying that Serbia was not a rich country and could not do big things, but that they had 'done this little thing to show they were grateful, and to keep the name of the Hospitals for ever in the countryside, so that the peasants would always remember.'*

* This fountain is still to be found in Mladenovac, but badly in need of renovation. Mladenovac, now a large provincial centre, is very different to the quiet agricultural town of sixty years ago. The fountain stands in a grassy, shaded hollow, but it is neglected—it would be a pity if it were also forgotten.

But to the south in Skoplje Lady Paget was not having a particularly pleasant summer. She and her staff had been in Serbia since October 1914—longer than any other unit. The winter of 1914-15 had been very hard on them with so many wounded, the typhus epidemic and finally, in spring, the multitudes of sick civilians. And the unit staff had suffered badly from illness, many of them with typhus.

There was a certain amount of disquietude among her staff, who by mid-summer felt they were not really needed, some even wondering if the unit should not disband and all return to England to offer their services where they might be more useful. But Lady Paget convinced the waverers of the certainty that the hour would come when they would be desperately needed. Without exception they were prepared to remain providing they would be engaged in useful work, and all acknowledged that it would be a tremendous shame to dismantle their magnificent hospital with its laundries, workshops, and outbuildings filled with every kind of equipment and stores. In addition Lady Paget was fortunate in having won the co-operation and confidence of General Popović, the civil and military governor of Skoplje, a humane and liberal man who took advantage of the presence of the British hospitals to inaugurate a higher standard of sanitation and medical care for his people.

Many of those in the unit, including Lady Paget, did however take some leave in England, but Lady Paget had not been back in Serbia for long when she had a severe personal blow. She lost her cousin, the Hon Richard Chichester, who was very dear to her. The son of Lord and Lady Templemore, he had come out with Lady Paget's SRF unit to act as secretary. At the beginning of August he went down with typhoid and died three weeks later in Belgrade.

While the summer of 1915 drifted by in the Balkans, the statesmen of both sides planned their moves. The military and strategic ramifications were becoming more varied and the permutations more complex. The chief targets for their deliberations were Bulgaria, Greece and, to a lesser extent Turkey, who had entered into the conflict in October 1914 on the side of the Central Powers.

But Turkey's first campaign, in the Causasus against Russia, was a disaster. An ill-equipped army of nearly 100,000 men was dispatched to the Caucasus in winter. Russian resistance, inadequate winter clothing, the ferocious cold and typhus, practically annihilated the Turkish army whose few survivors staggered home in a pitiful condition. Since that debacle the Turks had shown little inclination to resume action beyond their frontiers. Besides, they were preoccupied by the heroic but so-far frustrated attempts of the British to take the Dardanelles. And, since Serbia had not collapsed in the first phase of the war, there was no direct way for Germany to get military supplies through to her ally.

Thus the Serbs were not at the moment unduly anxious about the Turks. Their chief concern was their immediate neighbour, Bulgaria. The Bulgarians, under King Ferdinand, a German, harboured bitter resentment towards both the Serbs and the Greeks for the outcome of the second Balkan War in 1913. Bulgaria had been severely defeated in that harsh one-month conflict, which had been followed by the Treaty of Bucharest by which Bulgaria had been divested of almost all her recent territorial gains resulting from the 1912 defeat of Turkey. Above all, the division of most of the Macedonian spoils of war between Serbia and Greece rankled most deeply. Macedonia, with the important city of Skoplje, the ancient Slav religious and cultural capital Ohrid, and the port of Salonika, had been contested by all the Balkan countries, and now Bulgaria had only a small corner of it. Thus Serbia had good reasons for her conviction that Bulgaria's neutrality was a sham and that she would align herself with the Central Powers the moment it was propitious for her to do so.

Greece was divided on the issue. King Constantine, another German ruler, and brother-in-law of Germany's Kaiser Wilhelm, opted for the Central Powers who, he was convinced—and hoped —would win the war. But Venizelos, the brilliant and popular Prime Minister, firmly backed by the people, supported the Allies.

Earlier the Greeks, fearing a Bulgarian attempt on Salonika, had made a secret pact with Serbia whereby both countries would support each other for the possession of Salonika and Monastir, respectively. Should the Bulgarians attempt to invade the territory claimed by either Serbia or Greece, the two countries agreed to act together against the aggressor. This was the Serbo-Greek pact that the Serbs were banking on should the Bulgarians attack and invade.

Salonika and eastern Greece had only been liberated from Turkish domination during the Balkan Wars, and the Greeks had been fighting insurgent battles against their oppressor for a century. Though weary of it all, their fear of both the Turks and the Bulgarians made them turn towards the Allies. In 1913, with British encouragement, they had declared Salonika a free port. Thus, using this as a pretext, at the outbreak of war the Allies had quickly sailed into Salonika to use it as a refuelling base. Much later, when it was quite obvious that Salonika served as much more than a refuelling station for the Allied navies, and had become the important Allied military base for the eastern Mediterranean, King Constantine, encouraged by the Central Powers, formally and vociferously protested. In response General Sarrail, the French CIC of the Allied forces in Salonika, occupied the city and established a military government complete with curfew. Sarrail's action was risky, and certainly a violation of neutrality, but it worked, and it paid off.

Wartime friendships and alliances are fragile relationships dependent on the exigencies of the moment. Britain and France, as keen to keep Bulgaria out as the Central Powers were anxious to get her in, were making their tentative secret approaches to her. It emerged that they went so far as to offer to persuade Serbia to concede to Bulgaria a large part of southern Macedonia including Prilep, Monastir, Ohrid and Veles. News of this proposal to surrender territory so recently won at such great cost, was received with shocked dismay and incredulity by the Serbs. Some military leaders even protested that it would be vastly preferable to accept the overtures Austria was known to be making. However, the Allies withdrew their proposals, and Prime Minister Nicholas Pašić managed to soothe infuriated feelings and bring his government back into line with the Allies.

Nevertheless, during the summer, impatient with the lack of action and certain that the Austrians could be driven back, a few top army officers were urging the government to initiate an offensive against the Austrians. But the Serbs, usually hot-headed and impulsive, wisely refrained from any such move. Most of their 700 miles of frontier were with hostile neighbours—Austrians north and west, and the Bulgarians in the east. Italy, which had promised help, was holed up on the Isonzo front against Austria; the Russians were fully occupied along the eastern front before the relentless drive of the Austro-German armies; and the likelihood of Greece honouring her pact with Serbia was nil. The Serbs, barely recovered from their winter trials, and fearing a Bulgarian offensive from the east, were reluctant to engage on a large north and west offensive without the assurance of armed support. To repulse a full-scale determined enemy attack was beyond their resources alone. They needed reinforcements, equipment, arms and ammunition, and assured supply lines. Above all they needed their Allies.

It was the promised support, from the British and French, that everyone—Serbs and members of the Allied missions and relief units—so confidently awaited. After all, they felt, it was only a matter of clearing up the mess in the Dardanelles, then the troops would come. Since news was infrequent, unreliable and censored, few were aware of how badly things were going in the Gallipoli area. Thus there was little to dispel the confidence of the British and French in Serbia, or the Serbs themselves, about the eventual arrival of Allied divisions.

7

INVASION

On 5 October 1915 the peaceful interlude came to an abrupt end. During the night the Austro-German forces along the Danube began an intensive artillery bombardment of Belgrade, and within forty-eight hours over 40,000 shells had been lobbed on to the city. Then, in the wake of the shelling the enemy began massive assault crossings of the Danube and Sava rivers. The artillery of Vice-Admiral Troubridge's small International Force, after a brave response, was soon silenced. On 8 October, Belgrade fell.

Craigie Lorimer was a nurse at the British Fever Hospital in Belgrade, and had recently become engaged to Lieutenant Harry Fitch on Vice-Admiral Troubridge's staff. In a letter to her brother, Alec, she described Belgrade's fall: 'I suppose you've heard about the bombardment and evacuation of Belgrade . . . It began on the 6th October and to most of us it came as a surprise . . . On the 7th October, the bombardment was still going on and some poor folk from the civil population were brought in on stretchers—right through the day we were taking in patients as fast as we could.' Apart from a couple of orderlies they only had the matron, one doctor and three trained nurses to cope with the injured. 'While the doctor and nurses dressed wounds in the surgery a probationer and I received the patients in the wards, put them to bed, blanket-bathed and fed them. Later they came in so fast all we could do was to take off their boots and put them to bed as they were.'

Suddenly the water supply was cut off and the electricity failed. 'You can just imagine what it meant having to go round doing dressings by the light of a candle or table lantern and next morning we couldn't even wash the poor things, the water was so precious.' All that day and night the firing and shelling continued unabated. Craigie was so exhausted after forty-eight hours on duty that she just collapsed fully dressed on her bed and slept regardless of the gunfire.

The Vice-Admiral's staff had moved to Torlak, on the outer perimeter of Belgrade, and Harry Fitch was with him, much to Craigie's relief. But unexpectedly he turned up on horseback having ridden back to Belgrade at his chief's orders to see how the hospital was faring: 'I was so frightfully glad to see him I just didn't care who saw me kiss him right in the middle of the hall.'

Since the hospital was relatively safely situated and they had good cellars where they could shelter if necessary, it was at first decided not to evacuate the patients and staff immediately. But this decision was suddenly countermanded—any patients who could possibly walk were to be dressed and told to go to the nearest station, six miles away, while the others, the badly injured, were to be sent up to the Serbian Military Hospital then being run by a neutral American, Dr Ryan, who also happened to be in overall charge of all the relief hospitals in Belgrade. But there was as yet no question of the staff leaving.

Craigie and her colleagues, with certain misgivings, began to carry out this order, only holding back a few patients who were too dangerously ill to move. Then, without warning, and to their fury and chagrin, Dr Ryan ordered all the staff to evacuate the hospital. Next came the Vice-Admiral's naval surgeon who contributed to the confusion by telling them to stay firm; 'We nearly sent up a cheer we were so glad.' But, it was no use. Dr Ryan stormed in and insisted they obey his orders since, not only was he now in sole charge but he was also the one neutral consul left in Belgrade, briefed by various governments to act on behalf of the hospital staff when the enemy entered the city. There was nothing for it—this time he won and the staff, sad and dejected at abandoning their post, left with the one wagon they had.

It was an extraordinary walk in the dark with shells bursting fairly near and not a light anywhere to guide us. When we got out of the town we felt more or less safe from the firing but the road got worse and worse, simply thick with slimy mud and we made our way alongside thousands of poor refugees all with their faces set towards the south. Looking back from a hill outside the town I saw the last of Belgrade, standing out black against a red sky, and flames rising up in various places where aeroplanes had dropped incendiary bombs.

On the day that Belgrade fell one of the doctors from the Berry unit passed through Niš to find the town gaily decorated with French and British flags in excited anticipation of the arrival of the Allied troops from Salonika. 'Have you heard', one of the orderlies excitedly stopped Elsie Corbett, '2,500 French soldiers have arrived in Niš!' Someone else imagined they saw the flashes of artillery fire eastwards where the Bulgarians would come; and yet another heard that a British division was on its way from Macedonia. Once, on their way home from the hospital, Elsie Corbett and Kathleen Dillon met Crown Prince Alexander and had the temerity to ask him the news. The answer was not particularly enlightening: 'You know you must not believe all these silly rumours.' Rumours there were—wild ones, rumours of hope and of despair. A few days later the Allied flags were quietly taken down in Niš; the streets resumed their air of drab hopelessness, and the people lost their faith. The realisation had dawned that no Allied help was on its way.

For a while the gravity of the situation did not penetrate to the various scattered units. The staff were too busy getting ready for the work they had originally come out to do, namely to receive and to treat the wounded from the battle-front. Everything and everyone was primed and ready and on an emergency footing. Soon the wounded started coming in, a trickle at first, then in trainloads.

'Hurry up, twenty wounded coming to the Slatibor at 7 p.m.!', and Elsie and Kathleen went into top gear, preparing to receive the patients. Much later than the stated time, the wounded men arrived by hospital train from Belgrade in a frightful state. They had been several days on the 80-mile journey, and still had the original dressings on their wounds and still wore their muddy, blood-stained uniforms. Two died soon after admission, and the rest were in bad shape, several riddled with shrapnel which had resulted in appalling abdominal and head injuries.

The scene was much the same in all the hospitals. From mid-October the Berry unit started getting their share of wounded. At the Terapia, Dr Ada McLaren received the wounded who came from the station in the inevitable ox-wagon ambulances. She would check the nature of their injuries, sending them either direct to the ward or to the operating theatre where Dr Berry the surgeon, and his wife the anaesthetist, were ready and waiting. The less serious cases were diverted to a second Berry hospital, the Državna, under Dr Isobel Inglis and Dr Christopherson.

Among the cases Dr Berry handled that first day were severe perforating wounds of the brain and numerous compound fractures of the thigh. Since all the wounds had been inflicted several days earlier they were all badly septic. For the medically minded, here is Dr Berry's description of three operations he performed that first twenty-four hours:

> An extensive wound of the frontal lobe with much loss of brain substance was treated by being freely laid open, nearly half the frontal bone having to be removed with trephine and forceps; a large hernia cerebri ensued, but this gradually receded, and in a few weeks the patient made a good recovery and seemed but little the worse for his injury. Another, with a depressed but non-perforating shrapnel wound of the right occipital lobe, was on admission completely blind in both eyes; the depressed bone was removed. About three days later he had recovered his sight so far that he could distinguish the name on coins shown to him, and was doing very well indeed. Two days later he suddenly complained of violent pains in the head and died in a few hours. Another man . . . had been shot through the centre of the head of the left humerus; a conical German bullet was extracted from the lower part of the right axilla in the mid-axillary line. The patient made an excellent and speedy recovery, but how the great vessels of the mediastinum escaped injury is difficult to explain.

Further north, at Valjevo, Mladenovac and Lazarevac, much nearer the front, the Scottish Women's Hospitals units were soon extremely busy with the numerous wounded who poured in. But their good work was short-lived. As the front receded southwards before the powerful Austro-German thrust, and the Serbs retired to make a stand in the Šumadija highlands, the units were ordered to evacuate.

First it was the turn of Dr Beatrice McGregor's unit at Mladenovac. Lying directly south of the capital the town was right in the path of the enemy advance. Miss Pares, the administrator, and all the staff worked all night packing up their valuable equipment and medicines, and getting at least some of their patients into the ox-wagon ambulances. The severely wounded they had to leave in the charge of a Serbian doctor and some Austrian medical orderlies to await, it was fervently hoped, the mercy of the enemy. Thus they managed to get their entire hospital to Kragujevac, where they promptly opened up a small hospital for minor casualties and a huge dressing station. They had 600 beds and, counting all casualties from the severely to the slightly wounded, during their two weeks in Kragujevac they handled about 10,000 patients.

Dr Alice Hutchison was the next to go. Her unit was ordered first to Požega, but they had hardly settled there before they had hastily to pack up again and move on as another wave of Austrian forces poured over the western borders of nearby Bosnia. She managed to bring some patients with her but, as in Craigie Lorimer's hospital, they had been compelled to urge walking patients to return to their homes as best they could, and to abandon many wounded to the care of a skeleton staff of Serbs. With great difficulty, and forced to discard some valuable equipment, by fording mountain streams and short-cutting through trackless valleys, Alice Hutchison managed to get her unit to Vrnjačka Banja where she immediately opened a hospital and a dressing station. She was more than welcome as the battle casualties were pouring in, far beyond the capacity of the existing hospitals in the town.

Strangely enough the Lazarevac unit was the last to leave— strange because Lazarevac lies midway between Valjevo and Mladenovac and was nearer the firing line than the other two towns. One wonders whether in the chaos and confusion, the unit had perhaps been almost forgotten. Very much at the last minute, when they could already hear the dread boom of the guns, Dr Edith Hollway and her staff were ordered to leave. It was a narrow shave and a most uncomfortable departure. They had considerable difficulty in reaching their allotted destination, Kruševac, but, pushing their way through the endless stream of refugees, they managed without mishap. Immediately on arrival they set up a dressing station by taking over two huge storehouses, and got down to the urgent work awaiting them. But at one stage Dr Inglis dropped in and almost panicked when she saw Dr Hollway's dressing station becoming dangerously overcrowded. Fear of a typhus outbreak haunted her, a very valid fear because of the hordes of wounded men crowded together and the very limited means for bathing and disinfecting them adequately.

At last the expected happened. On 12 October Bulgaria, without any declaration of war, attacked Serbia, and on 13 October moved in across the entire eastern front. Then, on the fourteenth, as if to legalise the entire operation, Bulgaria formally declared war on Serbia. For a while the Serbs managed to prevent them penetrating too deeply into their territory but, towards the end of October, the Serbs found themselves in a very nasty position. After some stiff fighting the Bulgarians, on 19 October, finally broke the Serbian defence line by seizing Vranje, thus cutting the railway between Niš, the provisional capital, and the south. It was, *The Times* correspondent wrote, 'as if Serbia's backbone were broken.'

From the north the Austro-German armies were now moving steadily towards the Morava line, thus threatening Niš itself, and in the south the Bulgarians advanced unchecked towards Skoplje. Further afield in Greece, in the battle of wills between the Prime Minister, Venizelos, and King Constantine, the king was winning and he had no intention of honouring his country's pact with Serbia.

As the position steadily deteriorated in the north, and in the south the Bulgarians swept towards Skoplje, the anxious towns-people impatiently awaited the British and French troops from Salonika. Lady Paget knew perfectly well that the Allied troops had landed in Salonika, and each day a deputation of British and Serbs met the train from Salonika hoping against hope for the arrival of an advance Allied contingent. Like Niš, Skoplje had decorated its streets in eager expectation of the arrival of the Allies. But as day after day passed with no sign of the troops, the flowers and decorations wilted and faded, hope was deferred and apprehensions grew.

When the storm had burst, with enemy divisions pouring in from north, west and east, the Serbs, so sure that the Allied armies would come north from Salonika, had concentrated their defences in the northern part of the country, leaving the south virtually unguarded. By 16 October the situation was very tense in Skoplje. Lady Paget, feeling that it was time she was properly informed, went to the city governor, General Popović, and pointed out that she was responsible to her staff and patients. He was frank—the situation was desperate. The key position around Strumica in the east was exposed to great danger from the Bulgarian advance, and there was no promise of help from the CIC Allied forces in Salonika. He would, he said, be too humiliated to own to her the strength of the Serbian army in the south, and added that he had done everything possible to convey the urgency of the situation to the Allies in Salonika. With the inspiration of desperation the governor then begged Lady Paget to go herself to the Allied command. She was convinced that no general would listen to her, a mere woman, but should there be the remotest chance of anything coming of it she was prepared to go. Soon after she left him the governor frantically rang to tell her he would put a special carriage on the train for her to go to Salonika. She immediately took her courage in both hands and went.

At midday, 17 October, she arrived in Salonika and was granted interviews with the French and the British army commanders. She put the situation as forcibly as she could, but they made it clear that there was nothing they could do to help. Discouraged and miserable she took the train back to Skoplje next morning. Loaded on to her train were two motor lorries, well-intentioned gifts to help evacuate the unit. They had to be abandoned at the frontier.

Already the fighting was nearing Veles south of Skoplje, and the guns could be heard as Lady Paget made her way back up the Vardar valley to Skoplje from her fruitless mission. On her arrival she found chaos and despair in the city, and at the hospital an order with attached plans for the unit's evacuation. Lady Paget considered them, then rebelled and vetoed the lot. They would stay. It was only a matter of days before the area surrounding Skoplje would fall and she wisely foresaw the confusion and congestion on the roads and railway—anyway, the least she and her unit could do after the dismal failure of the Allies to help was to remain at their post with their Serbian patients, and prepare to be taken prisoner by the Bulgarians. Since she had done relief work for the Bulgarians during the 1912 Balkan Wars, and now had some Bulgarian prisoners as patients in the wards and, since she had known Queen Eleonora of Bulgaria personally, Lady Paget felt confident of reasonable treatment for her unit and the wounded Serbs in their care at the hands of the conquering Bulgarians. Skoplje fell to the Bulgarians on 22 October. Lady Paget and her staff had the doubtful distinction of being the first British relief workers to become prisoners of war.

A couple of weeks before the enemy forces had begun their offensive against Belgrade, Mrs Stobart had been told by Colonel Genčić that the situation was extremely grave, that the Serbian army was then taking up positions and that fighting was imminent. Not only did he feel that her help would be very much needed, but went further and asked if she would permit a part of her unit to accompany the Serbian army as a 'flying field hospital' at the front. 'Since it had always been understood', writes Mrs Stobart, 'that our mobile camp was to be utilised in this way if hostilities should be resumed, and, in fulfilment of the promise, which had been made soon after we had arrived in Kragujevac, I replied that I should be glad to perform service in whichever way was to the Serbian authorities most serviceable.' In fact she felt this request to be a tribute to her unit and to Britain.

It was then decided that Mrs Stobart's field hospital should have a detachment of about 18 from the unit including John Greenhalgh, a Serbian dispenser, a Serbian sergeant—a *narednik*—and 60 soldiers as ambulance men and drivers for the 30 ox- and horse-drawn wagons to transport the hospital tents and stores. Since the dispensaries would now be disbanded, 6 of their 7 motor ambulances were requisitioned for the column to transport the wounded, presumably from the front to the field hospitals.

One cannot help querying Mrs Stobart's later claim that she felt reluctant to leave the main hospital at Kragujevac for her field unit. Memories of her brilliant work at the front in 1912 in Bulgaria with her Convoy Corps must have stirred her too strongly to resist, or at least to question, the wisdom of Colonel Genčić's request. But, she says, the colonel insisted that she was more needed with the 'flying field hospital' and that no harm would befall the remainder of her SRF unit. After all, it had been established for six months, all the doctors and their staff knew their routine and were highly skilled professional people, and Dr Mabel King-May would be left in charge.

When she announced her plan to the unit all the staff wanted to come and it was hard to disappoint so many. In the end she took seventeen with her including two doctors—Catherine Payne and Beatrice Coxon. There was one interpreter and, of course,

John Greenhalgh the treasurer. The corps would be officially known as the First Serbian-English Field Hospital, attached to the Šumadija Army Division of 25,000 men.

On 2 October the entire column assembled, and the sixty Serbian soldiers were presented to their new commander who had been granted the temporary rank of major in the Serbian army. All the equipment was packed up and they entrained eastwards for Pirot lying very near what was soon to become Serbia's eastern front.

Back in London the Serbian writer and diplomat, Count Čedo Mijatović, clutching desperately at any Allied straw, was preparing an article, moving in its confused hopelessness, for the *Daily Express*: 'Our loyal and noble allies, French and English, are hastening to our aid, and already the simple rumour of their coming has redoubled the energy and bravery of our soldiers: yet—they may not come in time to secure for us the victory. As on the field of Kossovo, we are fighting now practically alone.'

8
The Retreat :
MASS EXODUS

'We are doctors and nurses—under no circumstances could you induce us to abandon the wounded in our hospitals. We were not sent out here to retreat upon the first approach of danger.' Sir Ralph Paget was dismayed at the vehemence with which the unit heads reacted to his proposals for eventual evacuation. But he had a clear brief from his superiors in London to ensure the safe evacuation of the British relief units and their tons of valuable hospital equipment. Earlier Colonel Genčić had assured him that he had at his disposal transport to move both the staff and the wounded to safety if necessary. But on the latter point Sir Ralph was sceptical.

And now he had dutifully presented the situation to the unit heads. Though he appreciated their laudable sentiments, Sir Ralph felt obliged to counter them, reminding his stubborn listeners that the extensive hospital equipment had been acquired at considerable expense from private donations 'for the use of the Serbs and not the use of the enemy; that its capture would materially benefit the enemy', and so on. But he was dealing with intelligent, determined women, who felt more beholden to the Serbs than to the Foreign Office, and who proceeded to refute his arguments. Was there any guarantee, they asked, that provisions would be made to evacuate all their hospital equipment, *and* the wounded? What about transport? Sir Ralph, remembering his own doubts on that matter, evaded the answer.

For the time being he did not force the issue, but decided to assess the situation through consultations with the Serbian government and military authorities. This meant visiting the various centres—Kruševac, Kraljevo and Skoplje—a gruelling tour which served to confirm his worst fears about the magnitude of the calamity.

During the subsequent weeks Serbia resembled a mad chess game. As the Central Powers advanced on all fronts, the Serbian army HQ, the government, the diplomatic corps, and eventually

106

the relief units, all leap-frogged from one place to another at an ever-increasing rate of disorganisation. And threading through the whole chaotic scene were hapless refugees and soldiers, gathering in numbers as they moved south from lost battles and occupied towns, jamming the roads and passes in their frantic leaderless efforts to flee the enemy.

Only one escape route out of the country remained. This led over the bleak Montenegrin and Albanian mountains to Scutari, thence to the coast where, it was hoped, Allied ships would take everyone to safety in Corfu and Corsica. A few managed to go south from Prizren, crossing into Greece via Monastir. But by early November this route was blocked by the Bulgarians who had occupied most of Macedonia.

Between early October and mid-November the Serbian army HQ moved first from Belgrade to Kragujevac, then to Kruševac, Raška and finally Mitrovica and Prizren before taking off over the mountains to Scutari, carrying their aged Field Marshal Putnik, deathly ill from asthma, in a sedan chair. The government's odyssey was similar: after leaving Niš on 4 October they retired to Kraljevo, where they remained for a month, then left in haste for Raška and Mitrovica. By then any semblance of a corporate governmental body had vanished, and individual members made their independent way to Prizren, then trekked to Scutari, most of them arriving in early December. The diplomatic corps more or less followed in their wake. Behind came the mass of people, mobs of young boys, soldiers, prisoners of war, and the unit members, all left to make their way as best they could.

The small British-Serbian gun-crew contingent from the International Force in Belgrade fought a gallant rearguard action all the way from the capital. After Priština they retreated through the rain and mud of the Kosovo plains towards Peć. Two of their guns were lost, bogged down in the terrible mud, a third fell through a rickety bridge, and the last they stripped and buried. Of the 103 British and Serbs of these gun-crews, 53 were killed or wounded. The remainder left Peć for Scutari on 2 December, arriving two weeks later in a shocking state, half-starved and totally exhausted. They had been fighting and retreating for sixty-seven days.

Before most of the nations joined the retreat Sir Ralph Paget had, with great difficulty, reached Skoplje where his wife had just returned from her abortive visit to the Allied command in

Salonika. Since again no transport was available to move the unit and their wounded, he found Lady Paget and her staff adamantly refusing to budge from Skoplje. There was little point in his remaining, especially since the problems of the recalcitrant units in the north demanded his return. His wife assured him that their large reserves of food and clothing were being distributed to Serbian troops and refugees as they passed through Skoplje.

On his way back Sir Ralph found Niš a ghost town; its people, following the example of the government, had simply left it. The remainder of his journey was hampered by increasing congestion on the railways—the 50-mile trip took 22 hours between Niš and Kruševac where more than 3,000 goods trucks laden with war material jammed the line for miles.

Colonel Genčić, helpless before the catastrophe engulfing his country, had entrusted the care of the British relief units to Dr Čurčin, the gentle medical liaison officer who had already established a close rapport with all the people in his charge. As Sir Ralph neared the end of his tour, Dr Čurčin received an urgent call from the railway commandant in Kragujevac, telling him that the last train was ready to leave—if he wanted to get the British units on it they must come at once. He rushed to the hospitals to order the women to leave immediately. The reaction on all sides was terrible; the hundreds of wounded were terrified at being left alone and helpless, and the doctors and nurses were shocked and deeply distressed by the order—this time from the Serbs—to leave their patients. Dr Inglis, who had been operating when Dr Čurčin arrived, came out immediately she got the message.

'Never before had I seen her in such a state', Dr Čurčin later said, 'she was pale and wretched. She tried to persuade me that it was not possible to do what I was asking them to do; that they could not leave the hospital in the prevailing conditions. I knew with whom I had to deal, and I was less willing to depress her than anybody else. I myself was deeply miserable, because I felt how, through this conflict of duties, a hostile atmosphere was developing between us.'

Dr Inglis yielded on condition that she could meet the Serbian doctor who was to take over the hospital and explain to him the serious cases. This was arranged and only at the last minute did Dr Inglis arrive for the train, which took them as far as Kruševac.

The sole assurance that had induced the women to leave Kragu-
jevac was Dr Čurčin's promise that they would be allowed, where
possible, to help the Serbian wounded by setting up dressing
stations near the main army centres along the southern route.
Thus, immediately upon reaching Kruševac, Dr Inglis and Dr
Hollway and their staff started treating the wounded again, while
Dr McGregor with her SWH party, and Dr King-May with the
Stobart unit, based themselves at first in Kraljevo.

Two weeks later all the unit heads were summoned to Vrnjačka
Banja for another meeting with Sir Ralph Paget. This time they
were prepared and delivered their ultimatum—they had no
intention of deserting their hospitals, nor of harrassing the Serbian
authorities further by insisting on evacuating their hospital
equipment when there was clearly no transport. This time Sir
Ralph gave in, but insisted on making the situation quite clear.

There was no chance of northern Serbia being saved, he told
them; therefore, the units must now choose either to move south
with the refugees via Mitrovica to Prizren, with the possibility of
establishing field hospitals there or if necessary, to proceed over
the mountains to Scutari, or to remain where they were, with the
certain knowledge that they would all soon become prisoners. He
now admitted that the hospital equipment could not possibly be
saved. The Serbs had no transport for their military supplies, their
army, or their wounded, let alone for the hospitals of the foreign
missions; in fact it was dubious if any transport would be found
for those unit staff who wished to go south. He would do his best,
but was very pessimistic about the outcome. He then went on to
warn the women that even the most basic provisioning for the
arduous winter journey through Montenegro and Albania would
be difficult if not impossible; nor could they count on supplies en
route and they would have to jettison all but essentials to make
room for limited rations from the hospital stores. The journey
would involve considerable danger and discomfort; therefore,
anyone undertaking it would do so entirely at her own risk. Finally
he suggested that only those who were exceptionally fit should risk
the undoubted hardships this route must entail, but he did urge
those few male orderlies of military age to make the attempt since
capture for them would mean being interned for the duration of
the war, whereas the women would most likely be repatriated
through the auspices of the International Red Cross. He ended his

109

address by asking the unit heads to discuss the matter with their staffs and then give him a list of those who wished to undertake the journey to Scutari.

Dr Inglis and most of the SWH staff elected to remain, among them Dr Hutchison, Dr Chesney, Dr Hollway and Mrs Haverfield. Some others, with personal reasons for wishing to return to England after their long tour of duty in Serbia, decided to go. Among these were Dr Beatrice McGregor and Mr William Smith, the unit transport officer, who was of military age. The Berry unit of Vrnjačka Banja decided to stay, again with the exception of a few, including a couple of men of military age. Jan Gordon came into this category and his wife, Cora, chose to accompany him. Most of the British Red Cross Hospital, including Kathleen Dillon and Elsie Corbett, firmly voted for staying. The remainder of Mrs Stobart's SRF unit, now under Dr King-May, after some deliberations, opted for leaving, at least for Mitrovica or Prizren, where they hoped to be able to link up with Mrs Stobart and her 'flying field hospital', and perhaps set up their hospital again further south.

When Dr Čurčin learned of the decision of the majority of the British women to stay 'a weight was lifted from our hearts, because not only did we not know whom to leave with the wounded, but also we had no means of transporting the Missions.' Dr Čurčin himself then took charge of those people who had decided to leave, about sixty in all, including Dr King-May's unit, which had gone in advance to open a dressing station at the medieval monastery of Studenica, a few miles off the main Raška road.

One glimmer of hope was the news that a small Allied division had crossed the frontier from Greece into Serbia—the 10th Division under General Sir Bryan Mahon with 13,000 men, and a French column half that number. Both followed the railway line leading north from Gevgelija, the Serbo-Greek frontier town; then the French went towards Strumica, where they managed to halt the Bulgarians briefly, while the British occupied the shores of Lake Dojran until they were savagely attacked by vastly superior enemy forces early in December and had to withdraw.

But for the Serbs this token support was useless. On 24 September the British Foreign Minister, Sir Edward Grey, had pledged England's assistance to Serbia 'without qualifications and without reserves'. Subsequently he claimed that these words were meant 'in a political and not in a military sense'. Which, to put it crudely, was a fat lot of use to the Serbs. Lofty political sentiments were no substitute for the military aid they so desperately needed.

By 15 November the remainder of the Serbian army was collected near Priština on the historic plains of Kosovo, scene of the nation's tragic defeat by the Turks in 1389. The Bulgarians coming up from Skoplje threatened to cut the road to Prizren and Peć, and thus the escape route to Albania, but it had to be kept open at all cost to allow the slow procession of gathering fugitives to get away. Thus these starving, exhausted soldiers made a last supreme effort to pierce the Bulgarian lines. They managed to hold the enemy at bay for six precious days, until their ammunition failed. Menaced by the Austro-German armies from the north and west and by the Bulgarians from the east, broken-hearted at the non-appearance of Allied reinforcements, and with their ammunition gone, the soldiers tossed their useless rifles into the ditches and turned to follow their king and people along the road they had struggled to keep open at such cost. The Serbs could do no more. They had been attacked by three powers, let down by the Greeks, and failed by their Allies.*

The Serbian general staff then called on the army to leave the country and face starvation and exile rather than fall into the hands of the enemy. No one was under any illusions what such a retreat would mean—the massive movement of about 200,000 men and the almost certain loss of all their equipment. Thousands of the men would succumb to cold and starvation before they could reach their destination in Albania, where the Allies promised them food supplies and ships to evacuate them to Corfu and

---

* If this seems hard on the Allies it is because of the importance of showing the impact on *contemporary* Serbia of Allied tardiness. With the wisdom of sixty years of historical hindsight a more dispassionate view results. In 1915 many valid—and invalid—factors contributed to the absence of effective Allied aid. Apart from the Dardanelles disaster and the Western Front, the global nature of the war by then forced Britain and France to deploy their armies far beyond the confines of Europe, eg to the Middle East, especially to guard the Suez Canal, the 'gateway' to the British Empire; while France was concerned with her North African colonies and the western Mediterranean. In the Balkans the Allies had lost Bulgaria to the Central Powers and, if King Constantine had his way, Greece could follow; therefore, to maintain Serbia's sinking morale the Allies had to go through the charade of promising armed support. Strategically it was perhaps by then the only choice, but for the Serbs in 1915 it was a tragic deception.

111

Corsica. The way would lead over some of the most inhospitable mountains in Europe with few towns, no roads except narrow mule tracks, and all in the deep snows of winter. Thus began the Great Retreat.

Two groups of 'Scottish' women, as the SWH members, Scottish or not, had come to be known, packed up and prepared to join the retreat along the Ibar valley via Raška and perhaps form a dressing station at Mitrovica or Peć. William Smith took charge of one party, while Dr McGregor led the second. A third group, the SRF unit under Dr King-May, was already in Studenica, but preparing to move on. In the background, hovering over them like a guardian angel, was Dr Čurčin, who was never to lose touch with the main groups of women the entire way to Albania.

By now it was almost impossible to get any form of transport. Dr McGregor leaving from Kraljevo bought, with the help of Sir Ralph Paget, ten ox-wagons, which were packed with food rations, blankets and basic medical equipment. William Smith's group, setting off from Kruševac during an artillery attack, had found eight ox-carts. The unit members discarded all but absolutely essential personal belongings. Of their departure into the unknown William Smith had this to say:

> We finally got away from the hospital about noon, joined the main road and became part of what was to become known as the Great Retreat. The road was a moving mass of transport of all kinds—motor-wagons, bullock-wagons, horse-wagons, men, and guns, besides the civilian population, men, women and children, all intent on escape . . . This procession had been passing continuously for days, stretching from one end of Serbia to the other, and one realised that this was something more than an army in retreat; it was the passing of a whole nation into exile, a people leaving a lost country.

Soon Dr McGregor's party was heading up the wild, lovely Ibar valley, while William Smith took the more easterly route towards Priština, both ways ultimately converging on Prizren and then Peć, which was to become the final rallying point for relief teams, government officials, the army staff and the diplomatic corps, before they launched off over the mountains to Scutari.

At first, until Raška, the Ibar valley road was manageable. Though packed with thousands of refugees, ox-wagons and even some motor vehicles, the way was wide enough and the going tolerable. But the forty-five miles from Raška to Mitrovica were extremely difficult and hazardous because of landslides and bridgeless mountain torrents where the water was rising every minute owing to heavy rain and snowfalls in the mountains. It was along this stretch of road that a tragedy occurred. One of Dr McGregor's staff, Caroline Toughill, was riding in one of the few motor lorries when the edge of the narrow road caved in and the lorry tumbled down into the river below. Mrs Toughill was so seriously injured that she died soon after. In a curious prophetic remark to a friend the day before, Caroline Toughill seemed to have foreseen her own death. A deeply religious person, she was moved by the splendour of the scenery along that wild valley to exclaim: 'Oh to be allowed to rest forever on such a hill and to be alone with God.'

Remembering this, her friends looked for a worthy resting place. Above the village of Leposavić they found, on the summit of a conical hill, a tiny Byzantine church with a small cemetery nearby. Here Caroline Toughill was buried. Her friends made a wreath of moss and berries, a Serbian surgeon carved a simple wooden cross, and the village priest conducted the funeral service. Officers, soldiers, Austrian prisoners, villagers and her unit comrades all assembled in the lovely secluded spot to pay their tribute as the simple pine coffin was lowered into the grave.

From Mitrovica all roads from the north converged on the plains of Kosovo, and by the time the 'Scottish' women reached this point the retreat had become an exodus through the cloying mud of the plains, sodden with snow and the torrential rain. If, in war, winter snows are the curse of Russia, autumn mud is that of Serbia. Wagons were bogged in it, starving horses and oxen, too weak to struggle, stood up to their knees in it, trapped in the morass. The refugees, soldiers and the British women fell and fought their way through the glutinous mire hour after hour, day after day in that terrible forced march. Mercilessly the piercing wind sliced through tattered clothing as snowstorms swept down from the mountains in a particularly bitter early winter. Defenceless peasant families cowered before the icy winds; soldiers dragged their useless field guns; monks left their monasteries bearing the relics of the medieval Nemanja kings, sacred to all Serbs; and the priests went from their churches carrying their ikons. With them, sharing their via dolorosa across the Kosovo plains, went the aged King Peter, half-paralysed with rheumatism so that, like the relics of his Nemanja forefathers, he would soon have to be borne by his people. Along too came his son, Crown Prince Alexander, shortly to suffer such agony from appendicitis that doctors must perforce operate on him in a simple army lazaret and then, to protect their patient from the cold, swathe him like a mummy to be carried by his soldiers into exile. Like an animated fresco from one of Serbia's great Byzantine monasteries—Dečani, Žiča or Studenica—the people joined the funeral procession of their nation. Trudging along on the sidelines, frozen with cold, desolate and starving, were thousands of Austrian prisoners, there because Vienna had chosen to ignore earlier approaches regarding their repatriation. Few would survive to reach the Adriatic.

Another disaster struck the units. Between Mitrovica and Peć one of the nurses, 'Ginger' Clifton, was accidentally shot. Two soldiers had quarrelled over a rifle which went off, the bullet hitting Nurse Clifton and penetrating both lungs. It was a danger-ous wound necessitating immediate medical attention and hospitalisation. Dr Mary Iles, who had arrived in Serbia from India only three weeks previously, and Dr King-May, did what they could and made one of the ox-wagons into an ambulance, but after thirty-six hours in the springless cart at zero temperature the doctors became very anxious, realising that their patient must be taken to a hospital quickly or the wound would be fatal. With great difficulty they got her to the army hospital at Mitrovica where she was admitted. Dr Iles, Nurse Bambridge and Dr McMillan, surrendering their chance of leaving the country, remained behind with 'Ginger' Clifton. Soon afterwards the Austrians took them all prisoner, but the patient was well cared for and she recovered completely. Later they were all repatriated and she resumed her nursing activities in another theatre of the war.

After the last-ditch army stand near Priština, when most of the soldiers joined the retreat, terrible scenes were witnessed all the way to Prizren. Deep snow lay everywhere; there was no supply column for the soldiers, therefore no food; the men and the refugees survived by eating flesh torn from the carcases of oxen

and horses that fell by the way. It was an ordeal to get a *komora**
into the densely packed column of trudging humanity, and those
who joined the retreat from side roads sometimes took days to
force a way in, every exhausted being in the column jealously
guarding every yard of his slow advance.

Nothing loath, at Priština forty British women found shelter in a
Turkish harem, invited by a Turkish merchant who extended to
them great courtesy and kindness. After their privations it was
bliss to be in warm clean quarters, no matter how strange and
exotic, and to be served little cups of black sweet coffee.

Soon after reaching Priština, Dr King-May and Miss Anne
McGlade learned that Mrs Stobart and her 'flying field hospital'
were camped on the outskirts of the town. Relieved to learn they
had come through safely, Dr King-May sent a message to report
on the state of the unit, and on Nurse Clifton's accident. In turn
she was told that Mrs Stobart intended to keep her column for the
time being, but two of her orderlies, Miss Sharman and Miss
Bingley, chose to rejoin the main unit.

One of the most pitiful features of the retreat was the flight of
thousands—some say 30,000—of young boys, those too young to be
in the army but old enough to march, that is from about twelve
to sixteen years old. Once Dr King-May's party passed a group of
about 1,500 of these unfortunate children, who were to suffer
appalling privations and loss of life long before they reached
Scutari. In the general panic and hopelessness the Serbian
authorities, convinced that the nation was doomed unless some of
the youth survived, with little planning urged these schoolboys
and cadets to join the exodus. Also, it was argued, if left behind
those boys nearing military age would be interned and thus many
might not survive the rigours of winter. Most were away from
home for the first time in their lives, they were lost and terrified,
separated from their families and villages, and there was no one to
assume responsibility for them. Not surprisingly some became
desperate young bandits and many of the weaker ones died of
hunger and neglect. They had no money, and were poorly clad for
the harsh cold. Sometimes small hopeless groups of these pathetic
youngsters were to be seen huddled together, weeping with fear
and loneliness. Around 20,000 of them would die before the

---

* *Komora*, or *komorra*, is a supply train of pack animals or ox-wagons etc.

winter was over: on the march, on the fever-ridden swamps of the
Albanian coast or on the island of Vido off the shores of Corfu to
which the ill, exhausted and emaciated survivors would be evacuated. Soon Vido, a lovely cypress-clad island, would be termed
'l'île des morts'. Fortier Jones, the American author and journalist
who had joined the retreat, wrote of them: 'they marched over the
country in droves. There were no officers to oversee them. They
were like the antelope, roaming over the wild hills along the Ibar.
They ate anything they could find, rotten apples, bad vegetables,
the precious bits of food found in abandoned tins . . .'

The long days dragged by and Dr King-May's party trudged
on, at last reaching Prizren where they could rest a little before
proceeding to Peć. Not far behind followed Dr McGregor and her
charges. All along the heart-breaking route hunger was now very
real for soldiers and refugees alike since all that was available was
what each person carried, most of which had long since gone. Now,
not only animals lay dead where they had fallen, but dead and
dying humans became a common sight, mostly the old, the ill and
the very young.

At Prizren the destitution and suffering among most of the
refugees were terrible to behold. The town's normal population
of around 20,000 had swollen to nearer 150,000, mostly destitute
people, who crammed the narrow streets and squares or huddled
around thousands of campfires on the outskirts. These homeless
invaders ransacked the shops and commandeered every vestige
of accommodation, food or potential transport. Prizren, a lovely
medieval trading city of rich merchants on the old silk route from
the east, with fine Byzantine churches and elegant mosques, was
ravaged by these desperate refugees who swept through it like the
rapacious hordes of old.

Thanks to Dr Čurčin the unit-women were housed in newly
built cholera sheds which were even heated—pure luxury after
the trials of that march. Now, together with William Smith's
party, which had come down from Kruševac, about sixty members
of the British relief units had got through, over fifty of them
women. Awaiting them was Sir Ralph Paget, who did what he
could to obtain some much-needed food supplies and ox-wagons
to transport their basic equipment and provisions, chiefly flour
and rice. Someone scouring Prizren returned triumphantly with a
few packets of *loukoumi* (Turkish delight), some dried raisins, and

even a carton of cigarettes bought from a small boy at an out-rageous price. No longer was there any question of re-establishing a hospital; it was now solely a matter of getting out.

Since the route south to Greece was now completely cut off everyone was ordered to proceed via Peć into the mountains to Andrijevica where, they were assured, provisions would be available. After Andrijevica came a high pass, then it was down-hill to Podgorica* in Montenegro and, so everyone was led to believe, a relatively easy stretch to Scutari, lying on the southern end of Lake Scutari in Albania, where help and supplies awaited them. The reality was going to be very different.

And so they all prepared carefully for this dangerous phase of the journey. They left Prizren, rejoined the lines of refugees and headed for Peć, where they would leave their ox-wagons and buy pack animals to negotiate the mountains. It was difficult for all the British units to keep together because whenever the slightest delay occurred, the endless column of refugees would surge for-ward to fill the vacated space. Once William Smith and his party were badly held up by the collapse of their starving oxen. In desperation he gave the animals to an Albanian peasant, which meant repacking everything on to the remaining wagons, by which time the rest of the party were miles ahead, so they had to travel all night. At last, still behind the main party, they collapsed totally spent at the huge Dečani monastery, which was crammed with soldiers and refugees. A kindly monk took pity on Smith's group and gave them tea and a room to themselves. Throughout the long night the carts lumbered into the monastery courtyard, and stretcher-bearers filed in carrying many wounded Serbian officers, some already dead from their injuries and the cold. The monks tended the soldiers and prayed for the dying.

The previous night Dr King-May, Dr Čurčin and the others had also stayed at Dečani, and continued on to Peć the next morning, and it was there that Smith's party caught up with them. Both groups managed to get quarters in the military barracks. Dr McGregor's people, who had joined up with William Smith and Dr Čurčin at Prizren, were also now in Peć. Finally, not far off, in another monastery just outside Peć, Mrs Stobart and her column, which had arrived direct from Priština, were quartered.

* Today Titograd, capital of Montenegro.

Immediately behind Peć rises a solid wall of mountains, seemingly impenetrable. But there is a way through — the Rugovska Klisura, a slender defile whose cliffs curve inwards forming Gothic arches overhead; on whose narrow ledge of track two men can hardly walk abreast, and with a wild torrent below. And for the refugees the rocky, uneven track was particularly treacherous because of snow and ice. Up and up it twisted, rougher and more dangerous as it ascended, packed with snow, and extremely precarious for both humans and animals to keep a foothold. Under the best conditions the passage through the gorge takes about ten hours before one emerges at the foot of the pass which then zig-zags up another 2,000 feet to a small plateau. Below the summit, at about 5,000 feet was a small timber *khan* or shelter, very rough but enough to protect the traveller from the deadly cold, with space for about thirty people sleeping on the floor. This *khan* was to be a goal for the units. Ox-wagons of any kind were out. No wheeled vehicles could possibly negotiate the Rugovska Klisura, let alone the narrow pass up to the plateau.

In Peć it took the units four days to prepare for the mountain agony ahead, as they searched the town for provisions. Fortunately they had enough money although the population, largely Albanian,* made fortunes from the sale of pack animals and harness. Dr King-May, with the help of Dr Čurčin and Fortier Jones, bought some rather miserable pack horses and mules, one between two people. Each person was limited to a maximum of six blankets with rubber sheeting to protect them from snow and rain; and a meagre food ration of two loaves of black bread, a little tea and coffee, a tin of Oxo and two small tins of condensed milk, which had to last until reaching Andrijevica. The women, considering the peaks before them, unanimously agreed to discard their impractical and cumbersome long skirts in favour of rough trousers fashioned out of surplus army blankets.

---

* This southern part of Serbia with the towns of Peć, Prizren, Priština and Mitrovica, has a large population of Moslem Albanians. Today Kosovo (called Kosmet until 1973) is an autonomous province with Priština as the capital and Albanian as the main language. Most of Kosovo's almost 1,000,000 Albanians —nearly 75 per cent of the province's population—are direct descendants from those who settled there in the seventeenth and eighteenth centuries after thousands of Serbs fled Turkish religious persecution and were given sanctuary by the Austrian Habsburg emperors in what was then part of Hungary and is today Vojvodina, Yugoslavia's second autonomous province.

'I fear that in crossing these two passes and generally on the road between Ipek [Peć] and Levareka, the personnel of the units must almost without exception have suffered severely from the cold, want of food and shelter, and other hardships, especially as towards the last seven days of November there was a heavy snowstorm', Sir Ralph Paget later reported. They did suffer. It was an appalling trek, yet all the women managed it. Dr Čurčin had this to say of his charges: 'I don't hesitate a moment in giving my opinion that the British women behaved better than anybody, better than any man. As regards powers of endurance, they were equal to the Serbian soldier, who, after having lost his unit, had to find his way where there was no way, and his bread where there was no bread. As regards morale—that power of the spirit— nobody was equal to them'. Later he adds: 'I must confess openly that my women fellow-travellers generally made me ashamed in all that concerns courage, endurance and good temper. The same is true of all the men of our company, Serbs or British. The woman did exactly as we did—and more; and they were always satisfied with less.'

Fortier Jones, who travelled with Dr King-May's party, was even more lavish in his praise for his courageous companions, and later wrote:

> Forty English women made the march that day. They made it without food and without drink; most of them made it on foot and in clothing intended only for the Balkan summer. I think it can be said that the party of English women stood it better than the Serbian refugees and fully as well as the Serbian army. Of course girls who entered the march mere girls came out in the evening old in experience. They saw things that generations of their sisters at home live and die without the slightest knowledge of—the madness of starvation, the passion to live at all cost, the swift decay of all civilized characteristics in freezing, starving men. They understand now better than any biologist, any economist, could have taught them the struggle for existence and the survival of the fittest. At the end they smiled, made tea, slept forty in a Turkish harem, and next day marched their thirty kilometres. They are the heroines of the Serbian tragedy, and they realized it not at all.

There was one girl who walked several days over the rocky path in the snow and ice wearing Serbian *opanci*, the thin peasant sandals, because her boots had been stolen, and Dr Čurčin only learned about it when the journey was nearly over. There was the nurse who broke her arm in falling on the road in the dark, but walked for weeks in great pain without mentioning it; and another nurse who made the entire journey with a severe wound on her foot and only occasionally, when the going was unbearably rough, did she quietly ask if she could ride the pack-horse for a little way, without saying why.

Dr King-May and her deputy, Miss Anne McGlade, were wonderful leaders, shining examples to their charges and of great assistance to Dr Čurčin, who marvelled how they never lost their nerve or their tempers; they were always calm, and grateful for any help or kindness. If Dr Čurčin failed to find food or shelter they assured him that there was plenty of everything and were always the first to spread their blankets on the hard ground. According to him each of the unit members seemed to compete with the others in unselfishness, courtesy and kindness.

Foreigners love to tease the British about hot-water bottles. Perhaps the legends surrounding them began during that retreat. Anyway, Fortier Jones was fascinated by these useful utensils. He soon noticed on that freezing journey that no matter where or how the women slept—in a deserted shepherd's hut, in the snow, under the pines—fires would be lit and water boiled for the ubiquitous hot-water bottle. In fact they even carried extra ones! 'They had thrown away their clothing, their precious souvenirs, they could not carry as much food as they needed; but they had extra hot-water bottles!' Fortier Jones's astonishment amused the women immensely, but he was converted to the wisdom of their fetish when they proved to him that not only did the hot-water bottle keep them warm in the freezing night but, in the morning, the water still retained enough warmth for a passable wash.

The units left Peć and it began to snow as they approached the Rugovska Klisura. They entered that formidable canyon, pushing on along the narrow path with the lines of refugees before and behind them. It grew colder as the track ascended and the snow became heavier. People fell on the treacherous ice and several times the pack-animals stumbled badly—once one rolled into the river below, fortunately where the bank was not so steep, and he and his load were rescued. That first day they marched well into the night, not daring to stop without shelter or warmth in that

(above) Plaque commemorating Dr. Katherine Macphail at the Kamenica hospital, which she founded for tubercular children on the hills overlooking the Danube near Novi Sad. Below the plaque are two nurses of the hospital; the one on the right, Sister Ljuba, trained under Dr. Macphail whom she remembers with gratitude and warmth *(MK)*

(left) Bust of Dr. Elsie Inglis by the great Yugoslav sculptor, Ivan Mestrović

(right) Sister Jean Rankin (left) and two other nurses from Lady Paget's SRF hospital in Skoplje, wearing the prescribed 'typhus uniform' – calico overalls from head to foot to protect them from the deadly lice *(Vivian Rankin Pithy)*

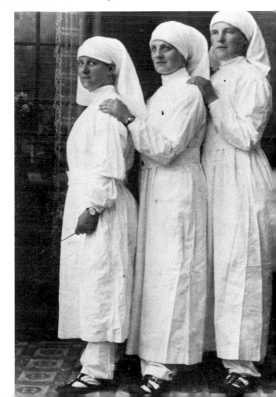

(*above*) Retreat: flight of the Serbian population before the enemy advance. This group is under the protection of a Serbian priest; (*below*) the retreat through Montenegro and Albania: a member of the SWH unit leads the second horse. A painting by William Smith, a transport orderly with the SWH

icy defile. Progress was slow, and at difficult corners the ponies had to be led individually, which sometimes meant a wait of an hour for those behind. As darkness came more horses fell; sometimes the crack of a merciful bullet was heard as an end was put to an animal's suffering, but often they were left to die where they had fallen on the rocks below. Leading a pack-animal in the dark on this narrow icy track was terrifying, but the women soon found that it was best to leave these mountain animals to their own devices, and they mostly found their way. Finally, well into the night the units reached a possible camping ground. As they settled down they looked back along the steep valley to see thousands of flickering campfires like earth-bound stars sparking the mountain sides for miles. Since there was no shelter they settled down in the deep snow. Wrapped in their blankets, warmed by each other and their hot-water bottles, the women slept the deep sleep of fatigue and mountain air.

By dawn the relentless march continued. The snow was blinding and wretchedly cold. Now they were up into the pass, beyond the point of no return. If a major blizzard caught them here the chance of survival was slim. Day after day they pushed on. Sometimes Albanian peasants helped as the horses slithered and stumbled on the rough icy path: 'One would take the pony's head, the other the tail, and all three would slide and slither down the icy descent in the cleverest fashion.'

Food supplies were now dangerously low and none to be found in this inhospitable region. Nearly a week later the women staggered into Andrijevica, and the lights of the little mountain town were the most cheering sight since Peć. Dr Ćurčin managed to find quarters at a squalid inn, but the promised food failed to materialise. With great difficulty and at excessive cost they bought a sheep to slaughter, and the military authorities gave them a ration of black bread. William Smith borrowed a huge pot from the innkeeper and, assisted by two others, chopped the sheep up and spent the day cooking—'the soup we made from that sheep was the finest ever made in the Balkan peninsula.'

After Andrijevica a fiercely steep ascent, reaching 7,000 feet, took them to the highest point in the retreat. After that it was still eighty miles to Podgorica, but the worst would be over, it would be downhill most of the way. Though short that awful climb was murderous, but they reached the top and found shelter in a small

Montenegrin *khan*, and all slept huddled together on the floor around a fire in the middle of the room. Several exhausting days later they descended to Podgorica—again no supplies, nor the assured transport for the last stage to Scutari. On they marched, down to Lake Scutari where a small boat took them across to the town of Scutari, their goal for so many weeks. But a shock of disappointment was their reward; their trek was still not over. Again they sought supplies—the promised Allied food and welcome. The latter was there but few provisions. Instead they were told to continue to the coast where they might find a ship to take them to Italy.

At Scutari Dr King-May and her companions were relieved to hear that one of their orderlies, Dorothy Brindley, together with some others, had reached Scutari three weeks earlier! Only on reaching England did Dr King-May learn the details of their remarkable short-cut.

Dorothy Brindley, a domestic science teacher from Staffordshire, had joined Mrs Stobart's SRF unit as a cook. When the unit had withdrawn from Kragujevac and then Kraljevo, she and some others had been sent on ahead to Raška to prepare for the arrival of the main unit. However, in the ensuing chaos no message reached them at Raška. Finally, Dorothy accepted an offer to join a small party led by Jan and Cora Gordon from the Berry unit. The Gordons had a good Austrian map, Cora spoke Serbian well, and both had travelled extensively in Serbia before the war. Disregarding all advice the little group left the stream of refugees, turning west via Novi Pazar towards Montenegro, 'a route which seemed to be quite unknown, and the mention of which provoked exclamations of horror at our temerity', Dorothy Brindley later recalled. They bought some pack-ponies and set off over a 4,000-foot pass which took them far from the crowded stream of refugees into the solitary wilderness of the Montenegrin mountains.

They walked and rode, slept in the open, in inns, once in a Moslem house; they were accused of being spies; they endured intense cold; tramped along trackless valleys through snow and mud, all on a spartan diet consisting mainly of rice and cocoa and a little maize bread bought in isolated hamlets. Some of the party suffered from dysentery and one from pleurisy, but in record time they reached Podgorica by this cross-country route. After telegraphing Scutari they made the long downhill trek to Plavnica on the lake then took a boat to Scutari. They then had a short rest before proceeding to San Giovanni di Medua where, after five miserable days of waiting, they boarded the *Harmonie* for Brindisi. On 6 December, one month after leaving Raška, the party reached London. It was a record—they arrived home three weeks before any other unit in the retreat.

Back at San Giovanni di Medua Dr Čurčin and his charges also had a miserable wait for a boat in the scruffy little port, where provision ships were supposed to have docked. Instead, all they found was the dismal sight of a harbour full of wrecks—eleven supply ships had been sunk a few days earlier by enemy submarines. For three days the units, housed in one room in a tiny inn, subsisted on bread made from sodden salty flour reclaimed from the sunken ships. At last an Italian ship, the *Brindisi*, docked and the captain reluctantly agreed to take them all to Italy. Though apprehensive at the prospect of submarines lying in wait outside the harbour, the unit members unanimously agreed to risk them. One night they boarded the ship which slipped silently out into the Adriatic. Next morning they landed safely in Brindisi, and twelve hours later were on their way by train through Italy and France to England. Their troubles were at an end. Since leaving Kragujevac they had been nine weeks and nearly 500 miles on the great retreat.

Shortly after the women reached England from the ordeals of their long retreat the Foreign Secretary, Sir Edward Grey, received the following letter from Miss (later Dame) S. E. S. Mair, President of the Scottish Womens Hospitals committee:

Dear Sir,

May I venture to ask you kindly to convey the very hearty thanks of the Committee of the Scottish Womens Hospitals for Foreign Service to the French and Italian governments for their generous action in giving free transport through their respective countries to members of our units returning lately from Serbia.

May I further in all courtesy point out that it was only on reaching our own shores that payment to London from these weary travellers was exacted.

I have the honour to remain

Yours respectfully (signed)

9

The Retreat: MRS STOBART'S FLYING FIELD HOSPITAL

When Mrs, now Major, St Clair Stobart left Kragujevac at the head of her 'flying field hospital', Colonel Teržić, CO of the 1st Šumadija Division to which she was attached, sent her a black horse that she might ride at the head of her column. From then on she was rarely out of the saddle since, she claimed, being mounted gave her more 'command mobility'.

From the day they left Kragujevac, Mrs Stobart and her column had in fact begun their part in the retreat. They had no sooner reached the Pirot region in eastern Serbia than their circuitous peregrinations, which were to last many weeks, began. As a section of the army fell back from the front the column was ordered to move; on reaching their allotted destination further orders drove them on again; once they were overlooked in the confusion and for a whole day hung around forgotten, only to learn that an NCO had omitted to deliver the order for them to leave for Niš that morning. They then rushed off in the evening to arrive at two o'clock in the morning of the next day. In charge of all this packing and unpacking, pitching tents and striking camp, sometimes three times a day, was the orderly Cissy Benjamin, a 24 year old ex-debutante who had left a fashionable social life in London to come to Serbia.

This hectic stop-and-start itinerary took them hither and thither as the Serbian armies began their ragged seesawing retreat from various sectors of the front. The weather worsened and the confusion increased. All this would have mattered less to the staff had they been fully engaged in treating the wounded. Instead, all their energy was spent packing and unpacking their extensive equipment, travelling in great discomfort over the awful roads in the rain and mud, and sleeping in the carts and ambulances. Until the Serbian transport system broke down completely, most of the wounded were sent direct by rail from the front to the main hospitals along the Morava river—Kruševac, Vrnjačka Banja, Kragujevac, and Kraljevo—bypassing Mrs Stobart's column. Thus the irony was that all the British units in these centres, including Dr King-May's, were overwhelmed with work and short-staffed, while the column which had set out so bravely, so eager to be on the spot to rescue the wounded at the front, was tending wounded below its capacity and the staff, both British and Serbian, were becoming weary and dispirited from the apparent futility of their wanderings.

Perhaps this is the point where Mrs Stobart erred in her judgement. Noble though it was to wish to be at the front to help the Serbian wounded, had she assessed the situation more cleverly she should perhaps have concluded that it might be more beneficial to the Serbs if her column rejoined the overworked unit at Kragujevac. There, apart from the boon of the extra medical staff, the ambulances would have been a godsend for transporting the wounded from the rail-heads, thus sparing at least some of the men that merciless ox-wagon ride. But, stubborn and proud of her new status and that of her column, and determined to repeat her success at Kirk-Kilisse, Mrs Stobart convinced herself and the others that their turn would come when the Serbs made their anticipated stand against the enemy once the Allied troops had arrived from the south to help them.

Finally, but briefly, their turn did come. One of their extraordinary moves took them very near the Belgrade front, when many wounded did pass through their dressing station. Her cryptic shorthand diary entry for 15 October reads: 'Pouring wet day and cold winds . . . Many wounded in aft. and eve. Dark and muddy & w'ded coming in pouring rain and wind. Evacuated them all day long to Palanka in cars.' But after several long days of hard work they had to withdraw south, and she sadly adds, 'from the moment of that first retreat we never advanced again.'

Gallant and dedicated as they were, her staff were worn out and irritated by the incessant daily moving and travelling in the atrocious weather. The doctors and nurses began to question the wisdom of their commander in her determination to keep the column going at all costs, and were convinced that they could do much more at the base hospitals.

Sir Ralph Paget was extremely annoyed at what he considered to be Mrs Stobart's precipitate action in galloping off to the front with so much valuable equipment and staff, and without informing him. In Nis he had no doubt learned about the column from Sir Charles Des Graz, the British Minister to Serbia, to whom Mrs Stobart had earlier gone to discuss her new command. On the occasion of a rare delivery of mail Mrs Stobart notes in her diary: 'Petty one [letter] from Paget re my incorrectness in not having wasted precious days consulting with him before arranged appointment command of field hospital. Called and wrote him soothingly.'

Nevertheless, in anticipating Paget's criticism of her to the Foreign Office, and to justify her action, Mrs Stobart took an extraordinary step. The next day her diary entry is :'Referent took me to Commander re cable to Ed. Grey & Govt. etc.' It seems she went over Sir Ralph's head and cabled the foreign minister himself. This partly explains why Paget, in his lengthy report on the British units in Serbia, makes little reference to the 'flying field hospital', doubtless saving his comments for an acid oral account on his return.

Relations were becoming transparently strained between Mrs Stobart and Dr Beatrice Coxon and, to a lesser degree, Dr Catherine Payne and one of the orderlies. Dr Coxon complained bitterly about the appalling facilities for the nurses, and argued that this continual moving and packing made it impossible for them to give adequate treatment to those wounded who came to them. Though Mrs Stobart was very brave and strong-willed and, regardless of her personal safety, recklessly rode all day near the firing line, she could be very obtuse regarding others, and sometimes disregarded the most basic conditions necessary for the doctors to do their exacting work. Once, after every item of medical equipment had been packed preparatory to their departure at dawn, she accepted a batch of seriously wounded men in the middle of the night instead of letting them be taken to the military dressing station nearby.

There was no open breach, just hairline cracks. The doctors, nurses and orderlies were dedicated, disciplined people, who certainly respected Mrs Stobart's remarkable achievement during the Balkan War, and were prepared to make many allowances. Not that they themselves were always docile—most of them were also strong-willed and independent and, worn down by the perpetual stress of the difficult circumstances, they must often have been touchy and over-critical.

One must be fair to Mrs Stobart. Some might fall back on the generalised presumption that women tend to bicker, and ask what does one expect with a woman in command. Column commander she might be, but Mrs Stobart had none of the awesome authority of an army major over his men. Whereas army discipline and an officer's authority—no matter how dumb the officer or how idiotic his orders—were absolute with harsh penalties for those who disobeyed, Mrs Stobart's authority, though real, was much more ephemeral, only backed by the self-discipline, good-will and respect of her British staff. That the Serb soldiers in her column obeyed implicitly was not surprising, since Mrs Stobart only had to report any recalcitrance on their part to Colonel Teržić and the matter was dealt with in drastic army fashion. But if a British orderly or doctor criticised or even opposed her she was powerless to mete out any penalty. All she could do was to let off steam in her diary: 'B. abominably cross . . . and forced me to separate from the Komorra while arguing with the little fool. Wdn't be chivvied bec. didn't want her to go back & wait for cars alone in the dark. Dr Coxon equally bad and supported her. Eventually the 3 cars caught up and they all got in thank God!'

In those days when class distinctions were more apparent and more accepted than today, most ordinary soldiers in Serbia were unsophisticated peasants while their officers, though also of recent peasant origins, were nevertheless from a more educated milieu, which ensured that their authority was accepted and generally trusted. Mrs Stobart, however, despite her wealth and well-bred county background had to contend with a group of women, most of whom, by the criteria of the time, were every bit her equal, while the doctors were professionally her superiors. This latter fact rankled deeply and probably explains the resentment of qualified medical women, especially doctors, that she harboured for the rest of her life. Imperious and distant though she was she did have her adherents among the staff—some had already served with her in the Balkan War—who remained uncritical and loyal to her to the end. And throughout all her trials she had the support of her husband who never left her side.

The column continued its erratic career, gradually drifting southwards. More wounded came in, again on the endless line of ox-wagon tumbrils. One night over a hundred men passed through the dressing stations. Some were dead on arrival—badly wounded men who had succumbed to the final combined assault of the cruel ox-wagon ride and the bitter cold. Alongside the road were now many dead. When there was time they were buried where they lay, their graves marked by simple wooden crosses. At least, conforming to Serbian tradition, they were buried by the wayside where for eternity they would have the company of travellers and wayfarers.

Occasionally couriers brought news and thus they learned of the Bulgarian offensive; that the Kragujevac hospitals were receiving thousands of wounded from the north; that a detachment of Allied troops had crossed the frontier from Greece; and that England had declared war on Bulgaria. Now the retreating Šumadija Division and Mrs Stobart's column were frequently engulfed by the tide of refugees—whole families, young boys and girls and the very old, all with their wagons and driving before them their precious flocks of goats, sheep, pigs and geese. Sadly the column made its way through deserted towns and silent villages with shuttered shops, empty houses, squalid muddy streets, all churned to a glutinous morass by thousands of horses, oxen, people, wagons and motor vehicles.

By October they were in full retreat, with the roar of the guns of lost battles behind them. They camped where they could, mostly by the roadside. Once they were attacked by enemy 'planes but no damage was done. But soon afterwards nearly sixty wounded were brought to them. They unpacked the surgical boxes and, by the light of storm lanterns, the doctors and nurses cut away the torn and bloody uniforms to dress the often terrible wounds sufficiently to get the patients on to Kruševac. As many as possible were carried in three ambulances, for the other three ambulances had been ordered to Kragujevac and had not yet returned, and they had no ox-wagons. To enable as many wounded as possible to be taken in the ambulances all the staff had to walk. It was a terrible walk along an appalling road, muddy, rutted, and riddled with jagged potholes, with broken bridges over streams and culverts. The Serbian orderlies lifted the wounded out of the ambulances and carried them over the broken bridges, while the vehicles were manhandled across the streams and gullies.

To report their whereabouts Mrs Stobart sent a courier to Dr King-May in Kragujevac and received a message back saying that the military authorities were evacuating them down the Ibar valley, where they intended to set up a dressing station at the monastery of Studenica, and that Dr Čurčin had been detailed to look after the British units during their evacuation.

Back with the army things had never looked so black. No one believed any longer in the advent of Allied aid, but Mrs Stobart was determined to keep her column together until all hope of a defensive stand was gone. On 2 November old King Peter passed through their camp and appealed to the men to hold fast a little longer pending Allied aid. 'But', writes Mrs Stobart, 'it was obvious that the Serbian army with its inferiority of artillery might check but could never stem the tide of the enemy advance.'

They pushed through towards Priština with the enemy on their heels—Mladenovac had fallen, then Kragujevac. Bitterly the women lamented their splendid hospital now in enemy hands, and wondered what had befallen their friends who had remained behind. Another batch of severely wounded men arrived. Under terrible conditions the medical women dressed their wounds and took the worst cases in the ambulances, sending the others ahead in the army ox-wagons. Now that the pressure was on and the wounded were coming to them the doctors and nurses were at their best, their disappointments and irritations forgotten as they calmly tended the wounded, moving quietly around the tents and ambulances, impervious to the tumult and chaos surrounding them.

On they went southwards towards Priština via a central route between the Ibar and the Niš road, always accompanied by the ceaseless rain and the endless sound of creaking wagons and the squelch of feet and hooves in the sucking mud. 'I looked behind me and saw only darkness and sorrow, columns and confusion', wrote Mrs Stobart. The oppressive silence of that retreat was heart-rending. There was complete absence of human sound, the silence of hopelessness and exhaustion, hour after hour, day after day: 'No laughter, no singing, no talking—the silence of a funeral procession, which indeed it was.'

Comparisons were later drawn between the Serbian retreat and Napoleon's retreat from Moscow. But the great difference was that Napoleon's armies were the invaders being driven out, while in Serbia, not only the army but thousands of civilians were being forced out of their homeland by the invading armies. An estimated 200,000 soldiers, the same number of civilians, 60,000 prisoners of war, 30,000 boys and hundreds of foreign relief personel took part in that retreat. Only the old and the very young remained behind, and those already trapped in occupied territories.

The day they heard that the Bulgarians had taken Niš, Mrs Stobart's column reached a narrow defile. Funnelling through it was an endless stream of humanity struggling to remain on the narrow road—army convoys, cavalry, peasants with their carts, all pushed day and night, a seething mass of panic-stricken people. Wagons became stuck in the mud, vehicles broke down, and everyone fought ruthlessly to keep their position in this narrow line of flight. Food was very short, shelter there was none, petrol was running out for the ambulances, and the enemy drew nearer from behind.

At the village of Brace they evacuated their wounded to a military hospital at Kursumlije fifteen miles away, then continued through Tulare where they buried their dead, and Čungula where they learned that Brace was burning behind them. Two weeks after their flight began a blizzard struck, and the sudden intense cold was frightful for the humans and lethal for the animals. The long exhausting march, the cold and lack of fodder were causing havoc, and horses and oxen lay dying all along the route.

They came to the 'field of blackbirds'—Kosovo, the ancient battlefield again strewn with the dead and the dying. 'Every few yards the corpses of oxen and horses and . . . bodies of wounded and dying men kept the image of death foremost in mind.' The luminous light of a pale wintry moon brought into relief the dark forms of the dying and the dead, and the waters of the flooded plain shimmered like sheet-glass.

At last they reached the outskirts of Priština, and it was here that Mrs Stobart took the final stand that later led to her being accused of 'deserting the unit'. She learned that Dr King-May and her part of the unit were quartered in the harem of a kindly Turkish merchant the other side of the town. This was the moment to reunite the unit, for the 'flying field hospital' had run its course since the Serbian army had given up; or she could have at least announced her intention of relinquishing her army command once they had all reached Peć, and of rejoining the main unit to lead it to Scutari. But she adamantly refused to take this step. Nothing was going to deflect her from her mission to lead the Serbian medical column, and she struck implacably to her principle that, since she came under Serbian army command, she was going to carry out her orders as the officer in charge of the column.

Dr King-May had sent Sister Stone and Dr McLaren to Mrs Stobart to report on the shooting of 'Ginger' Clifton, and the measures they had taken to get her into hospital at Mitrovica. Immediately this contact was made Dr Coxon, Dr Payne and two of the women drivers tried to press Mrs Stobart into consenting that they all join Dr King-May, but Mrs Stobart was obdurate: 'You can't desert now!' she fumed. And so they reluctantly agreed to stay until word came from Major Popović, the Army Medical Liaison Officer, about the immediate future of the column. But two of the orderlies, Miss Bingley and Miss Sharman, rebelled and returned with Sister Stone and Dr McLaren to join Dr King-May. Mrs Stobart's parting shot in her diary was: 'Bingley and Sharman leave to go to England with Dr May's party. No work here. Thankful rid of Bingley.'

For three nerve-racking days they hung around Priština, awaiting army orders. Once they saw three soldiers shot for sleeping in their army carts when on duty; and one of the nurses witnessed an incident of summary justice when four Serb soldiers were made to dig their own graves, kneel in them and then, tied to stakes, were shot. They were alleged to have been spying for Bulgaria.

By now there was open conflict between Mrs Stobart and the two doctors who repeatedly insisted that Mrs Stobart see Major Popović to clarify their situation regarding whether or not it would be wiser to join the others in Peć. Mrs Stobart's response was categoric: 'Of course not, when I receive an order I obey it, and I have an order to command this medical column.' But the column had been overlooked and Major Popović was nowhere to be found. An army orderly was horrified to come across them still in Priština: 'You should have left three days ago for Peć', he shouted in his agitation. At this Drs Payne and Coxon again insisted that they gave up the column and rejoin Dr King-May. Again Mrs Stobart won the round and made them promise to keep together until Peć.

Now it was clear that there was no longer any front, only a full-scale retreat. Mrs Stobart tried to get some ox-wagons since their two remaining ambulances had been sent on ahead, but their large dressing-tent had to be abandoned. Once assembled the column had enormous difficulty in rejoining the line of retreat. Finally they got into the line but hardly stopped day or night for fear of losing their place. The staff travelled in the ox-wagons and Mrs Stobart rode. Their way now led through scrub, forest and rocky country, and there was no road to speak of. The agony of fighting back into line made them hesitate to camp, even for a few hours. A lone refugee or a family might be allowed to squeeze into the retreat line, but not a whole column. By this time they had been without sleep for over seventy hours and Mrs Stobart had hardly been out of the saddle the entire time.

The last stage to Peć led them over gullies and streams, broken and blocked bridges and across ploughed fields. At last they arrived and camped in the grounds of a monastery just outside the town. Here they cut up some of their ox-wagons for firewood and, in the dim evening light, they saw looming over Peć the formidable mountains they would soon have to cross.

The next day, 30 November, Mrs Stobart called on Dr King-May whose party had also reached Peć and were preparing for their journey into the mountains. Predictably Mrs Stobart's reception was chilly. Now she had really burned her boats—come what may she chose to stick to her army column, and her unit could proceed without her, under the able command of Dr King-May, and Dr Čurčin, who would accompany all the British units over the mountains to Scutari. So, the break was made and Drs Coxon and Payne together with two nurses and three drivers rejoined Dr King-May. Of the original SRF unit only five remained with Mrs Stobart.

By now Mrs Stobart had given up begging the doctors to stay with her column—the breach was too great, and she clung to her army brief: 'I could not guarantee that I should return to London immediately. I was pledged to the army and to the column as long as my services were needed and I could not yet see what might be required of me, and it seemed wise that those who wished to make sure of being in London before Xmas should take the opportunity of Dr Čurčin's escort.'

Thus, by implying that the doctors' chief concern was to be in London for Xmas, and that they all needed the supervision of Dr Čurčin, she had her final say in the matter, and, after seeing the King-May party off, she washed her hands of them and set about preparing for her column's march over the mountains.

On 3 December her column started from Peć. Soon they were back in the familiar stream of refugees, winding their way into the awesome mountains. Mrs Stobart had ingeniously cut her remaining ox-wagons in half to make two-wheel carts out of them, better to negotiate the mountain trails. But it was no good, the trail was too narrow so they abandoned the carts and proceeded as best they could with pack ponies and the oxen, the latter to eat if necessary. Thus, the hospital equipment had to be sacrificed, so all that remained of her erstwhile proud 'flying field hospital' were the 60 or so orderlies and soldiers.

Mrs Stobart chose to avoid the claustrophobic Rugovska canyon by taking another mountain route— just as perilous and just as jammed with soldiers and refugees—over the wintry summits, through snow, ice, forests and rocky torrents, via Rožaj to Andrijevica. Stopping was always a problem since, on the one hand it was impossible to trek at night, on the other it was a dangerous procedure to camp on the mountain slope. But often they were forced to camp with logs jammed at their feet to prevent them from slithering down the steep slope.

Day after day they struggled on—far ahead and far behind the oxen, horses, and humans dragged their way through ice and snow. Once the fall of a man and his horse down the mountainside set up a chain reaction as those behind him slithered and fell, too, knocking down other men and horses as they tumbled like ninepins down the long slope. The food problem became acute and the track was lined with the bodies of oxen, horses, and even of men, dead from cold, hunger and exhaustion. No-one stopped to bury them; some had drifted far off the path to collapse and die in some lonely spot, out of reach and beyond help. No-one knows to this day how many died in those moutains, but over 50,000 soldiers and thousands of refugees and prisoners of war never reached Scutari.

Once Mrs Stobart heard a cry and turned to see her Serbian sergeant lose his nerve as his horse slithered and scrabbled, teetering on the edge of a sheer drop. As the horse slipped over the edge Mrs Stobart, yelling at the man to hang on, grabbed the reins and pulled desperately. Together they managed to rescue the horse and his precious load, and got down the hazardous path safely.

Desertions were beginning to occur in some of the army divisions. Many soldiers were plainsmen anyway, and hated and feared these hostile, alien mountains; all around the dead and the dying; and no sign of the promised help and supplies in Andrijevica or elsewhere. Given the circumstances there were few desertions, but some did turn back, two of them from Mrs Stobart's column. But, before they had got very far they were caught, and she reasoned with them, convincing them it was better to escape with her than to return alone into the arms of the enemy. Her appeal worked, and from then on she had no further problems with desertions.

Eventually they reached Andrijevica where, like those before them, they had hoped to find basic supplies, but their haul was a tiny bundle of tallow candles and fifty-six loaves of bread given them by the military camp. Now it was a matter of sheer survival as they pushed on over the high pass then down towards Podgorica.

Once they sheltered in a Montenegrin inn: 'going to bed was in those days a delightfully simple operation—men at one end of the room, women the other. No undressing, no washing, one rug on the ground to lie on and another to cover you, and once gone to bed you were generally asleep in a few minutes'; and she wryly comments that toilet facilities may have been a problem in Serbia, but they were not in Montenegro since they simply did not exist.

Their fifty-six loaves had to last her staff and sixty men until they reached the next military station, so they pushed on towards Podgorica—where again there were no supplies, and at last started the descent towards Lake Scutari. Mrs Stobart and her women staff could have taken the small ferry to Scutari, but she gallantly elected to march with her column round the lake. To their dismay the going round the mountainous shores bordering the lake was as bad as the way through Montenegro, sometimes worse. This last phase of their journey to Scutari took them through dense forests, along narrow paths muddy with melting snow. Once they scrambled over the bodies of three horses which had fallen on top of one another. The only relief in that terrible walk around the lake was the plentiful supply of wood so that the soldiers could make their roaring camp-fires at night, not only to keep warm, but to keep packs of wolves at bay.

Once the kindly Albanian monks of a small Franciscan monastery gave Mrs Stobart and her staff a frugal meal of maize, and shelter from the torrential rain; but in the small hamlets the people were terrified of these thousands of starving desperate

136

refugees pushing through the isolation of their poverty-stricken lives. The Albanian peasants, to whom hospitality is a sacred rite, who starving would share their last crust with a stranger, were hopeless and helpless before the magnitude of the disaster they witnessed daily as these homeless fugitives poured by in thousands through their austere, frugal land.

In pelting rain they finally reached Scutari. Mrs Stobart and her staff were put up at the British consul's home, a lovely house belonging to a Major Paget, an old inhabitant of Scutari, who called and told them to stay as long as they liked. After three months and 800 miles of hardship, continual marching, hunger and exhaustion, this unaccustomed luxury was a shock. Many old friends turned up in Scutari—Sir Charles Des Graz, the British Minister to Serbia, Colonel Genčić, Major Popović, and even their Divisional Commander, Colonel Teržić, who meanwhile had been promoted to Minister of War. Everyone was enormously impressed as Mrs Stobart's was the only column to have got through without any loss through death or desertion. With obvious relief Mrs Stobart wrote: 'They did not, I was humbly thankful to find, regret the experiment of having given to a woman the command of a field hospital column of the active army.'

For her the retreat was almost at an end. On 23 December they set out to catch the last boat, trekking across the marshy coastal plains to San Giovanni di Medua in time to see the boat sliding out of the harbour and, on the quay, an agitated Admiral Troubridge: 'Mrs Stobart, why are you so late? I've been expecting you all day. The last British boat has gone.' There was still a chance—a small Italian vessel, already overcrowded, would soon leave. 'I have been spending a very uncomfortable day telling 3,000 people that I can't find room on a boat that will only hold 300', said the admiral, 'but of course you shall have places.'

And so they sailed in this scruffy boat with no food, no hot drinks, no berths, but with hundreds of refugees and Serbian soldiers. It was a cold frightening voyage, but at noon on Christmas Day they landed in Brindisi.

From there they went via Rome and France to England where they found that none of their telegrams had arrived and no one came to meet them. Mrs Stobart's eventual reception was a deeply disappointing one, for on reporting to the headquarters of the SRF Committee she was greeted with a severe reprimand:

I was all the more surprised because, on my return to London from the ordeal of the three months retreat I was reprimanded by the Chairman of the Serbian Relief Fund Committee for having exceeded my instructions and having led my unit to unnecessary risks in accompanying the army to the Front. I shall never forget that interview with the Chairman. Thinking it my duty to report at once to HQ I went to London the morning after my return and, after three months of difficulties and starvation which in themselves, might have earned one would have thought some meed of sympathy I was met with a vote of censure.

Mrs Stobart's story with the wartime relief units ends here, except for one related episode. She undertook a lecture tour throughout America and she again trod on official British toes: though this tour was backed by the Ministry of Information, she crossed them by refusing their supervision. All the money she earned from her lectures, nearly £4,000, she gave to the Serbian Red Cross. Except for her steamer fare she had paid all her own expenses. On her return she called by appointment to see the minister of information but was left standing in the corridor only to be told that he was out. She left a message that another appointment be made but never heard from them again. After this rather shabby treatment she faded from the wartime scene, and turned her attention to a more inward expression of her personality, that of mysticism and spiritualism, to which she was to devote the remainder of her strange and restless life.

(*above*) In October 1915 the Serbian Army HQ escaped over the mountains to the Adriatic coast. Here they cross the ancient Sizar Bridge in Albania.

Throughout the entire retreat Serbian soldiers carried their aged and ailing Vojvode (Field Marshal) Putnik in a sedan chair

(above) Wounded being brought down from the mountains by mule 'ambulance' after the Battle of Kajmakčalan in autumn 1916; (below) near Rožaj Mrs St Clair Stobart's column huddles by the wayside awaiting the chance to push back into the retreating lines of refugees and soldiers

10

The Retreat:
FLORA SANDES JOINS THE ARMY

As the *Mossoul* steamed from Marseilles in the autumn of 1915, Dr Isabel Emslie, travelling to Serbia with the SWH Girton and Newnham unit, took note of one of her fellow passengers: 'Flora Sandes on board . . . she has been out in Serbia before as a Red Cross nurse, and has been home after typhus to collect money for the Serbs. A tall handsome woman with short grey hair and a faultless khaki coat and skirt.'

Fit and completely recovered after her convalescence in England, Flora was on her way to rejoin her Serbian hospital in Valjevo, but the news at Piraeus was ominous. The enemy was pushing down from the north, most of Serbia had fallen, and Lady Paget's unit in Skoplje was already in Bulgarian hands. Then, as the *Mossoul* sailed into Salonika on 3 November the hospital ship, *Marquette*, with many New Zealand doctors and nurses on board, was torpedoed and sank outside the bay with a heavy loss of life.

After landing at Salonika Flora wasted no time before setting out immediately by train for Monastir (Bitolj) with three of Lady Paget's staff who had been on leave in England—Lady Muriel Herbert, Elia Linden, and Dolly Miles. The four girls were met at Monastir by the British Consul, Mr Grieg, who urged them to return to Salonika without delay since the rest of Serbia would fall any day; in fact the last battle was then being fought at the Babuna Pass forty miles away, and it would only be a matter of time before Monastir itself was taken.

Flora, stubbornly desperate in her determination to return to the Serbs, had a wild idea of riding to Prizren over a hundred perilous miles north, but wisely gave it up when warned of the hazards of bandits and lack of food for her and her horses. Lady Muriel and her two companions, now having established beyond doubt that their SRF unit in Skoplje had been captured, reluctantly returned to Salonika. But Flora refused to give up. Mr Grieg, softened by her disappointment and impressed by her determination, suggested she go with him by car to Prilep, about twenty-five miles away at the foot of the Babuna Pass where, he said, there was a military hospital. Perhaps she could work there, anyway until the Serbs withdrew. Flora jumped at this offer and, leaving her luggage except for one case, a couple of blankets and her camp bed, drove off to Prilep with Mr Grieg.

They found Prilep milling with refugees and soldiers amid a resigned and sullen population. With great difficulty Flora got a room in a seedy inn that appeared also to be the town brothel. Feeling very alone and strange she pushed her way through crowds of drunken soldiers to her grubby little room which, she noted in her diary, 'contains (besides my camp bed) a rickety chair, and a small table with my little rubber basin, a cracked mirror and my faithful tea basket. From the cafe below comes a deafening chorus of Serbian soldiers . . . The view from my window is not calculated to inspire confidence either. It looks on to a stable yard full of pigs, donkeys and the most villainous looking Turks squatting about at their supper.'

To bolster her courage Flora put her loaded service revolver on the table beside the bed before lying down fully dressed to sleep. No sooner had she dozed off than she was rudely awakened by raucous shouting and pounding on the door. With revolver in one hand and a torch in the other she sat tense and scared, then yelled at the noisy interlopers in a mixture of English and broken Serb to get the hell away from her door. This seemed to redouble the efforts of the intruders until Flora began to fear the dreaded Bulgars had indeed arrived. Eventually the noisy drunks gave up and left her in peace, but she had little sleep that night.

Next day, on the way to the military hospital, Flora met an American doctor who warned her that the food was so extremely scarce in Prilep that, to get a square meal, you took your meat in one restaurant, your potatoes in another, and your coffee in a third.

Despite these inauspicious beginnings Flora was delighted when her services were gratefully accepted at the military hospital. Though she found few wounded, many cases of dysentery crowded the inadequate wards where hundreds of patients lay on the floor and proper nursing was out of the question since equipment and medicines were practically non-existent. All Flora could do was to bathe the feverish patients a little, dole out some simple medicines from her own stocks, and calm the men as best she could.

Flora was just getting settled in when she was asked to join the 2nd Regiment Ambulance Unit, an invitation she accepted with alacrity. But the hospital staff and patients, sad to see their English friend leave, warned her that life with the unit would be very tough and bet, doubtless motivated by wishful thinking, that after three days of freezing in a small tent in the wintry hills she would be glad to be back with them.

On joining the 2nd Regiment's unit Flora's first army issue was a small bivouac tent, and all the soldiers gathered around to welcome this tall, slender, good-looking recruit. During the nights that followed, sitting round the blazing camp-fires, the soldiers would often regale Flora with lurid tales of the Komitadjis, who would swoop down on them once the Bulgarians had overrun Serbia. 'The Komitadjis, who are they?' Flora asked the first time they were mentioned. And, with all the skill of born story-tellers the Serbs related the ancient tales of the Hajduks and the more modern ones of the Komitadjis.

The Hajduks, national folk heroes of medieval times, imbued with a Robin Hood code, were insurgents who led a permanent guerilla war against the Turks. Their exploits, real and imaginary, are preserved in numerous folk ballads. By the nineteenth century the Hajduks had become the Komitadjis. 'Komitadji', from the Turkish meaning a 'member of the committee', was the name given to detachments of Bulgarian and Serbian guerilla fighters of the nineteenth and early twentieth centuries who, commanded by merciless chieftains, terrorised the Turkish authorities in Macedonia and elsewhere. Bearded, heavily armed, daring and patriotic, they at first perpetuated the old Hajduk tradition. But, once the Turks had been driven out, the role of the Hajduk/Komitadji was virtually over. However, to quote the Yugoslav author Stojan Pribičević: 'following the law of inertia, these 'komitadjis' have continued their existence long after their special task was over.'

In the uncertain fluctuating political scene before and immediately after World War I some Komitadjis degenerated into lawless bandits, pillaging, robbing and terrorising the remoter mountain districts of most of the Balkans; others played a more sinister role by becoming the secret force of unscrupulous political parties, intimidating political rivals by all the weapons of terror including blackmail, kidnap and assassination. Thus, regrettably, the proud heroic Hajduks, who later became the fierce, well-organised Komitadjis fighting their effective guerilla campaign against the Turks, had entered their third phase, that of being at best robber bands attacking for pure gain, at worst political assassins bent on indiscriminate bombings and terror tactics.

Most Serbs remain true Hajduks at heart—loyal to their code of honour, hospitable to the friendly stranger in their midst, and imbued with a passionate love of their homeland that will always rally them to the side of any able leader when an alien power threatens their country.

Deeply touched that this Englishwoman had chosen to be among them, everyone did his best to make Flora comfortable. The 'ambulance' or field unit consisted of one largish tent where the patients lay two to a bed or on muddy straw on the ground in their trench-stained uniforms, until they could be moved to the base hospital. A few boxes of dressings, a small table to write at, about a dozen tents for the soldiers and ambulance men, and three ox-wagons, comprised the entire outfit, which was stationed in a rocky valley a few miles from Prilep.

Only slightly wounded men were coming in from the Babuna battle, those in fact who could make their own way since it was impossible for stretcher-bearers to carry seriously wounded men down the exposed mountain paths; it was far too difficult and dangerous. The few badly wounded who did get down suffered dreadfully in the wagons during the days of jolting over the stony mountain roads with only the rough dressing done on the battle-field from the soldier's own kit. By army regulation, each soldier carried one dressing in his pocket and this, no matter how severe his wounds, was all he had until he reached a field station.

Discipline was good among the soldiers but Flora was amazed and impressed at the easy familiarity between officers and men. 'I could never have imagined English officers and men mucking in, singing and eating together like the Serbs do', she commented. This relaxed relationship was a heritage of the old Hajduk era—the bond of guerilla bands waging their wars against the oppressors when natural leaders emerged and were followed with total faith and respect. Robert Seton-Watson, in a lecture delivered at King's College, London, in 1915, had this to say about the Serbian army:

144

No one . . . can fail to be struck by the almost ideal relations which exist between officers and men, the charming blend of discipline and comradeship . . . Just as it is customary to address the troops as a whole as 'heroes', so the officers summon their men to the fight, not as 'men' but as 'brothers'. After the day's work was over, it was pleasant to see officers and men together dancing the Kolo, the famous national dance of the Serb, and yet to realise that this—according to Prussian standards— monstrous familiarity did not for a moment impair the strict discipline which is indispensable to every army.

The warmth and kindness that surrounded Flora from the moment she arrived moved her deeply. Being a rebel against the conventions of her times she had endured and accepted the solitariness of the outsider. But here she was completely accepted; she felt at one with them. As she sat with the soldiers round the ritual camp-fires her Serbian improved as they smoked, discussed the war, told their war stories, and mourned the failure of the Allies to come. This fact could so easily have made Flora feel uncomfortable but the men spoke without rancour, always careful to spare her feelings. They went to endless trouble to help her with their complicated language and, with their natural innate courtesy, always ensured that she had the best place by the fire, and the tastiest morsel on the rare occasions when they grilled a goose or even a pig on the spit.

At last the expected order came to withdraw and they pulled back to within a few miles of Monastir. Here Flora was transferred to the regimental field unit attached to army headquarters, and for the first time she met her regimental commander, Colonel Milić. After a few words of greeting and thanks he announced that the regiment would soon have to retreat through Albania: 'We must then abandon the ambulance units because we cannot take them or the wounded over the mountains.' He talked on, discussing dispassionately the immediate grim future of his land and of his regiment; how their temporary defeat would drive them into the unknown of exile. But one day they would re-form and return to liberate their country. Turning to Flora he added, 'You had better leave now while it is still possible—you can still get over the frontier to Greece.' 'But I want to remain with the 2nd Regiment', Flora exclaimed in dismay. Apparently unmoved,

Colonel Milić explained carefully and patiently, 'We must leave the wounded here, and it will be a harsh fighting retreat through Albania since the Bulgarians will not let us go so easily.'

The threat of being pushed across the border into the sanctuary of Greece distressed Flora deeply. Never had she been so happy, felt so accepted, and so understood as she had during this short time with the 2nd Regiment. After all, she pleaded, she was a trained first-aid worker, there would be wounded if there was fighting, and she could help even without hospital equipment. Perhaps in his wisdom Colonel Milić divined something of this young woman's torment. For a while he was silent, lost in thought, almost as if he had forgotten her. 'Well', he mused at last, 'perhaps we could take you into the army.'

Flora gaped. What on earth did he mean? That she could actually become a soldier? Suddenly, on an impulse, Colonel Milić walked up to her and, removing the small metal '2' from his own epaulette, he pinned it on to Flora's smart khaki jacket. 'There—you are now a private in the 2nd Regiment, 1st Serbian Army.'

Dumb with excitement she glanced down at the little silver '2' on her jacket, then looked up into the gravely smiling face of her colonel. 'We will, of course, have to confirm your recruitment with the Divisional Commander', he said, 'but it should be all right.' Then, as a special compliment, he lent her a white half-Arab mare, which she called 'Diana' and, as a tribute to her as an Ally, not as a woman, he decreed that she might ride and have a batman, normally the privileges of an officer.

Would the soldiers accept her as one of them? Feeling rather apprehensive Flora joined them as usual that night by the fire. Nothing had changed except perhaps the bond was deeper—she had become *naša Engleskinja* (our Englishwoman). Though it was wonderful to Flora that these soldiers accepted her as one of them, it was not so strange to them that a woman had become a combatant soldier. There were many precedents in their violent fighting history. Dragutin, a small stocky Serb who had volunteered to be Flora's batman, was soon fussing and bothering about her, proud of his unusual charge. But the matter still had to be confirmed by the Divisional Commander, Colonel Vasić.

Several days later Flora rode with Colonel Milić to headquarters where, in a large room, she found Colonel Vasić and an Allied officer, Captain O'Grady from the British Military Mission. After the introductions Flora stood aside as the officers discussed the tactics for the impending withdrawal. Then Colonel Vasić pushed his maps aside and turned to Flora: 'Are you really certain that you wish to remain with the regiment? I ask because this is your last chance to get out. You would be wiser perhaps to take the train tonight to Salonika. It might well be the last one.'

Flora was not going to be packed off so easily. Trying to sound as detached as possible she told Colonel Vasić how attached she had become to the 2nd Regiment, what an honour it was for her, an Englishwoman, to be with it but, because she genuinely had the interests of the Serbs and the regiment at heart, she would indeed catch the train if Colonel Vasić felt that she, a woman, would be an encumbrance. However, if he thought she could be of the slightest use, she begged to be allowed to stay.

Colonel Vasic then went on to warn her that the coming months would be full of danger and uncertainty; there would be no ambulance unit, the retreat through Albania would be terrible— nothing she had gone through so far would compare with the hardships that lay ahead. Many would die in the retreat, and there would be much fighting. Yes, Flora replied, she did realise that the times ahead would be very difficult and dangerous, but she was very fit and she did so much wish to remain with the regiment.

Colonel Vasić frowned and fiddled with his papers while Flora waited in trepidation; then he looked up and spoke the words that sealed Flora's fate and determined the entire extraordinary course of her future: 'Very well—Colonel Milić speaks highly of you, and tells me how much you are respected by the Regiment, and your presence will, I am sure, encourage the soldiers since you will represent our Ally, England. I thank you and wish you luck.'

Captain O'Grady shook her hand warmly and wished her all the best as Flora stumbled out of the room with mixed emotions, not the least being the shattering anxiety of whether she was worthy of being a soldier among these brave men.

Westwards from Skoplje and the Vardar valley the Bulgarians advanced in overwhelming numbers, four to one against the Serbian strength, and much fresher and better equipped. Position

147

after position was lost and the Serbs, falling back little by little, had now been fighting a rearguard action for six weeks in rain and bitter cold. A blizzard was blowing when the general order was given to retreat. Before the ambulance unit was disbanded and, during an artillery attack, Flora watched from high ground the distant lines of soldiers retreating across the snow. Flora never forgot that sight: 'The grey November twilight, the endless white expanse of snow, lit up every moment by the flashes of the guns, and the long column of men trailing away into the dusk, wailing a sort of dirge . . . something between a song and a sob—it was a most heartbreaking sound.'

When Flora joined the regiment, Captain O'Grady and the British consul had given her some small gifts to distribute to the soldiers—a case of woollen Balaclava helmets, one of cigarettes and another with jam. After some consultation Colonel Milić suggested she give them to the 4th Company which had had a particularly bad time in the Babuna fighting. Feeling a bit self-conscious and accompanied by the Company Commander, Lieutenant Jović, she distributed her largesse—a spoonful of jam and two cigarettes per man and one helmet between seven! But the men were delighted and touched, these peasant soldiers who received nothing from the outside world, no mail, no news, no food parcels, to make their hard life a little more bearable.

Suddenly one evening the 2nd Regiment was ordered to withdraw from Monastir and to move westwards towards Struga at the north end of Lake Ohrid on the borders of Albania. As Flora rode 'Diana' along the icy, slippery road she froze with the cold and was nauseated by the 'horrible looking corpses of bullocks and donkeys and ponies'. She was even more appalled at the amount of abandoned ammunition and rifles lying by the roadside.

To help combat the piercing cold Flora carried a thermos flask of hot tea laced with cognac, and at an old Turkish blockhouse near the frontier she offered a shivering gendarme a drink from her flask. He accepted gratefully then, to her surprise, cried out as he gulped from the flask, nearly dropping it in his consternation at finding the contents piping hot. He could not fathom the mystery but concluded that the tea had somehow been warmed by being on the saddle against 'Diana's' sweating body.

In the half-light of a grey winter dawn they pushed on through the snow around the north end of Lake Ohrid via Struga towards the bleak Albanian mountains—'and altogether we looked the most hopelessly forlorn army imaginable, setting our face towards the dark, hard-looking range of snow-capped mountains which separate their beloved Serbia from Albania. It was the last town in Serbia, and we were being driven out of it into exile . . .' As they marched on into the mountains the physical suffering was nothing compared with the homesickness and despair of the soldiers as they turned their backs on their homeland and headed for the coast that lay far beyond the mountains.

Just after Struga, which was being shelled by the advancing Bulgarians, the regiment camped and, after their first night in Albania, Flora awoke at dawn to find the entire regiment sitting up with their shirts off busily hunting the 'first hundred thousand' lice; and longed to be free to do the same herself. On that first morning of their retreat Flora shared some bread and cheese with a half-starved soldier who, with ten others, had received no army rations at a remote outpost, and had just rejoined the main regiment. To her surprise he carefully pocketed the food. 'Aren't you going to eat it?' Flora asked. 'Not now—I want to share it with my comrades.'

On the Albanian side of the frontier they found poverty-stricken hamlets and Flora was shocked by the hostility of the unfortunate inhabitants, who were terrified and apprehensive as the Serbian army poured through, followed closely by the Bulgarians. Throughout a long and violent history foreign armies had meant pillaging, looting and death to the villagers.

As they climbed into the mountains one of the officers showed Flora how to handle a small mortar and even let her fire it towards the distant approaching Bulgarians. Once Flora heard a far-off wail carried by the wind—'Hourra! Hourra!', the spine-chilling cry of the Bulgarians as they charge. A shiver of fear ran through Flora like an electric shock.

Once the regiment was halted and deployed, ready for an attack. Flora made her way to the 4th Company, and they took cover among the rocks. At this point Flora had no rifle, only her revolver, but one of her comrades sometimes lent her his rifle while he had a quiet smoke. They lay up, firing at the Bulgarians all day until the shooting died down at dark. After her baptism of fire Lieutenant Jović took Flora formally into the 4th Company.

On they went, up and up the steep pine-clad slopes in pitch darkness and pouring rain, everything cold and soaking wet, and Flora learned that to climb into a frozen saddle was one of the lesser joys of life. The ascent up the 5,500-foot high Mount Chukus (Čukus) became much steeper nearer the summit, forcing them to leave their horses and scramble on foot through the dense mountain scrub, over rocks and boulders, slithering and stumbling in the mud and snow. Twelve hours later they finally camped among the pines in the pouring rain at the top of the mountain. Flora was so wet and frozen that she crawled out of her tent to dry her soaking feet. She stuck them too near the fire and burned her boots! Later she realised that she had escaped a severe reprimand when, soon afterwards, she witnessed an officer upbraiding a soldier who had burned his coat: 'Do you think you were the only one who was cold?' the officer raged, 'Why didn't *that* man and *that* man burn their clothes?'

The evening after they had camped at the summit of Mount Chukus the rain vanished to reveal clear night skies and a brilliant moon. 'We spread our blankets on spruce boughs around the fire and rolled up in them. It was a most glorious moonlight night, with the ground covered with white hoar frost, and it looked perfectly lovely with all the camp fires twinkling every few yards.' Flora lay on her back looking up at the stars. 'What are you thinking about?' one of the soldiers asked. After a moment Flora answered, 'When I am old and decrepit and done for, and have to stay in a house and not go about any more, I shall remember my first night with the 4th Company on Mount Chukus.'

At last Flora was issued with a rifle. It felt odd, and not at all pleasant, to be armed and licensed to kill, and it made her very uneasy at first. But the distance helped make the act of shooting to kill more impersonal and she eventually overcame her qualms, though never a deep inner revulsion.

Food was nearly exhausted and the men subsisted on corn cobs roasted over the fire or beaten into coarse flour for bread. One evening the regiment, sporadically engaged in fighting, slowly made its way on foot down the other side of Mount Chukus. Fortunately the moonlight helped, though Flora cursed as she slipped down the steep muddy slope in her smooth-soled boots. But she made it and finally they all reached the place where the horses, which had been taken down in advance, awaited Flora and the officers. Thankfully Flora mounted and then rode all night through a narrow defile with a sheer drop on one side and a cliff on the other until at dawn they reached Elbasan, a small shabby town with muddy cobbled streets in the Albanian highlands. Again the inhabitants were hostile and refused to sell food for the men or hay for the horses. It was still freezing cold but the regiment pushed on through a torrential downpour into the Shkumbin river valley to find the river in full spate, and the beautiful old bridge no longer spanning the wide torrent. With the aid of planks and logs Flora and the officers managed to get the men across before fording the wide swift river on horseback, arriving exhausted on the other side where they camped in the bracken of the hills.

Already, in the short time since being attached to the 4th Company, Flora had shared with her comrades a day's fighting, followed by a 12-hour march which had begun at 3 o'clock in the morning, then the climb to the top of Mount Chukus in pelting rain, two more days of continuous fighting, then the trek down the mountain—all on a diet of a few corn cobs and a little weak tea! But by the time they had crossed the Shkumbin river the pursuing Bulgarians seemed to have given up the chase, so Flora and her comrades were able to rest for four days—until Christmas Eve.

That 1915 Christmas Eve morning Flora found in her pack 200 francs so she and a couple of officers went up into a small Albanian hamlet where they managed to buy a few unleavened loaves of coarse bread. They rested a while outside a small house and an old Albanian woman brought Flora a bowl of sour milk and, in return, Flora gave her a small mirror which sent the old lady into ecstasies of wonder. Then she asked Lieutenant Jović whether Flora was a woman or a soldier. 'She is an Englishwoman, but a Serbian soldier', he replied, leaving her very baffled. With the loaves from the village and the remnants of some cognac they celebrated the western Christmas, and Flora delighted everyone by playing 'God Save the King' and carols on her violin. This poor instrument, which she had insisted on bringing with her, suffered considerably and, Flora admitted, 'the damp had not improved its tone'.

During their Christmas celebrations news came that Skoplje had been taken by the French. For a while, until the news proved false, everyone was jubilant. In fact, the first reliable news was only available when Durazzo was reached. While the main part of the Serbian army, most of the civilian refugees, the 'Scottish' women and Dr Čurčin's charges were enduring the grim retreat over the Montenegrin and Albanian mountains through northern Albania to Scutari, thence to San Giovanni di Medua, that part of the army that had been engaged in southern Serbia was routed through central Albania via Elbasan and Kavaia to Durazzo. The latter route was a good deal shorter with no high mountain passes to cross; but it was a fighting retreat as the Bulgarians pursued the army most of the way. The worst parts were the last ones, the terrible trek across the sodden, muddy river flats between Kavaia and Durazzo, then the grim slog through the marshes of the coastal plains, across two wide unbridged rivers to reach the port of Valona in southern Albania to embark for Corfu.

The food problem worsened. In the small Albanian hamlets what little food there was sold at famine prices. The men lived solely on their coarse corn-meal bread made from corn cobs, but even these were running out. The sound of guns had vanished, but now valuable horses and pack animals were lost through exhaustion and starvation. Flora had long since lost 'Diana' and was now mounted on a rough mountain pony. Even if ill, the men had to keep going since no one could be carried.

Flora had never felt so totally exhausted in her life. Every nerve, every muscle ached. She now understood what her exhausted soldier patients had meant when they complained that 'everything hurts'. She wrote: 'You seem to be nothing but pain from the crown of your aching head to the soles of your blistered feet.' As they struggled down from the highlands towards Durazzo the weather became mercifully warmer, but everyone was by now at the brink of total exhaustion.

Finally they reached Kavaia, at the edge of the coastal plains. Flora had never seen mud like that in Kavaia, the streets were a liquid black mass, the men waded through it above their knees, and it seeped over the edge of the officers' top boots. Every few yards were dead and dying horses which had floundered in the mire.

That last bitter stage, almost within reach of their goal, was the ultimate nightmare—many men collapsed, often dying where they fell from exhaustion and exposure. The last day's march was interminable, from five in the morning until eight that night. As they stumbled towards their destination they could hear the boom of naval guns in the distance as the Austrian navy shelled Durazzo.

On New Year's Eve, the last day of 1915, they staggered into their camp ten miles from Durazzo. Several days later Flora rode into the town and the first person she saw was a 'real live English sergeant-major' walking down the street, who was very astonished at the exuberant welcome he received from a Serbian 'soldier'. He took Flora at once to the headquarters of the British Adriatic Mission where she was given a tremendous reception amid considerable amazement and admiration. From their limited stores the British officers gave her cases of 'sundry luxuries'—bread, butter and jam—to take back to her regiment.

Meanwhile the Serbian Orthodox Christmas, which falls nearly two weeks after the western one, had arrived, and the survivors of the various Serb regiments, including Flora's, celebrated their festivities for three days. And, as a special celebratory bonus, Flora was made a corporal and invited to dine with the colonel of the regiment and his staff at the officers' mess.

Soon after her arrival in the camp near Durazzo, to Flora's amazed delight, she received a telegram from her friend, Emily Simmonds, asking her to come at once into the town where she was in charge of relief for Serbian refugees. Flora immediately obtained leave to ride into Durazzo where she learned that Emily was at the house of the Serbian crown prince Alexander, whither she had been commanded so as to be presented to His Royal Highness. On learning of Flora's presence in Durazzo, Prince Alexander extended the invitation to her and, in a quiet informal ceremony, he decorated the two women with the coveted Serbian Order of St Sava in recognition of their selfless and heroic services to Serbia.

Emily, idealist and pacifist, was taken aback and not wholly approving of her friend's transformation into a soldier. But their close mutual respect and friendship prevailed over their differences and Flora got leave to give Emily some invaluable help in her relief work with the Serbs, especially during their hazardous evacuation to Corfu and Corsica.

11

PRISONERS OF WAR

While the sixty British women were slogging their way in the retreat towards Albania, and Flora Sandes was approaching her army career, those who remained behind awaited in some trepidation the arrival of the enemy. As we have seen, the first to be overrun were Lady Paget and her SRF staff in Skoplje. To a great extent this chapter belongs to them. Though the restrictions and uncertainties that faced the British units in the north when the Austro-Hungarian troops occupied the region were difficult and occasionally disagreeable, they experienced none of the extreme hardships, tensions and privations that were the daily lot of Lady Paget's unit. From the day the Bulgarians arrived Lady Paget faced a variety of difficult and delicate situations which demanded all her tact, diplomacy and quick-wittedness.

By mid-October that cold wet autumn of 1915, when the arrival of the Bulgarians was imminent, considerable tension built up among the staff and patients, 'Nerves and tempers varied like a barometer before a typhoon', said Lady Paget later, 'unceasing rain chilled our bodies and souls and mud plastered everything with ugliness and desolation.' She had taken a calculated gamble in electing to remain with the Serbian wounded at the splendid SRF hospital to await the conquering Bulgarians. Two years earlier her relief work in the Balkan War, when Bulgaria was Serbia's ally, had brought her in contact with many Bulgarians including Queen Eleonora, a skilled nurse and tireless relief worker. She had been generous in her praise for Lady Paget, who now banked on this former collaboration and mutual respect to enable her to maintain the hospital, and thus continue tending the Serbian wounded and the thousands of hapless refugees thronging the stricken city.

On 22 October the Bulgarians entered Skoplje, took over and established martial law. Within a week the city faced total famine and chaos. The retreating Serbian army had driven before it all the livestock including sheep, cattle and horses, destroyed bridges and railways as they went, and burned all the crops. What little remained was commandeered by the Bulgarians for their troops, leaving nothing for the unfortunate civilians and the refugees pouring in from the countryside. The SRF hospital stores contained considerable stocks of clothing, but only limited food supplies including 300 sacks of flour.

The first four weeks of occupation saw four successive Bulgarian commandants of Skoplje, all suspicious of the foreign missions. With so many changes of command Lady Paget had little chance of establishing contact with any of them, and once narrowly escaped a nasty situation. One day the commandant ordered her to inspect a mass grave which, he alleged, contained the bodies of Bulgarian victims of Serbian atrocities. He wanted, he claimed, an independent witness to confirm that Serbian allegations about Bulgarian atrocities were lies, that in fact the reverse was true. Under guard she was escorted to the grave beside which lay several exhumed bodies. But, just in time, she noticed two cameramen and quickly drew back since, she now realised, the intention was to photograph her beside the bodies for propaganda purposes. The few she saw showed no signs of brutality—rather they seemed what they most probably were, soldiers who had died in battle.

As the victors settled in, Lady Paget with considerable difficulty convinced the Bulgarian authorities that it was in their interest to allow her unit to administer relief to the starving refugees, who included people from all the Macedonian minorities—Serb, Turk, Bulgarian, Greek and Albanian. But the unit soon ran into trouble when Bulgarian groups accused them of favouring the Serbs, a charge which resulted in temporary suspension of relief operations and renewed attempts by Lady Paget to start them again. She explained to the commandant that her unit followed a policy which she believed to be reasonable, namely 'to give to all who were absolutely destitute and without resources, regardless of nationality'. Gradually the Bulgarians came to appreciate the principle upon which the unit worked, and to trust its administrator, which led to a smoother relief operation to the benefit of all concerned.

In the subsequent winter months Skoplje was in the grip of famine and sub-zero cold. The hospital was crammed with wounded, including many surgical cases necessitating ten to fifteen hours a day in the operating theatres; and at night the

Sisters, each with a single candle, made their rounds in wards of fifty beds, doing painful and complicated dressings by the light of that small spluttering flame. With no form of heating whatsoever the wards were deadly cold, and the spartan staff accommodation 'through the coldest and darkest days of winter, except for a solitary candle had neither light nor warmth'.

Daily they endured the exhausting experience of extorting the barest essentials from the authorities. After the commandant, or mayor, besieged by a thousand applicants, had been reached and persuaded of the absolute necessity of some commodity, he would sign an order which was then submitted to the supply officer, who would protest violently at the amount authorised and reduce it to a fraction. This was then followed by a battle for transport, for the unit's ambulances were immobilised through lack of petrol, and ox-wagons were as rare as taxis. Should no transport be available the entire performance had to be repeated the next day, since permits were only valid on the day of issue. 'Lucky was the day when permits, ox-carts and stores all coincided, and the hospital fires and lights all brightened up for a bit.' So acute was the fuel shortage and so bitter the cold that the staff tore down their new wooden sheds for firewood.

Informers were a constant nuisance as they plagued the commandant with tales of the purest fantasy, for example that among the refugees getting relief were Serbian soldiers dressed as women, and that military information was being exchanged. Unfortunately, the Bulgarians, paranoiacally suspicious, tended to believe them. One day, thoroughly fed up, Lady Paget stormed into the commandant demanding that sentries be placed on guard at the distribution centre to prove that nothing irregular was taking place. Reluctantly he agreed, the sentries duly arrived, and the unit had less trouble from the informers.

A horrible feature of that grim winter was the number of unburied animal carcasses—horses, oxen, mules—everywhere, even around the hospital precincts. The skins had been removed by enterprising Turkish shoemakers, but 'the bodies lay there bloated and purple in the snow, while roving bands of pariah-dogs and flights of carrion-crows tore them to pieces. It was difficult to go more than a few hundred yards without finding a ditch choked with putrefying carcasses.' No one could bury them, the ground was too frozen; there was no fuel to burn them, and so they remained. But, far worse: 'It was not only the beasts that had to await over-long for burial; the corpses of soldiers did not count for much more when there were so few to look after the living.' Bodies overflowed the mortuary in the first days after the last battle for Skoplje, and were laid out in nearby sheds. The town authorities undertook to remove them for burial; but it was not until the hideous smell of death and putrefaction pervaded the area that, to their horror, the medical staff found that not only had the dead not been removed but the mortuary was choked to the entrance with rotting corpses.

Though the intense cold helped keep epidemics at bay, it caused untold misery. Hundreds of refugees and lost soldiers, trying to reach Skoplje, froze to death in the drifts or arrived crippled with severely frostbitten feet. One party of men had no bread for nineteen days and no food at all for five. Many were raving mad with hunger. Sometimes the SRF distribution unit dealt with 4,000 people a day, handing out a half-kilo of flour or rice per adult and a quarter-kilo per child. Many women and children arrived in rags having *walked* the entire way from Prizren or Priština, over sixty miles through snow and mud, and the unit would clothe them completely. Orphaned children of all ages wandered in alone, ill and emaciated; they, too, had walked across the frozen country, surviving solely through the kindness of Bulgarian and Austrian soldiers who gave them scraps of food. Pregnant mothers in rags came for something to wrap round their future babies; other young mothers stood for hours with babies in their arms, awaiting their pitiful flour allowance; sometimes the unit even paid the rents of these unfortunate women to prevent them being evicted. Once, one of the tragic boy contingents turned up, 105 of them, 'shoeless, destitute and covered with lice'. They had tramped through the snow from Prizren. Fearing typhus Lady Paget, with Bulgarian permission, brought the boys to the hospital where they were bathed and disinfected and their tattered rags sterilised.

At the end of November Lady Paget faced another crisis, this time from her own staff. The continual overwork, tension, privations, cold and malnutrition were taking their toll and, above all, the decreasing number of Serb patients and the increase of Bulgarians were negating any reason for staying. The unit argued that approaches should now be made to the Bulgarians regarding their repatriation through the International Red Cross. Lady Paget agreed and approached the commandant who, much to her relief, was understanding, promising that once the railways were reopened and troop movements permitted it, the unit staff could be sent home.

Then in December the entire delicate structure of relations with the Bulgarians was thrown completely out of gear by the sudden arrival, one foggy morning, of the Germans. In no time they swarmed all over the place, commandeering everything in sight, upsetting friend and foe alike. Over a thousand soldiers quartered themselves in the hospital outhouses, exhausted the vital hospital water supplies and took all the hay, leaving the unit's draught animals to starve to death.

Lady Paget took a chance. She called on the Bulgarian commandant and complained bitterly about the German behaviour, reminding him that the British staff were *his* prisoners and that he should assert himself more since he was in command of Skoplje, or the Germans would take over completely; anyway, she ended, it was his responsibility to see that his prisoners were treated correctly. It worked. Soon the Bulgarians, thoroughly offended by the Germans, hardly concealed their dislike for their ally. Matters came to a head when the German High Command under General Mackensen arrived, and the army medical corps tried to seize the hospital, bursting in, ordering everyone about, and announcing that all the British would be interned in Germany for the duration of the war. Again Lady Paget flew to the commandant, and together they drew up a plan of mutual self-defence. Until the British staff were repatriated the Bulgarians would ostensibly take over the hospital, appointing a Bulgarian medical director. Nothing would change regarding the running of the hospital, except that the Bulgarian flag would fly from the mast. Overnight the plan was put into effect but the Germans, furious at being deprived of the hospital, stepped up their petty harassment of British and Bulgarians alike.

Individual German officers and soldiers behaved perfectly, often helping the overworked staff; all the offensiveness came from their HQ. The unit CMO, Dr Maitland, by now so experienced with typhus, won the grudging respect of the Germans when he undertook to examine their own typhus patients. While the German doctor stood at a safe distance, 'spectacled, masked, and her-

158

metically sealed against infection', Dr Maitland calmly sat by the patients, examined them carefully and lectured the nervous Germans on handling typhus cases and the necessary disinfection procedures.

Regarding their repatriation, Lady Paget had written privately to Queen Eleonora begging her to use her influence since the strain of work was now telling seriously on the staff. At last, on 5 January 1916, the railway to Niš was reopened, but the commandant warned the British that it would still be several weeks before their repatriation could begin. Those weeks were extremely difficult and the general health of the staff deteriorated seriously— already six were stretcher cases. Then, quite unexpectedly, with little notice, the unit was ordered to prepare for their departure. Before dawn on 17 Febuary the unit left for Sofia in a convoy of ten Bulgarian motor ambulances.

Of their departure Lady Paget wrote: 'It was not easy to leave the hospital, though it held for us the memory of so much pain and hard work. It had been brought forth in sorrow, when typhus held the land in its grip. It had arisen up out of the filth and disease in which we found it, by the labours of a few, till by degrees it had become one of the finest and best-equipped hospitals in Serbia.' They had so hoped to hand it over to the Serbs.

In Sofia the staff were put up in hotels by the Bulgarian Red Cross and Queen Eleonora showed her concern by sending a lady-in-waiting to check that all arrangements were satisfactory. From Sofia the unit went by Bulgarian hospital train through Romania to Russia, thence by boat to England, finally arriving on 3 April 1916, seventeen months after they had arrived in Serbia.

On her return Lady Paget, who had proved such a remarkable administrator and who had, except for a short convalescence in England after a severe bout of typhus, been at her exacting post longer than any other British unit head in Serbia, learned 'that the terms of mutual civility upon which we lived with the Bulgarians have given rise in certain quarters to criticism and misunderstanding, it being specially suggested that I acted injudiciously in allowing myself to be a guest of the Queen of Bulgaria while a prisoner of war'. She had never, she pointed out, been a guest of the queen but, together with the rest of the unit, had accepted the hospitality of the Bulgarian Red Cross in Sofia.

Doubtless these petty allegations wounded this gentle sensitive woman deeply. For the remainder of the war she withdrew from the public scene but never lost her love and friendship for Serbia. She retained this for the rest of her long life, rendering many services to that country. Today there is still in Belgrade, near the large general hospital, a small street named after her—Ledi Pažet Ulica.

Far north of Skoplje, in Vrnjačka Banja and Kruševac, an ominous silence hung over the streets and squares. After the recent pandemonium of shelling and fighting, the hectic passage of army convoys in retreat and the tangled chaos of the flight of civilian refugees, the noiseless hiatus jarred the nerves of those who had remained behind. As they went about their medical duties the unit staff wondered when the Austrian troops would arrive and what would transpire when they did.

On 8 November 1915, Alice Hutchison took some orderlies down to Vrnjačka Banja station to pick up some beds that had arrived from Valjevo. Needing a few extra hands she turned to some men attired in what she had come to regard as 'prison garb' and asked them to help. 'But, Madame Doctor', whispered an orderly, 'they are the enemy!' Sure enough they were armed. Dr Hutchison was momentarily taken aback but, shrugging her shoulders, pressed on with her request. The men courteously helped load the beds then their officer announced that they would be moving into Vrnjačka Banja the next day. A couple of days earlier, following a nasty bombardment in Kruševac, Dr Elsie Inglis on her way to the hospital rounded a corner to find an Austrian regiment lined up and white flags hanging out of many windows. Kruševac had fallen.

Merging those who had remained behind into two groups, Dr Inglis put one lot in charge of a hospital set up in a former girls' school with much of the excellent SWH equipment from Kragujevac; the second group took over an annex of the Serbian army's Czar Lazar Hospital. Two days after their arrival the Austrians occupied the former hospital with all its equipment. 'Of course they took it', mourned the Serbian director, 'you had made it so beautiful.'

Except for confiscating this hospital the Austrians did not interfere with the work of the foreign units. Dr Inglis and her staff were free to come and go as they wished, to tend their patients, even to wander around the countryside. Their work was now centred in their part of the Czar Lazar Hospital where they had over 900 patients. Dr Edith Hollway alone had 300 in a former hospital storehouse, the 'Magazine'. Since they had too few beds they pushed two together to take three patients and put mattresses on the floor. In her 'Magazine' Dr Hollway ingeniously bedded patients on deep rows of shelves which ran in four tiers the full length of the building, with the slightly wounded on the top tier.

Again Dr Inglis feared typhus. The conditions were very dangerous with underfed, exhausted patients, overcrowding, intense cold and insufficient fuel and water. She appealed for another building for use as an isolation ward. 'There is no other building', was the terse Austrian response. So, once again the 'Scottish' women improvised. They made a small bathroom in the corner of the 'Magazine', installed two disinfectors, and took over the laundry. Then, every five days they systematically worked round the ward, bathing and disinfecting. They had not one case of typhus while the Austrians were rumoured to have many.

One medical task Dr Inglis refused point blank—to take charge of a hospital for women suffering from venereal disease. At first sight this refusal seems odd, even shocking, coming from enlightened women doctors, but theirs was neither a callous nor a purely moral standpoint; it was rather that they felt the Serbian wounded had prior claim to any available medical care. 'It was very difficult to refuse with our modern vision of the solidarity of womanhood', writes Dr Inglis, 'but the Hospital was not open for the safety of the women, but for the protection of the German army.'

Food was a constant problem. The main diet was a scanty ration of bread and beans; and some rice and condensed milk from the stores were boiled up to make a small supplement. Mrs Haverfield, the administrator, braving snowstorms and sleet, scoured the countryside for milk and eggs, buying from the peasants what she could, but she never found much. The misery and depression of the civilian population and the wretched state of the Serbian prisoners as they passed through Kruševac on their way to prison camps in Hungary, combined to make this a most miserable time for the unit staff. In addition, the total lack of news drove them to live on the wildest rumours: 'The English at

161

Skoplje, the Italians at Pojega [Požega], and the Russians over the Carpathians—we could not believe that Serbia had been sacrificed for nothing', Dr Inglis later recounted.

On 9 and 10 November the Austrians had occupied Vrnjačka Banja. As elsewhere, they behaved correctly and allowed the units to carry on with their work. But, much to the delight of the patients, and the awed consternation of her staff, Alice Hutchison was soon on a collision course with the occupiers over the interpretation of the Geneva Convention, bravely combating the slightest infringement of the provisions regarding her patients or the status of her staff as prisoners of war. When, at the end of November, the Austrians ordered her unit to Kruševac, she firmly refused to yield one item of her equipment until she had obtained a receipt so that it might be paid for after the war, according to the provisions of the Convention.

When Dr Hutchison's unit reached Kruševac she was appalled at the accommodation of Dr Inglis: 'Picture over twenty people— including the head of the Hospital—dining and sleeping and eating and washing in one room.' Dr Hutchison's unit was only a few days in Kruševac before being dispatched to an internment camp at Kevavara on the lonely Hungarian puszta, where they remained for nearly three months, thirty-two of them confined to two small rooms. Their incarceration was uncomfortable, but not too harsh and they even went on long walks, much to the fury of the armed guard who had to accompany them. 'After one expedition our guard got so tired that he complained to the captain though we had only been about six or eight miles. He reported that it would not be so bad if we would only walk, but we "flew like geese over the mud".'

On Christmas Day they had a small tree and a good meal since they had managed to buy two geese at black market prices. They sang carols and a subdued version of the national anthem, at which point Alice Hutchison surreptitiously, but triumphantly, produced the Union Jack, confessing that since the day the enemy had arrived she had worn it wrapped round her under her uniform.

On 4 February their repatriation journey began. They went by train via Budapest, thence to Vienna where, with the help of the International Red Cross and the neutral Americans, the unit proceeded to Switzerland. At Bludenz, waving their precious flag out of the window, they crossed the frontier to freedom.

While Alice Hutchison's unit was being hustled out of Serbia the Berrys, Elsie Corbett, Kathleen Dillon and their colleagues, were working more or less normally in Vrnjačka Banja. Though, as in Kruševac, certain controls were imposed, the Austrians behaved admirably and their commanding officer, Prince Lobkowitz, a familiar figure in prewar London social circles, was known personally to several of the British unit members.

There was much to do at first tending the seriously wounded from recent battles and civilian patients, including many children, victims of their lethal games with abandoned ammunition. But as the weeks passed fewer patients were admitted, and the Serbian wounded as they recovered were taken off to prison camps, the more serious cases being transferred to Austrian army hospitals.

On 16 January, twenty-four women, including Elsie Corbett and Kathleen Dillon from the Red Cross unit, were transferred to Kruševac and placed under Dr Inglis, who could only accommodate them all in one small room. But they managed and helped the 'Scottish' women in the wards. Three weeks later, the day after Elsie Corbett had celebrated her twenty-third birthday, the general repatriation of all the British units began with the departure of the entire Kruševac contingent under Dr Inglis. A week later the Berry unit followed from Vrnjačka Banja. They all took the same route via Vienna, where they were given great help by a distinguished Anglo-Austrian, Sir Rudolf Slatin, known as Slatin Pasha in the Sudan where he had served Britain as a provincial governor. Now he was back in his homeland for the duration of the war. At Bludenz near the Swiss frontier, all the unit staff were detained for several weeks, apparently as some kind of security precaution, but they were allowed to walk quite freely around the lovely alpine countryside. Finally they went on to Zurich, where they at last found British newspapers, 'which stunned us with their casualty lists'. They crossed France by train to Le Havre, then went by ferry to Southampton, and their journey was over—they were home.

Some of the women reappear in Serbia with units attached to the re-formed Serbian army during the triumphant return to Serbia; others, like Alice Hutchison, resumed their private lives or medical duties in Britain. But soon after reaching England, Dr Inglis began forming a large SWH unit, destined for Russia to serve

163

with a Serb army division attached to the Russian army. This division, comprising Serb volunteers from Austrian territories, was based near Odessa and badly in need of a medical unit. In autumn 1916 the unit sailed for Archangel, then continued by train to Odessa. Among those who served in Russia with Dr Inglis were Dr Lilian Chesney and Mrs Evelina Haverfield. It was a terrible campaign culminating in Russia's collapse into revolution. In November 1917 Dr Inglis, now known to be mortally ill, her staff, and the remnants of the Serbian division, were evacuated by the British navy from Archangel. On 27 November, the day after docking at Newcastle, Dr Elsie Inglis died. The funeral that followed in Edinburgh, one of the most impressive ever seen in Britain for anyone other than a monarch, was attended by members of the diplomatic corps, hundreds of medical women, suffragettes, politicians, thousands of ordinary citizens from north and south of the border, and every Serb in Britain. All lined the streets to pay homage to this truly noble woman. Soon afterwards the Elsie Inglis Memorial Hospital was founded in Edinburgh; in Belgrade another hospital would bear her name—the commemorative plaque is still there—and Ivan Mestrović cast a splendid bronze bust in her memory. And today, sinking into the undergrowth of an obscure grove in Mladenovac, is still to be found the memorial fountain dedicated by the townspeople to Elsie Inglis and her Scottish Women's Hospitals units in Serbia.

An apt and generous tribute, paid a year earlier to Dr Inglis by the historian, Robert Seton-Watson, in *New Europe*, provides an appropriate valediction:

History will record the name of Elsie Inglis, like that of Lady Paget, as pre-eminent among that band of women who have redeemed for all time the honour of Britain in the Balkans. Among the Serbs it is already assuming an almost legendary quality. To us it will serve to remind us that Florence Nightingale will never be without successors among us.

(right) Headstone of the Hon. Mrs. Haverfield's grave at Bajina Bashta. The latter part of the inscription reads: 'She worked for the Serbian people with untiring zeal. A straight fighter, a straight rider and a most loyal friend. RIP' *(MK)*;

(below) the urgency of escape from the enemy, and the frozen ground, made it impossible to bury the dead who were left where they fell

(*overleaf*) Sergeant-Major Flora Sandes, with a Serbian officer in Salonika. In the fierce battle for Hill 1212 in autumn 1916 she was severly wounded by a hand grenade, and later she was decorated with the coveted Karakjordj Cross for bravery in action

(*above*) Flora Sandes, in her eighties, at her cottage in Suffolk shortly before she died in 1961. (*Mrs. Lilian Vidaković*); (*below*) Mrs. St Clair Stobart leading her column through the snow near Rožaj in December 1915. Since they could not negotiate the mountain tracks the ox-wagons had been abandoned in favour of pack horses and mules, and a few oxen, chiefly for food

12
EVACUATION AND REHABILITATION

As about 150,000 exhausted soldiers and refugees headed slowly through the treacherous bogs of the Albanian river flats towards Durazzo, Alessio and San Giovanni di Medua, the British, French and Italians struggled frantically to establish supply lines and bases, no matter how crude, for distributing food and clothing. That they had so far partially failed was due neither to indifference nor to negligence. On the one hand the Austrian navy, unhindered, was shelling the coastal towns and torpedoing supply ships; on the other, Albania's terrible roads, the absence of railways, the malarial swamps and the lack of any harbour facilities such as wharves, jetties and lighters for landing troops and supplies, obstructed all the Allied plans for feeding, sheltering and eventually evacuating the Serbian army.

Italy, recently lured into the war on the side of the Allies by promises of future Adriatic concessions, had taken over the command of this area, much to the private regret of some Allied officers and members of the Durazzo-based British Adriatic Mission (BAM), now under Vice-Admiral Troubridge who had so recently escaped from Serbia with the retreat. The lack of effective naval action against the marauding Austrians was blamed by some on the Italians, but they were finding it extremely difficult to keep the sea communications open to Brindisi. Meanwhile the strategic and supposedly impregnable Lovčen Pass, just over the border in Montenegro, had fallen to the Austrians, posing an immediate threat to Scutari and thus the evacuation of the Serbs.

Only one possibility remained. The unfortunate Serbs would have to trek again, this time sixty miles south through the mire of the coastal plains to Valona, a small Albanian port not far from the island of Corfu. Laffan, a Cambridge historian attached to a British ambulance unit in Salonika, later wrote:

Those who went through the whole retreat say that the last stages through the marshes and mud of central Albania were the worst of all. Hope deferred, the continued starvation and the heartbreaking nature of the country broke down the resistance of the strongest. The whole retreat from the banks of the Morava to the harbour at Valona was one *crescendo* of sorrow and calamity. When at last Valona was reached thousands still died neglected before they could be taken off by the French and British ships.

Valona, with its rugged fjord-type bay, though also menaced by enemy submarines, provided a modicum of shelter for Allied supply ships. But navigation was hazardous because of steep rocky shores, and harbour facilities nil. Supplies and equipment had to be landed by a makeshift system of pontoons, while provisional jetties were built to embark the Serbs for their short uncomfortable voyage to safety in Corfu.

On 23 December, with an Italian destroyer escort, the British transport *Myrmidon* anchored in Valona harbour. On board were a detachment of Royal Engineer sappers to build the necessary jetties, a couple of Serbian Relief Fund officers, some transport vehicles and over 600 tons of SRF supplies, mostly foodstuffs such as rice and flour for the approaching Serbian army. Tugs and lighters should have been brought from Naples, but had not arrived, so two small pontoons were found and the unloading began immediately. For some reason the Italians had received orders from Rome to halt the Serbs at the Viosa river only twelve miles away in distance, but a day away in time because of the appalling swamps that barred the approaches to Valona. From the *Myrmidon* Captain Finlay wrote in his diary on 28 December:

> We are discharging bags of flour, but there is such a shortage of lighters at the end of the day we find we have discharged 25 tons. At this rate it will take 250 days to discharge the "Myrmidon" and meanwhile the Serbians whom we have come to feed are in sore need. Imagine the conditions . . . There is a train of 100 mules, each one carries 2 sacks, one on each side of it, and it takes them all day to reach the Serbians, to do the 12 miles over those awful tracks . . . There are 100,000 Serbs to be fed between here and Durazzo.

After the Herculean efforts at unloading the supplies it was very frustrating to watch the precious bales of food pile up on the Valona beaches because the only means of reaching the starving Serbs was by slow mule train. But the enterprising British and Italians managed to speed up the delivery by using a shallow-draught coastal steamer, the *Julanda*, to sail up the Viosa estuary to where the Serbian army waited huddled on the river bank. But the supply operation suffered a severe loss when the *Palermo*, bringing a vital forty-man bakery team to turn the flour into much-needed bread for the Serbs, was torpedoed and sunk with all lives lost. Soon after this disaster the Italians allowed the Serbs to move on to Valona, but with strict orders that the soldiers be transported immediately to Corfu while any civilian refugees must go north again to Durazzo.

On Christmas Day 1915, Captain Finlay went ashore at Valona with a party of six to explore the area. Near the beach they passed through an Austrian POW camp. The prisoners were in rags, most had no footwear, many were deathly ill, weakened by starvation, exposure and exhaustion, and the death-rate was fifty a day. 'You can't imagine how terrible they look', Finlay reported, 'their eyes are ghastly, and their cheeks sunken, and they are pale like ghosts of men. In the shelter the mud is a foot deep, and they lie on the ground without covering through the cold night, wondering if they will see the morning.' Eventually these unfortunate men, about 10,000 in all, were rescued and taken to Sardinia where they spent the remainder of the war in internment camps.

From 11 January the Serbs began arriving at Valona where they immediately boarded the *Myrmidon* and other transports, and were taken to Corfu. Despite Italian injunctions regarding civilian refugees, 'that regulation became a dead letter and in any case great numbers of civilians have arrived in the guise of soldiers', wrote Professor Bosanquet of the SRF in Corfu. After being clothed and fed these refugees were sent on to Corsica where newly formed units of the Scottish Women's Hospitals and the Serbian Relief Fund awaited them.

By 11 February 110,000 Serbs had been transported to Corfu, and only 20,000 remained to be taken aboard at Valona. Corfu acted as a clearing base for sorting out the wounded and ill from those whose recovery was chiefly a matter of food and rest. From Corfu, civilians and invalid soldiers were sent to Ajaccio in

Corsica and Bizerta in Tunisia, while the basically fit troops were kept back pending their transport to army camps in Salonika. The saddest task was coping with the hundreds of boy refugees, transported from the Albanian coastal hamlet of Fieri to Corfu during the first weeks of the general evacuation. 'They are a lamentable little remnant of the youth of Serbia', reported Captain Gooden, the British liaison officer, 'At Fieri they were already reduced to a small fraction, but death has been busy amongst them since.' From Corfu a small SRF team under Mr E. P. Warren took charge of the survivors on the island of Vido.

Vido, enclosed in the arms of Corfu bay, served as a combined lazaret and mortuary for the wretched boy refugees who had managed to get that far. At Fieri they were dying like flies from illness and exhaustion, so the Italians quickly transferred them to a reception camp on Vido, which came to be known as *l'île des morts*. Tuberculosis, enteric and dysentery decimated these starving boys, and nightly the aptly styled *White Sepulchre* sailed out to sea from Vido to commit hundreds of bodies to the depths. No reliable figures are available for the numbers who died during the retreat and after reaching Albania, but they run into many thousands. After the end of hostilities the Serbian government, obviously embarrassed by its hysteria in encouraging these cadets and schoolboys in their unsupervised mass escape, played down the tragedy and in 1920 issued absurdly low, and over-exact, 'official figures'. Not only had the boys no official escorts to report back casualty figures, but the Serbs were in no position to be filing casualty lists. They were not doing the evacuating, nor were they responsible for the refugee centres, hospitals etc in Corfu, Vido and Corsica—the French, British and Italian authorities were. In charge of receiving all the Serbian refugees were the various Red Cross, SRF and SWH teams, and it is their estimates, together with those of the Allied military staffs, which must be considered more realistic than the later Serbian figures.

Even the estimates of the army casualties on the retreat vary considerably. It was estimated that the Serbian army was about 200,000 strong when the order came to leave the country, and by summer 1916 the re-formed Serbian army in Salonika was about 130,000 strong, which leaves 70,000 unaccounted for. Of these, many thousands died on the retreat, or from exhaustion and disease during the first weeks in Durazzo, Valona and Corfu; many died in rearguard battles during the retreat; many lost their lives in the snow as, separated from their regiments, they tried to reach Skoplje, Monastir and Greece; a good number were taken prisoner by the Austrians and Bulgarians; and a few simply deserted. Probably 40,000 deaths during and immediately after the retreat is as good an assessment as any. And the toll of civilian refugees—old men, women and children—in the retreat is anybody's guess. Whole families, even small communities, vanished without trace, never to be heard of again. Thousands, tens of thousands?

As the thousands of Serbian soldiers poured into Corfu the fuel shortage became acute, the food distribution chaotic, and barrack accommodation very inadequate. To add to the general misery, this island of sun was drowned in torrential rain that continued unabated for six weeks, seriously hampering the unloading operations in the congested harbour, and deeply affecting the morale of the unfortunate Serbs. Complaints and grievances multiplied and, as the French grew thoroughly exasperated with the Serbs, Captain Gooden sadly wrote in his diary, 'one wishes the excellent French would exchange their sarcastic suggestions for definite instructions.'

Even after their arrival the daily mortality rate among the Serbs was about a hundred, due mainly to dysentery and exhaustion. Nevertheless, Gooden optimistically noted that though the Serbs were 'utterly worn out . . . none the less they prove to have great powers of recovery, which augurs well for their final restoration to strength'.

Once the soldiers had recuperated they were to be sent to Salonika, which was already designated as the Allied base for the future offensive north into Serbia. But the Serbs, understandably dubious about Allied promises, were very mistrustful about this impending transfer. On 1 March Captain Gooden reports that hints have been made to the Allies by senior Serbian officers that it must be ensured that when the army is moved to a new base 'it shall find a really adequate preparation awaiting it in the way of accommodation, provisions and equipment' since never again can the officers urge their men on with the old cry that 'at the next place (always the *next* place)' provisions will be awaiting them. To placate them in their anxieties the French agreed to send an advance detachment of Serbian officers to Salonika to check that adequate facilities awaited them.

173

A difficult additional problem concerned the thousands of Serbian cavalry- and pack-horses still stranded in Albania. Serbian officers continually plagued the Allies about these animals until most of them were brought to Corfu. Later Gooden adds a note in good-humoured exasperation: 'Those Serbian horses again!' Apparently they had to be tethered with wire halters since 'Serbian horses regard rope halters as a dainty goodnaturedly added to their rations.'

Further north in Durazzo, Flora Sandes, with a month's leave from the army, was resting and also helping her friend, Emily Simmonds, the dedicated Anglo-American nurse who had been running a one-woman rescue operation for Serbian refugees. Emily had escorted large batches of lost civilians, mostly women and children, in Italian, British and French ships to refuges all over the Mediterranean, running the gauntlet of enemy shipping to Brindisi, Corsica and Marseilles. Sometimes she worked for the Red Cross, sometimes for the Serbian Relief Fund, and just as often on her own initiative. Once, in Brindisi she found a couple of thousand stranded refugees who had not eaten for two days. Without hesitation she slashed through a jungle of red tape, rushed around the town buying foodstuffs, then issued the rations herself until some sort of official system was established.

From Durazzo, Flora's regiment was ordered south to Valona to embark for Corfu. Already word had gone round about the trials of that week-long trek. Allied medical officers examined the men to weed out those who were unfit since some troops could be taken by sea from Durazzo. No one was anxious to trudge through the mud for a week to Valona: 'You can't imagine', said Flora afterwards, 'how many men suddenly discovered they were crippled with rheumatism or bad feet!' In the end, on 10 February about sixty soldiers from the 4th Company, including Flora, boarded a small Italian coaster during an Austrian air attack, and sailed to Corfu.

They arrived in pouring rain, to find that their camp lay about eight miles from the town. To their dismay the ritual camp-fires were forbidden—doubtless to prevent the olive groves from being laid waste. There was no hay to sleep on and only bully beef to eat, but this was too indigestible and unpalatable for men weakened by months of semi-starvation. Above all the Serbs yearned for their basic diet, bread. A Serbian peasant can live perfectly well on his coarse, rich maize bread, but is miserable without it. One day Flora, distressed by the misery of her comrades, hitched a lift in a lorry to Corfu and spent the day in the rain going from one official to another—from the British to the French, then to the Italians and back again to the French—doggedly seeking some bread for her 4th Company. The bakery was stocked with bread, but no amount of pleading got Flora a crumb; she lacked the appropriate forms. Exhausted, dejected and soaking wet, she made one last attempt with the French authorities. Fighting back genuine tears she pitched such a pitiful tale of woe that the French relented and gave her what she wanted, with the proviso that she 'must not make a precedent of this unofficial way of doing business'! Weary but triumphant she returned to her delighted comrades with bread, meat and two demijohns of wine.

Gradually, with rest and regular food, the men began to recover. Again Flora acted on their behalf when she bullied the SRF and Red Cross into issuing clothing for her regiment. Professor Bosanquet was full of amused admiration: 'I wish I could show you . . . Miss Sandes, the nurse who retreated with the Serbians, with a gang of Serbian Red Cross men shifting hundreds of bales in the successful attempt to find underclothing enough for 3,250 men of the 2nd Regiment—*her* Regiment; thereby it became possible to draw fresh uniforms for the whole of these men who were still in the filthy rags they had worn since the retreat.' Through her energetic efforts Flora's regiment was the first of the Serbian army to be fitted out from head to foot with new British uniforms. No wonder she was soon promoted to sergeant.

Meanwhile in Britain accounts of the plight of the retreating soldiers, of the boys on the island of Vido, of the many civilian refugees and of the planned re-formation of the Serbian army at Salonika, led to renewed efforts in the SWH and SRF committees to recruit units for service in various corners of the Mediterranean. There was no shortage of volunteer medical women, nurses and VADs, many of whom had already served in Serbia, France or Belgium. Dorothy Brindley, back at her teaching post after her escape from Serbia with Jan and Cora Gordon, responded immediately to a telegram from the SRF committee, and was soon on her way with a SRF unit to Salonika; Dr Katherine Macphail, recently repatriated with Dr Inglis's group from Austrian intern-

ment, enrolled again for medical work in Corsica. Florence Maw
and Dot Newall, who had been with Mrs Stobart's unit and had
retreated with Dr King-May, went to Corsica, and so did Sister
Rankin, formerly with Lady Paget in Skoplje. Elsie Corbett and
Kathleen Dillon were soon on duty again, this time with a motor
column attached to the SWH in Salonika. Among the many
newcomers to work for the Serbs were Maurice Wilson and his
sister, Francesca, later renowned for her relief work during two
world wars, and the books she wrote about it; and Olive Lodge,
who became a scholar of repute on Montenegrin peasant life and
customs.

Generous funds allowed the SWH and SRF to dispatch superbly
equipped units with X-ray equipment, splendid canvas tents and
ward marquees, ambulances and lorries, ample clothing supplies,
the latest surgical instruments and something quite new, orthopaedic apparatus for helping rehabilitate paralysed and limbless
soldiers.

Dr Mary Blair, with a SWH team of sixteen medical women,
nurses and VADs, had been sent out in November 1915 to reinforce Dr Hutchison's unit in Valjevo. Since the enemy offensive
in Serbia had prevented them from reaching their destination,
they had set up reception centres at Gevgelija and Florina to care
for Serbian refugees, mostly women and children, who had fled
across the border to Greece. Then, in January 1916, Sir Edward
Boyle, the SRF representative, suggested to Dr Blair that she take
charge of a hospital in Corsica for Serbian refugees who had
survived the retreat. Dr Blair accepted gladly and at the end of
January her small group—the nucleus of the fifth SWH unit—
sailed to Ajaccio where they opened a reception camp and hospital,
first in an old convent, later in the Villa Miot, for civilian refugees
and invalid soldiers. Of the first soldiers to arrive, Dr Blair wrote:
'what a pitiful sight they were—broken men; many could not
stand up, so worn out were they— some footless, some wounded,
all filthy, but game to the last.'

Then came the boy refugees, whose condition shocked Dr Blair:
'Many of them had had no change of clothes for three months;
their ages ranged from six to eighteen years.' One of the unit
members, Dr Helena Jones, worked closely with these boys, many
of whom owed their lives to her devotion and medical skill. Some
time later, when the stronger boys had recovered, about 3,000

were sent to various institutions and lycées in France, and over 300 went to England where some universities, including Oxford and Cambridge, admitted about thirty who had completed their high-school studies in Serbia. while others were accepted by public schools. Several boys' hostels, financed by a special SRF committee chaired by Mrs Carrington-Wilde, were opened in a number of towns—Oxford, Cambridge, Aberdeen and elsewhere; and many boys were adopted by private families until the end of the war.

At Ajaccio, among the many diseases the units had to contend with were typhoid, malaria, pneumonia and tuberculosis; and at Sallanches in the Haute-Savoie a 100-bed TB sanatorium, put by the French at the disposal of the SWH for the many refugee tubercular cases, was under the able direction of an experienced doctor who ran her own hospital in India, Dr Matilda Macphail.

Ajaccio, remote on its wild romantic Corsican shore, had seemed secure from the chaos and misery of war until that sad invasion by ill and haggard refugees and, in charge of them, a group of determined medical women demanding this and commandeering that, and generally making their presence very much felt to the intense annoyance of the *préfet* and his good friend the British Consul, Mr Henry Dundas. Dundas was so furious at the intrusion and audacity of his countrywomen that he dashed off a long, petulant and malicious letter of complaint to the Foreign Office. He begins: 'Dr Blair (Lady Dr) Head of the Scottish Women's Hospital, influenced by the Administrator—and especially the latter, are behaving foolishly towards me.' He goes on to wail about their arrogance towards him, about them accusing him of interfering in hospital matters—which he no doubt did; about Dr Blair's insistence on ' "having it out", as she puts it', with the *préfet* and so on. 'Dr Blair and Miss Culbard of the Hospital, and Miss Bankhardt (believed by many to be an adventuress) of the Serbian Relief Fund, seem to think that they have a right to "beard" the Prefect in his den and to argue and wrangle with him to their hearts' content.' Clearly he blames all his sorrows on the administrator, 'Miss Culbard, a suffragette (I understand), is at the bottom of all the discontent in the Hospital.' In the margin of this letter a Foreign Office official has jotted an appropriate comment: 'I don't know Mr. Dundas personally, but he seems to have little sense of proportion.'

177

In a letter clearly meant to counter the consul's querulous reports, Sir Edward Boyle of the SRF wrote to the secretary of the SWH in Edinburgh:

> As Head of the British Mission here, I should like to inform you how entirely satisfied I am with the arrangements that have been made, and how creditable I think they are both on the medical side, to Dr. Blair, and on the administrative side, to Miss Culbard . . . We find ourselves faced from time to time by difficulties in one way or another, and I should like to place on record my sense, not merely of the ability with which your ladies do their work, but also of the judgement and the self-restraint which they display under all circumstances. All their colleagues here find it a pleasure to work with them.

Soon afterwards the French authorities intervened decisively with the *préfet* and the women had no further trouble from that quarter. We have no more of Mr Dundas, who presumably was left to fume impotently in his consulate.

Co-operation between the SWH and the SRF was particularly close at Ajaccio, so much so that, as Sir Edward Boyle wrote, 'in the eyes of the French and of the Serbs here the two form part of one British Mission.' Later, in addition to the Villa Miot there was a fever hospital and four dispensaries in villages where some Serb families had been sent and where, with SRF backing, they were given work and small plots of land and were enabled to grow vegetables, spin wool and weave carpets. This was good for the Serbs' morale; they earned a little money and produced vegetables for the hospital.

At Bizerta in Tunisia many thousands of Serbian soldiers were in French hospitals, barracks and rest camps. There Maurice Wilson, the SRF representative, did valuable work in distributing clothes and setting up workshops for the disabled soldiers. Later his sister, Francesca, and Margaret McFie joined him from Ajaccio. On one hand, the two young women found the situation tragic at Bizerta because of the numerous shockingly disabled soldiers: 'Some were yellow and withered with prolonged dysentery or had the unnatural pallor of epilepsy, others were paralysed after fever, crippled through frost bite, or had all their vitality burned out of them by malaria. There were blind men and men

178

without hands or arms. Some of them were tremblers, shaking day and night without pause.' On the other hand, it was impressive and heartening to see the many workshops where hundreds of disabled Serbs struggled to learn crafts and trades with Serbian master-craftsmen as instructors: shoemaking, tailoring, carpentering—something that would help these crippled men adjust to life when they one day returned to Serbia.

Overnight in Corfu the cold wet winter surrendered to a brilliant spring of clear skies and lush green vegetation, with a leaden sea transformed to startling blue—a new season that heralded renewed hope. Most of the Serbs had made a remarkable recovery. Regular food, routine medical treatment and a couple of months' rest, had restored over 100,000 starving, battered soldiers to a disciplined army of fit and healthy men. British uniforms and French rifles had been issued, regular army training and exercises had become routine, and they were now ready to go, 'to resume their endless task of war once more', as Laffan puts it. By mid-April 1916 the first units were standing by ready to embark for Salonika.

13

The Return:
SALONIKA TO MONASTIR

'We are rather cramped for space', wrote Dr Louise McIlroy, CMO of the SWH Girton and Newnham unit, 'but we are near the sea and across the harbour we can see the snow-clad top of Mt Olympus, beloved of the gods.'

It was spring 1916 and Dr McIlroy's unit, which had arrived in Macedonia the previous autumn, was firmly established under canvas on the outskirts of Salonika. The Girton and Newnham unit came under the French War Office and was now attached to the Armée d'Orient, the French Expeditionary Force based in Salonika. It had begun its career in 1915 administering a large army hospital for the French at Troyes in the Champagne district of France; then the French had assigned the unit to serve in Macedonia because, being entirely under canvas, it was extremely mobile. On arrival at Salonika in November 1915 the Girton and Newnham unit, led by Mrs Harley, sister of Field Marshal Lord French, had been dispatched immediately by the French to Gevgelija on the Serbo-Greek frontier to set up a base hospital.

Oddly enough, in the same transport they had found themselves in the company of the 10th British Division under General Sir Bryan Mahon, which was on its way to the south-eastern sector of the Bulgarian Front. Even odder—and more than ironic—was the fact that the Girton and Newnham unit, going to the help of the Serbs and the French, found that the British 10th Division had no field hospital of its own. So much for the British War Office's outright rejection of the voluntary enlistment of women surgeons and physicians for any kind of war service!

Gevgelija had been crowded with Greek soldiers and Serbian wounded. There the casualty station was beyond description—a makeshift horror at the military barracks where conditions were atrocious. Dr McIlroy and her assistant, Dr Isabel Emslie, found the exhausted army surgeons operating 'by the light of thin tallow candles and without anaesthetics; the suffering was past telling and was only equalled by the boundless courage of the patients'.

Within a day, by taking over a local silk factory, the unit had prepared their base hospital, even with electric light powered by a generator ingeniously rigged up by the radiologist, Edith Stoney, when she had installed her X-ray plant. Twenty-four hours later they were ready for the stream of battle casualties and starving refugees.

For a month they worked without respite, tending Serbian refugees and French soldiers, mostly Senegalese troops, before being recalled to Salonika where they found a fine site for their hospital within the perimeter of the so-called 'Birdcage', a fortified zone contained by the Allied armies in the event of an enemy attack.

Britain and France had agreed to share equally in providing the Serbs with rations, ammunition and transport, and each nation undertook to supply hospitals capable of admitting 7,000 patients, Britain sending hospitals for the Serbs, the French guaranteeing the stipulated number of beds in their own field hospitals. 'Have you heard', Dr McIlroy had come in to Dr Mary McNiell with a paper in her hand, 'the British War Office appears to believe it has "given" us to the Serbs! We are part of the French army, even if most of our patients are Serbs. But it seems that Britain has promised the Serbs 7,000 beds, of which our 300 are now reckoned part!'

Of the many remarkable women in the Girton and Newnham unit, several stood out. Mrs Harley, its head, was already 63 years old, but wiry and energetic—'with well-chiselled nose, pale piercing eyes, she was slight and graceful and, as she adored everything *militaire*, was always attired in full uniform'. Apart from her distinguished brother, Lord French, who was CIC British forces in France, Mrs Harley had a sister who was a noted pacifist, emancipationist and socialist, Mrs Charlotte Despard. It was rather to be expected that the two sisters were not on the best of terms.

The CMO, Louise McIlroy, a very attractive woman with dark hair, lively grey eyes and a lovely speaking voice, already had a successful career behind her as a gynaecologist and surgeon. Her engaging charm and ready wit made her immensely popular, and much in demand as a speaker for public functions. Both patients and staff adored her.

One of the younger doctors was Isabel Emslie, a passionate amateur ballet dancer and dramatist, and later a distinguished psychiatrist. But perhaps the most brilliant member of that outstanding unit was Edith Stoney, an X-ray specialist and former Cambridge mathematics wrangler, who had left a double career—associate lecturer at Newnham, and lecturer in physics at London University—to join the SWH, first in France, then in Macedonia. Since the SWH Committee had turned down her request for a portable generator she simply bought one herself, an action that was soon justified by the dearth of electricity at Gevgelija and Salonika. Thus it was that, in addition to setting up her X-ray plant, she could light the entire hospital: 'The electric light was needed in the pharmacy until the doctors had finished', she wrote from Gevgelija, 'and it was often late before I could stop the little engine and pack it up warm for the night . . . When I creaked up the ladders in stockinged feet to the loft where fifty-four of us slept, there could be no thought of washing, with ice already in the jug; it was often an inch and a half thick by morning. Instead of undressing, one piled on every scrap of extra clothes one had, and put one's waterproof under the mattress to stop the draught up through it.'

From January 1916 Miss Stoney ran the X-ray unit at the Salonika hospital and assisted British and French doctors from the army hospitals, illuminating the hospital with electricity from her little engine and treating patients with radiant heat and vibratory massage. Isabel Emslie remembered her as a mere wisp of a woman with periwinkle-blue eyes and a vivacious personality who 'gave the impression of a reed that might snap in two when the wind blew—she had the slenderest ankles I have ever seen'. But her physical endurance was astonishing for so fragile a body: 'I have seen her carry huge loads, scramble up tent ropes, and sit astride the ridge of the tents in the biting wind repairing electric lighting wires.'

Salonika was exotic and colourful. From afar the city, with its ramparts and magnificent harbour, its gaily coloured roofs and many minarets and cupolas, was strikingly beautiful but, within the city confines, it was squalid and crowded, swarming with people of all types and nationalities. Then came the Allied troops to add more colour—Italians in their smart, slate-green uniforms; the French in blue; the British and re-equipped Serbs in smart khaki; French colonial troops, the Senegalese, very tall and very black with bright red fezzes; the Indo-Chinese with large conical hats and, most stunning of all, the crack Greek Evzone guards with their white, billowing shirts, red facings, flared breeches and pompommed shoes. The favourite meeting place was Flocas, the *confiserie* renowned to this day; and in the back streets were a myriad bars, night-clubs of dubious entertainment, *bordellos*, and noisy all-night restaurants where Salonika tradesmen made fortunes from the misfortunes of war.

All through that spring and summer of 1916 Allied troops poured into Salonika, mobilising for the campaign that lay ahead. The Serbian army, 130,000 strong, disembarked from Corfu; French infantry and cavalry divisions arrived as did British transport columns and munition trains, two more SWH units— the America unit, and the SWH Motor Ambulance Column—and various SRF detachments. And all the while, behind the scenes, a Greek drama raged between Venizelos and his liberal supporters who wished to join the Allies, and King Constantine and his cohorts who favoured the Central Powers. But when in May 1916 Greek royalist forces yielded Fort Rupel—a key position dominating the Struma valley—to the Bulgarians, this was too much. The Allies then proceeded to blockade Greek ports, and General Sarrail proclaimed martial law in Salonika, virtually occupying the city.

'Flora Sandes has arrived in Salonika', announced Isabel Emslie to her friends at the SWH hospital, 'and what is more she's a Serbian soldier, in fact a sergeant. I must say she looks very fit and smart.'

For among the first Serbian troops to arrive in Salonika was the 2nd Regiment and Flora with her 4th Company. The attractive woman sergeant aroused considerable interest, and even the blasé Salonikans stared as the slender NCO, flanked by handsome Serbian officers, strolled through the city. Soon Flora unwittingly caught the fascinated attention of a debonair Frenchman. Colonel Descoins was a senior French staff officer with whom Captain Gooden, recently transferred from Corfu, dealt regularly on joint staff matters. One day the colonel vanished. Gooden searched the city to call him to a meeting; finally he found Descoins strolling aimlessly around a shopping arcade, 'in his worst form of inattention to business . . . He has not been himself since the arrival of Sergeant Miss Sandes in her riding breeches—or rather he has been less able to pretend to be a serious person. No reflection on the gallant Sergeant, who didn't take any particular notice of him.'

Soon after the Serbs had settled in their camp at Salonika Flora took a couple of months leave in England, returning in mid-summer in time for the severest trials of her army career.

The Macedonian campaigns did not involve the appalling battle losses suffered by the French and British on the Western Front, nor the tragic futility of the Gallipoli landings, but neither was it the 'side show' it was often termed at the time, much to the hurt annoyance of the troops involved. Much of it was tedious waiting for action against the enemy, and much of it was sporadic but deadly fighting along the Struma and Vardar Fronts, resulting in heavy casualties because of the harsh, open terrain that afforded no protection from shell and rifle fire. But, above all, the enemy was malaria.

Less than twenty years earlier Sir Ronald Ross had determined that malaria was transmitted to man by bites from the *Anopheles* mosquito, and though quinine was found to alleviate the fever no known prophylactic existed. Up to the war Salonika had been free of malaria, but not of this mosquito, so when troops returned from the marshy, malaria-infested Struma valley, the vicious cycle began, as they in turn infected the local *Anopheles* which then spread the fever like a plague. Malaria, with its characteristic debilitating and recurrent fever wrought havoc in the army until the end of the war. From 1916 until 1918 it caused more casualties, including a heavy death-rate, than enemy action. During the three years, 1916-18, the total number of admissions for malaria—including re-admissions because the fever was recurrent—was over 160,000; alone in 1918 the number of days lost due to the disease was nearly 2 million.

Dr McIlroy's staff found their work extremely exhausting in the torrid heat of that particularly hot Macedonian summer. Patients raved with malaria and dysentery fevers—often both combined—of sometimes 108°F, and there were never enough icepacks or iced water for all the fever and heat-stroke patients. The victims suffered agonies of thirst and it was not unknown for a patient in his delirium to dash out into the nearby sea. The death-rate was appalling. Then the hospital staff began to suffer and great numbers of troops, nursing sisters and doctors were invalided home, some to suffer ill-health for years to come.

General Sarrail, who commanded the French troops and was CIC Allied Forces in Macedonia, was tall and handsome with a shock of white hair, a considerable dandy and popular with women; but as a commander he was arrogant, authoritarian and incompetent. Considerable tension existed between him and the Serbs, chiefly because Sarrail adamantly refused to allow the Serbs to have their own base HQ since, he insisted, they came under French command.

Despite these high-level clashes the Allied army plans for the impending autumn offensive were taking shape. The Serbs were to take the left flank of the northwards thrust towards Serbia, ie along a line east of Monastir to include the Moglena mountain chain; the French would take up positions along the Moglenica valley; while the British would dig in along the Struma valley, and their supply columns would move up with rations and ammunition for all the attacking forces.

From Salonika a narrow-gauge railway skirts the edge of the Vardar plains to Vertekop, then climbs steeply up the mountains to Ostrovo, and along the lake to Sorović. In 1916 this 90-mile trip from Salonika to Ostrovo took 24 hours! The summer was fiendishly hot at Vertekop, but a few miles further on, Edessa was an oasis of waterfalls, vineyards and orchards.

Suddenly the unexpected happened. Before the Allied armies were properly deployed the canny Bulgarians launched a pincer attack, in the west from Monastir and in the east from the recently surrendered Fort Rupel along the Struma valley. But the Serbs, joined by a French division, reacted with a lightening counterattack, while the British rushed their supply columns into position.

At this critical juncture two more SWH units arrived in Salonika—the SWH America unit, and the First SWH Motor Ambulance Column. The name of the former derived from the fact that funds for its upkeep were largely subscribed in the United States. Many of its staff of sixty women doctors, nurses, orderlies and drivers came from Australia and New Zealand. The CMO, Dr Agnes Bennett, was an Australian in her mid-fifties, who had been the first woman to graduate with honours in science from

Sydney University. Later she studied medicine at Edinburgh, gaining her MB in 1899, the same year as Elsie Inglis. She had been in Edinburgh again, preparing her MD thesis, when war broke out; so she immediately rushed to Egypt, where the Australian and New Zealand forces were based and joined the NZAMC as a captain. Then in 1916 she transferred to the SWH to take charge of the America unit. A solid, rather reserved woman, she was a fine doctor and unit chief whose unshakeable calm won the complete confidence of her staff. Two other doctors were Australians—Dr Lilian Cooper, a brilliant surgeon, and Dr Jessie Scott. Dr Mary de Garis, the deputy CMO, came from New Zealand. In a rather sweet letter a Serbian patient, writing in English, describes her: 'Miss Dr. de Garis is a woman of medium build, physically well developed, energetical and of serious look.' The America unit had a transport section of lorries and ambulances to enable it to be as mobile as possible, to carry the wounded, and to move the staff and equipment when necessary. This was headed by another Australian, Mary Bedford.

In May 1916 Mrs Harley had left the Girton and Newnham unit and returned to England to persuade the SWH committee to let her take a completely independent motor ambulance unit out to Macedonia. The eternal ox-wagons and the sufferings of the wounded without proper ambulances had impressed upon her the value of such a column in that area. Dr Elsie Inglis, herself preparing to take a unit to Russia, backed Mrs Harley, and so the motor ambulance column was formed with Mrs Harley as its administrator. Elsie Corbett and Kathleen Dillon, anxious to get back to help the Serbs, were put in touch with Mrs Harley who recruited them at once. They immediately took a crash course—almost literally—in the driving and maintenance of Ford vehicles, 'hounded through London on a skeleton chassis by an instructor who was sure that all accidents were due to hesitation rather than speed'. Soon the SWH Motor Ambulance Column with eighteen members, including Mrs Harley and her daughter Edith, was ready to embark for Salonika.

They arrived about the same time as the America unit, and Colonel Sondemeyer, Director of Medical Services for the Serbian army, dispatched both units to Ostrovo, the ambulance column being stationed a few miles from the America unit. Ostrovo, a mountain town ninety miles from Salonika, lies near the shores of a large lake amid scenery of stunning splendour. The America unit tents were erected in a hollow between gently sloping hills, with clusters of shady elms nearby, and surrounded by a country-side sweet-scented with wild cyclamen, orchids and irises, and invaded by clouds of multi-coloured butterflies. From the hillsides the thin evocative sounds of reed pipes played by shepherd boys completed this Arcadian scene. To the north rose the majestic barrier to Serbia, the Moglena mountains now dominated by the enemy.

The units had barely settled in when all hell broke loose. Before going to bed that first night in Ostrovo Dr Bennett and her staff, watching star-shells curving into the dark sky, guessed they marked the prelude to the offensive. Sure enough, early next morning the silence was shattered by the thunderous boom of artillery and, as the unit ate a hasty breakfast, the offensive began. With that tense calm that conveys controlled urgency, Agnes Bennett issued her orders—everyone at their posts, operating tents to be in readiness, ambulances to be primed and ward tents ready for the casualties that must soon come.

Not far from Ostrovo the 2nd Regiment, including Flora and her 4th Company, were camped at the foot of the mountains. The morning that the offensive began Colonel Milić, Flora's CO, tried to deceive her. Knowing that Flora had earlier requested leave to ride to Ostrovo to visit her countrywomen at the SWH hospital, he asked her:

'I thought you wanted to go to Ostrovo, Sandes?'

'But we've been ordered to stand by for action', she replied, somewhat surprised.

'We are only going to hold some lines of communication near the reserves; we'll not be near any fighting. You have plenty of time to stay away for several days; I'll give you a horse to start now, if you like.'

But Colonel Milić, who always spoke German with Flora, under-estimated her progress in Serbian when he turned to one of his staff and said, 'You know we are going right into the thick of it, and it's such a pity for her to be killed. I'd like to keep her out of it.'

Everyone, including the colonel, had to laugh when Flora, slowly in her best Serbian, thanked him for his thoughtfulness but she preferred to stay with the company. It was the last time Flora saw her colonel, for two days later he was killed by a stray shell.

The Serbs began the advance by making a spectacular charge up the slopes to take the Gorničevo pass into the Moglena mountains. Their way took them over stony, exposed terrain where the only shelters were semi-circular piles of rocks, hastily scrabbled together by the men to provide some cover. As the Serbs dashed up those terrible slopes, the Bulgarians, finding themselves in danger of being cut off from base, fell back rapidly from their newly won positions and, followed by the French, the Serbs stormed into the small town of Florina.

It was grim in those mountains, scorching hot during the day, freezing cold at night when the soldiers lay on the barren slopes in clothes soaked with sweat that slowly froze as the night chill descended. Flora's company was in that first ferocious drive, and she describes those early days of her initiation into battle:

> Incessant fighting, weariness indescribable, but hand-in-hand with romance, adventure and comradeship which more than made up for everything. Days and weeks went by during which one never took one's boots off; always on the alert, contesting one mountain top after another. Daily increasing casualties among officers and men . . . In the 'Iron Regiment'—our nickname—I served my apprenticeship with a vengeance, and my tough and hardy comrades, most of them young veterans of two previous wars, taught me how to be a Serbian soldier.

While Flora fought her way with her comrades into the mountains, Kathleen Dillon, Elsie Corbett and the other drivers at Ostrovo, who had been startled out of their sleep that first morning by the infernal din of machine-gun fire and shells screaming overhead, were having their baptism of fire. The ambulances were immediately ordered to move towards the battle lines, and Elsie's was one of the first to leave. Within a mile of the lines she picked up her first two casualties and brought them back to Dr Bennett. That afternoon the ambulances were held back because of the intense bombardment, but when the Serbian commander sent for them and Mrs Harley refused to let them go, the girls were so outraged that Elsie and two others risked charges of gross insubordination by simply going, driving all night over dreadful mule tracks pitted with shell-holes, to and fro from the lines to the hospital, delivering many wounded. It says something for Mrs

Harley that she held her peace, but it was the first of several confrontations which would eventually lead to her resignation from the unit.

On 13 September the Serbs took Gorničevo and all that Elsie found of a hamlet at the top of the pass was smoking ruins and 'a few keening women and an old man grubbing about among the ruins of their homes, and I never saw a more tragic sight'. As the Serbs pushed on, the increased distance between the Front and the hospital made the ambulance trips over that rugged country far more hazardous—sometimes it took 4 hours to go 20 miles. The girls never stopped night and day, doing all their own repairs —mending flat tyres, cleaning blocked carburettors, changing plugs, and cooling the boiling engines. Night driving could be hell —the Ford lights operated off the engine, dimming as the motor slowed, and on those trails the enforced snail's pace meant in effect driving in the dark.

Soon everyone was advancing through the country freed by the Serbs—lines of British supply lorries, mule trains, columns of carts driven by Serbs; French cavalry mounted on dusty, sweating horses; and 'Serbs providently leading sheep or goats with them, one with a lamb over his shoulders, and one with a black bantam on a string.'

Then came the battle of Kajmakčalan. Kajmakčalan, an 8,000-foot mountain, dominates the Serbo-Greek frontier and the Moglena mountains. Since occupying this region in 1915 the Germans and Bulgarians had systematically fortified the mountain's summit, enabling them to reign inviolable over the entire surrounding area. No one, except the Serbs, believed it remotely possible to capture Kajmakčalan.

Thus began the heroic two-week battle, one of the greatest of the war, when in the second half of September the 3rd Serbian Army 'fought a battle of giants for the heights' without adequate artillery support, and relying on British supplies brought up with immense difficulty over the trackless foothills and up the precipitous slopes. Determined to demolish this fortified barrier to their homeland the Serbs fought the Bulgarians ferociously and bitterly in the maze of trenches, tunnels, dugouts and stone barricades that crowned the summit. Both sides suffered terrible losses as they fought the savage hand-to-hand battle every inch of that mountainous way. By the end of September the battle ended as the Serbs forced the Bulgarians from their formidable bastion.

189

Agnes Bennett's hospital in Ostrovo was one of the main casualty clearing stations, in fact the nearest to the Front, and the wounded came in hourly by ambulance, or in hammock-stretchers slung either side of mules, straight down from Kajmakčalan. Many wounded were in a bad way, 'gangrene was rife, and the constant amputations were a terrible trial for all concerned in the operating tent.'

Depleted though they were by their fearful losses the Serbs continued their headlong pursuit of the enemy down the northern slopes to the Crna River valley into their homeland. Nothing checked their rush. They captured one Bulgarian position after another, forging towards a point from which to drive the invaders out of Monastir. On 10 November the battle for Monastir began, a savage four-day conflict that forced the enemy behind their second line of defence just beyond the town, but the Serbs relentlessly pushed their attack, first aiming for a critical strategic point known on army ordnance maps as 'Hill 1212'.

Winter was in the air as Flora's company approached Hill 1212 on 15 November 1916. Already the ground was frozen as they stopped that night to spread their groundsheets on the snow. It was deadly silent with not a whisper from the enemy, now so very near. Until dawn—then the sudden crack of rifle fire, and the ominous sounding 'Hourra! Hourra!' of the Bulgarians as they charged.

Higher up a dense mist concealed the enemy. All the elements of a classic and very nasty surprise attack caused a moment's panic in Flora's company. 'Forward! Forward!' shouted Lieutenant Dodić and, after a fractional hesitation, Flora and her comrades raced forward up the slope. Just then a group of Bulgarians emerged from behind a barrier of rocks, hurling handgrenades.

Suddenly Flora felt as though the mountain had crashed on her —everything went black; she could see nothing, but something soft swept across her face and instinctively she grabbed it, hanging on for dear life. Later she learned it was the lieutenant's greatcoat and, though he felt every button rip off, he had no idea what he was dragging behind him until he reached the cover of some rocks and looked back to see Flora lying in snow that was reddening beneath her. Under the noses of the Bulgarians he crawled back and Flora momentarily recovered consciousness to hear him urging her: 'Stretch out your arm—please, Sandes!' She could not—it was smashed—so he crawled another yard, grabbed her wrist and, despite her obvious agony, with superhuman strength dragged her back to cover. The next hours were a nightmare for Flora, and for her comrades who never expected to get her back alive. At last they reached the first field ambulance where her wounds were roughly dressed and the bleeding stopped. Apart from her smashed arm Flora had over a dozen wounds on her back and down her right side.

From there it took the brave stretcher-bearers two hours to get her to the next dressing-station. After a grim scramble in a snow storm they made it with Flora now in agony as the first numbing shock wore off. There, while her wounds were disinfected and dressed, for the first time since being hit she broke down and, burying her head in the chest of the surgeon, wept like a child. But she had more to endure—another thirty-six hours on the stretcher before she was brought to Ostrovo.

Elsie Corbett was the first to see Flora. Dashing into the others she shouted: 'Flora Sandes has been brought in, badly wounded. We must do something!' Mrs Harley herself took over and got Flora into the SWH hospital. Next morning their best driver took her down to Edessa where she was admitted to a small field hospital. Flora never ceased to be thankful for her countrywomen who proved such superb drivers and nurses, and so marvellously gentle when they moved her. Finally she was driven to Salonika where, much to the consternation of the British duty officer, she was admitted to the 41st General Hospital, a British military hospital.

About a week later, Crown Prince Alexander's aide-de-camp came to her ward and, in the presence of the senior hospital staff, awarded Flora the Karadjordj Star for bravery in action, the most coveted decoration in the army, and the first time a woman had ever won it. A British war correspondent wrote an article about the event, which begins: 'In a clean comfortable bed, amidst comfortable and quiet surroundings, lies a comely, motherly-looking little lady'. A more inappropriate introduction to Flora would be hard to imagine!

'When will you come back to us?' her despairing batman had asked Flora as she was borne away on the stretcher. 'Don't worry, I'll be back in a week or so', Flora managed to answer. But it was six months before she was fit, after two months in a hospital in Salonika followed by nearly four in Bizerta in Tunisia.

Thus Flora missed the last phase of the advance when her regiment stormed and took the next strategic point, Hill 1378, which posed a threat to the Prilep road, the one remaining Bulgarian escape route. It was then that the enemy yielded Monastir rather than run the risk of being cut off. On 19 November a Serbian patrol swam the Crna river and rode triumphantly into Monastir just ahead of a French cavalry division coming up from the south. Monastir had been won, the Serbs were back on their own soil.

Owing to the incredibly involved chess-game of war, the political situation in Greece, strategic priorities of various Fronts, and a myriad other reasons, some valid, some involving crass ineptitude, it was to be nearly two years before the northwards offensive was resumed. Monastir remained in Allied hands but it paid a heavy price as the Bulgarians dug in again and subjected the small town to incessant artillery attacks throughout those many long months.

For failing to sustain the offensive General Sarrail was severely criticised, above all by the triumphant disappointed Serbs who, at the height of their victorious drive, had been checked on the threshold of their country.

14

The Return:
MONASTIR TO BELGRADE

The generals conferred. Since winter was setting in, they said, and no further reinforcements could be spared, and since the Serbian troops were exhausted after their epic advance, further fighting was out of the question for the time being and the advance would be halted, at least until the following spring. And so the waiting began; waiting punctuated by short, nasty skirmishes all along the Front; a wait that was to endure until autumn 1918 before the full-scale offensive was resumed. But no one in 1916, least of all the Serbs, anticipated an interval of nearly two years as they fortified their newly won positions around Monastir, preparing for the final phase of their return to Serbia.

And so another bleak wartime winter passed. In December 1916 Mrs Harley resigned from the SWH Transport Column, which was then merged with the America unit's Ambulance Column under the able command of Mary Bedford, already known throughout the region as 'Miss Spare Parts' because of her tireless quest at all levels and by all means for the spares so vital for keeping her ambulances going on the terrible roads. Her remarkable success was evident from the fact that, during the entire winter, her ambulances were out of action for only two days.

All the time that the battles had raged in the mountains, and the ambulances had toiled ceaselessly to and fro bringing in the wounded direct from the field dressing stations, Agnes Bennett and her staff in Ostrovo were on duty in the operating tent and wards. Often men were dying on arrival, some were already dead, and many who still lived had terrible injuries which required all the skill of Agnes Bennett and her surgeons. One man had thirty-five severe shrapnel wounds, another had half his chest blown open, and one had both his legs in shreds, yet these skilful doctors saved their lives. Once, a particularly heavy artillery attack began, with shells falling very near, just as Dr de Garis began operating

193

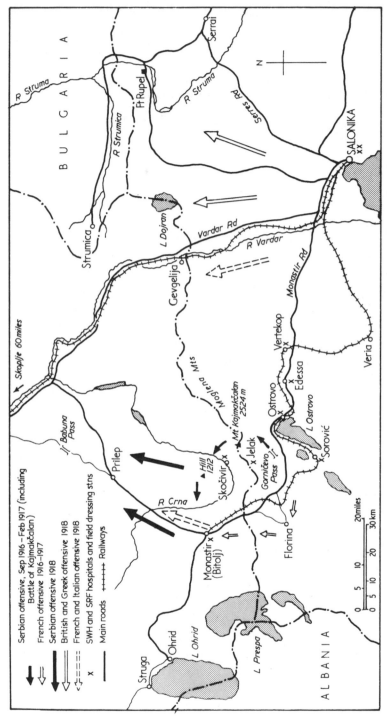

Map C The Serbo-Greek regions of Macedonia indicating the areas
of the offensives of the Macedonian campaigns 1914–18
(*lower inset of general map on page 8*)

Serbian offensive, Sep 1916 – Feb 1917 (including
       Battle of Kajmakčalan)
French offensive 1916–1917
Serbian offensive 1918
British and Greek offensive 1918
French and Italian offensive 1918
x   SWH and SRF hospitals and field dressing stns
       Main roads   ++++++ Railways

to remove a bullet from the back of a man's palate. Not a tremor of fear disturbed the calm efficiency of the staff as they went about their allocated tasks—the operation could have been taking place in a London hospital.

The America unit was the Serbs' main field and transit hospital. When patients could travel they were transferred to the French evacuation hospital near Ostrovo station, then taken by ambulance train to Salonika. Dr Bennett never had an empty bed; as soon as patients moved out the next lot were lined up for admission.

The Serbian victories at Kajmakčalan and Monastir had been days of gladness in the wards, when the patients were transformed with joy. From somewhere the obligatory *guslar* arrived to intone his poems of triumph, and the fitter men, their deep natural voices harmonising magnificently, sang the sad nostalgic songs of their homeland. Soon the hospital staff knew many songs, above all 'Tamo daleko', composed on Corfu after the retreat, a song that lives on to this day.

The distance between the Front and the hospital had been worrying Agnes Bennett; the drive was exhausting for her intrepid drivers, and an ordeal for the wounded. So she dispatched an advance hospital of thirty beds north to Dobroveni under Dr Lilian Cooper, with several volunteer staff and three ambulances. Then in January Mary Bedford based her transport column at Jelak, perched amid pine forests 5,000 feet up on a shoulder of Kajmakčalan, where it was attached to a field dressing station. From this eyrie the girls 'scoured the mountains for wounded' and became familiar figures along the trails and improvised roads. From the Front a few miles north, the enemy's intermittent shelling and sniping ensured a regular flow of casualties throughout the winter.

In January 1917 Mrs Harley set off independently with her two daughters, Edith and Florence—the latter a former Queen Alexandra nursing sister—to do relief work in the stricken town of Monastir. There the inhabitants, mostly women and children, subjected to daily artillery attacks lived a twilight life of fear in their cellars, with little food and no medical attention. Mrs Harley moved into a Turkish house, whose main practical comforts were a primus stove and an old Serbian 'cheecha' (correctly čiča, an 'old man' or 'uncle') who acted as cook and general handyman.

Mrs Harley was soon organising relief and, at her own expense, opened an orphanage for over eighty children.

On the afternoon of 7 March, after a busy day, Mrs Harley was sitting by the window in her house having a cup of tea when a shell burst nearby. As a reflex action everyone threw themselves flat on the floor. Then Edith scrambled to her feet and saw her mother still in her chair. 'Mother, get down, please!' she pleaded. But there was no response. Mrs Harley was already dead—a piece of shrapnel had struck her in the middle of the forehead as neatly as a perfectly aimed bullet.

The shock of Mrs Harley's death reverberated throughout all the Allied camps and hospitals, and when her body in its un-adorned pine coffin was brought by train to Salonika and placed in a large tent at the SWH Girton and Newnham hospital, an avalanche of flowers and wreaths came in from every Allied unit and HQ. People of all nationalities, ranks and professions—soldiers, high-ranking HQ staff, civic dignitaries, hospital staff, French, British, Serb and Greek—streamed through the austere army tent to pay their respects to this brave woman, killed on active service.

Her funeral was impressive, conducted with full military honours and all the martial ceremony that she would have loved. Escorted by Serbian royal guards, British and French military bands, attended by Prince George of Serbia, the British Com-mander, General Sir George Milne, and other army chiefs, and with French soldiers carrying huge laurel wreaths, Mrs Harley was laid to rest in the Allied war cemetery, the only woman among thousands of fallen soldiers.

In Monastir a street was named after her, and in July 1917, during a splendid religious ceremony, the Serbs unveiled a memorial they had built over her grave. The inscription, roughly translated, reads:

> On your tomb instead of flowers
> The gratitude of the Serbs shall blossom
> For your wonderful acts your name shall
> Be known from generation to generation

If the Macedonian campaign stagnated in 1917, political intrigues and local crises did not. Certainly the most important event for the

Allies occurred in June when King Constantine admitted defeat in the face of growing opposition and a mini-putsch in Macedonia, and handed over to his younger son, Alexander, a pleasant young man more interested in fast cars than in politics and unlikely to be a headache to anyone. This turn of events meant that finally Greece stepped out of her uneasy neutrality and joined the Allies, declaring war on the Central Powers.

But the most spectacular show of the year was the great fire at Salonika in August, which seems to have started in a bakery. Aided by a stiff breeze it swiftly spread through the narrow alleys of the old quarter and was soon out of control, blazing through the city. Louise McIlroy and Isabel Emslie watched the spectacle for a while from the city ramparts until it became unpleasantly clear that the fire-fighting facilities were totally inadequate and that the fire was moving rapidly towards their hospital, very vulnerable with its canvas tents and marquees. As the wind grew stronger the fire streaked along streets of wooden houses towards the rows of tents where the staff stood by with buckets of water and wet rags on sticks to douse the sparks already showering down on them. But at midnight the wind changed, blowing the fire back on to its own ashes and it was soon out. Many Allied drivers, including the SWH women, did valiant work evacuating terrified women and children, and the Australian, Olive Kelso King, was awarded a Serbian medal for valour for rescuing Serbian refugees. There were few casualties fortunately, but the city was a ruin— shops and hotels were gutted, whole streets of houses were now heaps of rubble, and the superb Byzantine church of St Demetrius was also completely destroyed; but the Turkish quarter with its mosques and minarets was hardly touched.

In the previous April a small advance SRF hospital had been sent up to Monastir from Sorović to help the unfortunate population, now subject to a new horror—asphyxiating-gas shells. Dr W. E. Haigh led this team of five volunteers, which included Dorothy Brindley, back on the scene after her escape from Serbia a year earlier. At one end of the town, in a house with sturdy cellars, they opened a hospital with twenty beds and an outpatients' department.

Very soon the hospital had to be enlarged to forty beds, and in the outpatients' department about eighty people were treated daily, mostly suffering from shrapnel injuries, gas afflictions, malnutrition and dysentery. Then on 4 August the town had its worst attack—heavy shells, incendiaries and gas shells rained down for over six hours, until Monastir was in flames. Dorothy Brindley (now Mrs Milić) recalls the horror of that fire, ignited by the incendiaries, that swept through Monastir towards their hospital: 'We had all the patients in the cellars and no way of evacuating them to safety. It was really a most helpless and alarming situation. We could see the fire advancing rapidly, fanned by a strong wind. Then, within a couple of hundred yards of us the wind changed and the danger was past. We were very lucky.' This happened only four days before the fire in Salonika.

Despite the daily perils and the unremitting hospital work, this small unit found an outlet for light relief, so good for morale under such daily stress. They created a newspaper, the *Monastir Monitor*, and the first issue, in July 1917, had an editorial, numerous advertisements and news flashes, all couched in satirical vein, for example: '*Salonika:* It is hoped that by the aid of a new micrometer which has just been delivered our Staff will be able to determine the movements of the Macedonian Front with precision.' A quiz on various topics included a mathematical riddle: 'Directrice A exercises a pressure of 4 pounds to the square inch on subordinate B. Assuming that the pressure is constant and that the coefficient of friction varies inversely as the distance between A and B, consider the possiblity that the line of B's movement will be straight, and determine the locus of resignation.'

Ostrovo, the Arcadian site of the America unit, had revealed a most alarming flaw—it was infested with malaria. This became very apparent during the summer when many people, staff and patients, went down with fever of a particularly severe variety. Some suffered so badly that they had to be invalided home and in November, Agnes Bennett, after enduring several debilitating bouts, was forced to give up and be invalided back to Australia, her place as CMO being taken by Dr Mary de Garis. The next victim was Mary Bedford, who also had to leave, and Kathleen Dillon replaced her as head of the transport column.

At the end of November everyone, especially the 'Scottish' women, was distressed and shocked to learn of the death of Dr Elsie Inglis. This sad and chilling news heralded the fourth wartime winter, which drifted into 1918 with still no sign of the promised offensive.

Though Flora Sandes returned in spring 1917, she was still not fit and had to be admitted to hospital in Salonika for another operation, after which she was sent to England to recuperate. Soon after her arrival she met three other veterans: Mrs Haverfield, back in England after being in Russia with Dr Inglis; the in-indomitable Emily Simmonds, still working for the Serbs; and Anne McGlade, who with Dr King-May had led the Stobart unit during the retreat. This formidable quartet got together to raise further funds for the Serbs—for mobile canteens and gift parcels for the men at the Front. It had upset Flora deeply that none of her comrades ever had the letters or the small comforts such as socks, cigarettes and so forth, that Allied soldiers received regularly.

Flora was roped in to give fund-raising talks, a prospect that half-paralysed her with stage-fright, but her instant success bolstered her self-confidence. She even went to France to address British troops behind the Western Front, and was a tremendous hit. Between them the four women collected £5,000, and the Sandes-Haverfield Canteens were launched. Gift parcels were soon on their way to Serbian soldiers, particularly to Flora's regiment, much to the boundless delight of the recipients; and Anne McGlade, who spoke Serbian well, went out to Macedonia with the first of the mobile canteens. These were intended for all Serbian troops, but expressly to include the 'cheechas'—men too old or infirm to be at the Front, but able to serve as camp orderlies, muleteers and general rouseabouts, forever on the fringes of the army, but often forgotten and neglected among the combatant soldiers.

In 1918 Flora returned to Macedonia with a friend, Miss Coates, to drive one of the canteen Fords, and they found Anne McGlade already running the main canteen near the Divisional HQ north of Kajmakčalan with Emily Simmonds, who had reappeared among the Serbs, often dropping in to help. Flora, claiming to be fit at last, was anxious not to miss the offensive which now seemed imminent; but she nearly did miss it—she again had to enter hospital, but was out a week before the offensive began on 14 September 1918.

The Allied forces, now commanded by General Franchet d'Esperey—Sarrail, much to everyone's relief, having been re-called at the end of 1917—suddenly surged forward all along the Front. Serbian, French, Italian, British and Greek armies on the

Vardar and Struma Fronts launched massive concerted attacks, taking position after position, driving the Bulgarians back until the British forces crossed into Bulgaria to seize the strategic town of Strumica, which precipitated Bulgaria's surrender. The pent-up energy of the Allied soldiers, their fury and frustration from all the months of waiting, of vicious stalemate battles, of heat, cold and malaria, were released in a surging vengeful rout of the enemy who had kept them penned up behind a pitiless, hostile Front for so long.

The Serbs again took the lead. Night and day they pounded northwards, sweeping through the Moglena mountains, up to Prilep, conquering the Babuna Pass, and on towards Veles, Skoplje, Vranje and Niš. Bringing up the rear and formally attached to the Serbian army, came Kathleen Dillon's ambulance column but, even motorised, it was difficult to keep pace with the Serbs. Kathleen's diary reads thus—Prilep: 'in our cars we can't keep up with the army which is marching and fighting at the same time!' Babuna Pass: 'over the Babuna Pass—and down and down and down—hairpin after hairpin bend, a perfect nightmare of them'; and Veles: 'The enemy only cleared out the night before last, so the station buildings are burning still.'

On 26 September, after British divisions had taken Strumica, a Bulgarian staff officer came to British HQ asking for armistice terms, and four days later, on 30 September, the Bulgarians capitulated. But though the war might be nearly won, it was not yet over.

Just before the September offensive the America unit lost Dr Mary de Garis, one of those driven out of Macedonia by malaria. She was replaced by Dr Isabel Emslie from the Girton and Newnham unit. Not yet 30, sociable and lively, she was a first-class doctor and would soon prove an excellent CMO.

Ahead Kathleen Dillon and her drivers had made a bitter discovery, that the hospital conditions in Serbia were appalling, quite as bad as in 1914. In Salonika the Serbs had had the use of the French and British hospitals, but now they had only three SWH ones. Firstly the Girton and Newnham unit had been instructed to remain in Salonika to continue the valuable orthopaedic work they had just begun. When on furlough in Britain in 1917 Dr McIlroy had spoken eloquently at fund-raising dinners of the need for artificial limbs, even wooden stumps and hooks for arms, to begin the immediate rehabilitation of limbless Serbs. This appeal had led to the most modern orthopaedic equipment being sent out to Salonika, and the establishment of a separate orthopaedic annex. Then a new SWH unit, the Elsie Inglis unit with Dr Annette Benson as CMO, had recently arrived in Salonika and was to be assigned to Skoplje, and later to Sarajevo. Dr Lilian Chesney, who had meanwhile been in Russia with Dr Inglis, was back among the Serbs with this unit. Finally, the third SWH hospital, the America unit at Ostrovo, was now ordered north to Vranje, midway between Skoplje and Niš. This development meant in effect that two SWH hospitals were to bear the brunt of the initial care of the wounded in Serbia.

To check the arrangements for their hospital, Dr Emslie and the unit administrator, Mrs Green, made a preliminary trip to Vranje. They were stunned with shock at what they found in the premises allotted to them—a huge army barracks, indescribably filthy, packed with French, British, Bulgarian and Serbian wounded who were feverish, delirious and often dying. Dr Emslie was even more shaken by her visit to the operating theatre: 'it was ghastly, and nothing I had imagined in pre-Listerian or even in mediaeval days approached it in frightfulness . . . A few saws and knives were lying about, and pails full of bits of legs and arms lay around the table and were black with greedy flies. The surgeons, with their sleeves rolled up and waterproof aprons black and red with old and new blood, worked steadily without anaesthetics.'

The two women rushed back to Ostrovo to get things moving. Everything was loaded onto thirty goods wagons for rail transit to Monastir from which the entire hospital was taken to Vranje on British transport lorries. The unit's ambulances and lorries came on by road, following the route of the army, over the Babuna Pass with all the pitiful litter of war cluttering the roadside—ammunition, discarded enemy packs, dead horses and mules, wrecked vehicles—and the sad familiar lines of returning refugees now plodding slowly home.

On 27 October the unit reached the dreadful satanic barracks which was to be their base for a long time to come. With its extensive outhouses, storerooms and stables, the building was potentially ideal for a hospital, but the task of realising that potential was formidable. Cleaning, scrubbing and disinfecting began immediately with gangs of 'cheechas', and slowly the transformation took place. The convoys of lorries arrived safely, the only mishap—a rather awful one—occurring on arrival when one lorry 'met its Waterloo in our backyard, where the lid of our cesspool gave way under its weight and down it sank into the abyss'. Later, with difficulty, it was retrieved.

Meanwhile, ahead of the America unit, Kathleen Dillon, Elsie Corbett and the others were running an endless shuttle service for the wounded, picking them up at dressing stations, then taking them to the nearest hospitals which were not hospitals but grim human depositories. From Babuna they drove up and down those fearsome hairpin roads, bringing their patients to a hospital in Prilep; as the army advanced up the Vardar they took the wounded to Veles, then on to Skoplje where a hospital of sorts was being run by Princess Narishchkine, alleged to be the mistress of Prince Alexander.

At the beginning of October Kathleen's drivers reached Kumanovo, from where they had to bring the wounded back to Skoplje in torrential rain, again to the Narishchkine hospital, which was then the only one and full to overflowing, with no medical staff or equipment. Four orderlies and the courageous Princess did their best for 360 wounded and dying men. 'It was a nightmare place full of suffering there was no hope of relieving,' said Elsie Corbett. Later the SRF would again come to the rescue by taking over Lady Paget's former hospital to resume the work left off when she and her staff became prisoners in 1915. And the Elsie Inglis unit would also later do sterling work in Skoplje before being transferred to Sarajevo.

Next, Kathleen Dillon's column was dispatched to Vranje, fording the Morava river to reach it since all the bridges were down. Ahead they could see the flash of artillery fire—the enemy had only been driven out of Vranje the previous night. The towns-people, hysterical with joy, rushed out weeping, cheering, hanging garlands of flowers on the Fords, and entreating the exhausted girls to eat, to drink and to celebrate. Three days later the ambulances were ordered to Niš, still picking up the wounded from the army dressing-stations along the way and delivering them, to the nearest so-called hospitals. Now, having far outstripped the supply lines, Kathleen's petrol supplies were exhausted and the ambulances reached Niš on their last drop of fuel through the familiar autumn mud of Serbia's sodden roads. By dint of threat and forceful persuasion Kathleen managed to obtain some benzole; it was a poor substitute for petrol but it got the invincible Fords to Leskovac. Again they endured a smothering welcome. Drowned in flowers and suffocated by the embraces of the wildly excited populace, they fled into a cafe with 'the crowd surging after us, clasping us round the necks and climbing on the tables to get a better view'. A desperate wail was heard from the midst of the frenzied citizens: 'It is awful to be Scotch on an occasion like this; you do feel so embarrassed!'

To the girls the celebration seemed premature as they brought more patients to another ghastly hospital—bare, waterless, cold and filthy, no blankets, only a little straw for the wounded, ill and dying men. This time Kathleen took action. She called in the celebrating townspeople to help, and to their credit they responded magnificently, bringing beds, blankets and food, but it was still not enough for again there were no medicines or surgical equipment, and few medical staff. And now a new and sinister threat, the deadly influenza epidemic, was spreading insidiously throughout the country.

Always just ahead of Kathleen Dillon's ambulances was Flora Sandes with her regiment. By now a seasoned veteran she had kept up with her hardy comrades despite her recent wounds and operations. Occasionally, when a horse was available, she would ride out the particularly long and arduous stretches. From the northern slopes of Kajmakčalan Flora's regiment had moved off one day down into the valley and across the Crna river to join the main Serbian army in the relentless pursuit of the enemy. Into the foothills they went, fighting all the way; once they were blocked by blistering grass fires blazing along the hill-crests, started by the Bulgarians to conceal their withdrawal. Sometimes Flora and her Company hauled themseves up almost sheer gully walls as they pressed on through the rugged hills and ravines towards Prilep. Heat and thirst were their main discomforts—they were allowed one full water-bottle a day and very meagre rations, but Flora found she was too exhausted to eat and at the end of each arduous day, when a halt was called, everyone dropped to the ground, asleep in an instant.

One day, Flora leant against a rock gingerly peeling off her socks to reveal her raw and bleeding feet. She had good English walking boots, she had soaped her socks until the soap ran out, then she had begged oil from the machine-gunners to oil her socks, but to no avail—the daily marathon marches over that rocky broken ground tore her feet to pieces. A comrade looking on exclaimed when he saw her damaged feet: 'I won't moan about my feet any more. I wonder that you can walk at all!'

They fought their way down to the Vardar then, on the way to Niš, they learned that Bulgaria had surrendered and their advance became a victory parade through the villages and towns. The people mobbed them, pushing fruit, wine and bread into their hands, and showering them with wild flowers. An old man came up to Flora and shoved a piece of bread into her hand saying, 'There, lad, take this, you must be hungry.' She probably looked it—thin, sunburnt, weary and ragged like her companions. They reached the Morava region where most of the men had been recruited, and Flora's heart ached for the mothers searching for their sons. They had come miles from their villages, carrying simple provisions and asking, pleading, crying: where is my Dušan, or Milan, or Štefan? One old peasant woman grabbed the arm of Flora's neighbour in the column; 'Have you seen Marko?' she pleaded. 'Oh, he is behind somewhere', was the reply. 'Is he really behind?' Flora asked him when the old woman had disappeared. 'How could I tell her now that he died of hunger in Albania? She will find out soon enough.'

Though the Bulgarians had surrendered, the Austrians and Germans had not, but they were weakening, and Czech and Hungarian battalions were surrendering *en masse*. Nevertheless, unpleasant clashes took place all the way. At Niš, the enemy left from one end of the town as the Serbs came in at the other. There, for the first time since their fighting advance had begun, the regiment stopped a while. Again the townspeople fêted them and, to her acute embarrassment, Flora became a celebrity overnight. Since both her colonel and commandant came from Niš, they took her to their families; once she was even the guest of Vojvoda Mišić, Serbia's Commander-in-Chief. Later, as Flora rode away with her colonel, the people showered them and their horses with garlands of flowers and ribbons; the colonel teased Flora saying that they looked more like a bridal couple off on their honeymoon than a colonel and his sergeant riding back to camp.

Beyond Niš the regiment met more stiff resistance from a pocket of Germans in the hills—bridges were shelled and a persistent artillery barrage plastered the roads. Then, beyond Ćuprija, Flora was forced to confess that she was half dead with a raging fever and, despite torrential rain she was ordered to ride back to that town to be admitted to hospital. Almost in a state of collapse on arrival, she found another atrocious hospital, worse than the one she remembered at Valjevo four years earlier. Hundreds of men lay on the cold stone floors, many wounded, all of them with influenza, dysentery or pneumonia. At the sight of this gruesome lazaret Flora's batman came to her rescue by installing her with a private family, who received her with warmth and kindness, putting her into a clean, warm bed where she promptly fell asleep for three days. When she awoke, feeling much better, sitting beside her she found Miloje, her pack-horse attendant, who had steadfastly refused to abandon her among strangers. He insisted on staying and proved a loyal and efficient nurse, but his morbid tales of the local hospital made Flora resolve to organise the local people to help. As soon as she was better she made her first speech in Serbian: 'A week ago', she told them, 'you were throwing flowers at the soldiers and calling them heroes, but now you are letting them die of neglect and forgotten on the bare floors of your hospital. Please help them!' It had an immediate effect and under Flora's supervision the hospital was cleaned up and the women brought in blankets, beds, food and water for the men.

Back in Vranje the America unit were having a sad and difficult time. Maybe the war was nearly over, but not its tragic aftermath, which was very apparent in Vranje. They were engulfed by tragedy: the tragedy of the ill, the dying, and now the lethal influenza in their midst; and the tragedy of homecomings when soldiers found their houses destroyed, their families missing or, worse still, learned that their wives or children, or both, had died a few days before from influenza. 'Nearly everywhere there was weeping and wailing instead of laughter and gladness.' Now the influenza demoralised the people who besieged the overtaxed nurses and doctors, beseeching them to help, to come to their homes, to work miracles.

In addition, Mrs Green was having formidable problems with the promised transport of food and medical supplies from the depot in Skoplje—she needed daily rations for 600 people and was not getting them. She knew perfectly well that the supplies were in Skoplje, but it required tenacity, persistence and coercion to jolt the apathetic officials out of their innate inertia, not to mention their occasional dishonesty.

The misery of the living even affected the dead. Though by November the hospital was running more or less normally the death-rate was still high, and the mortuary always full. At first the bodies were laid out in their uniforms, but when—despite a guard —the uniforms vanished, Dr Emslie decreed that they be removed from the dead and given to the destitute living; the bodies were then wrapped in army blankets, but again the dead were stripped. Then the staff used rough cotton shrouds, but even these disappeared.

11 November 1918, Armistice Day—a day like any other. While Belgrade had its victory parade and official speeches, in Niš Elsie Corbett, oblivious to her surroundings, fought a high fever and the piercing agony of a severe mastoid abscess. By her sat Kathleen Dillon, keeping a posse of avid Serbian surgeons at bay, and chasing out village women who gloomily predicted that the poor young *Engleskinja* was dying. Nearby in Ćuprija Flora Sandes perspired and tossed through the crisis phase of influenza; down in Vranje, Isabel Emslie commented: 'we heard it was Armistice Day, but nobody seemed happy about it, and we hardly seemed to realise what it meant'; and from the Elsie Inglis unit, now in Skoplje, Elinor Rendel wrote to her mother: 'no one took any interest in the news except ourselves'; for Anne McGlade, handing out 500 mugs of tea and soup a day to starving refugees in the Niš region, it was just another sad autumn day. And so the British women and other relief workers continued their war against hunger, disease and death, for which there could be no armistice, only victory or defeat, and sometimes the respite of a truce.

Elsie Corbett's abscess burst of its own accord, and ten days later she emerged rather shakily to accompany Kathleen to Belgrade. There they met Flora Sandes—'properly to the fore', to quote Elsie— looking rather thin and tired, but the centre of jubilant attention wherever she went. From all corners of Serbia British medical women, in groups or individually, were converging on the capital from their relief activities. Dr Lilian Chesney was there, up from Sarajevo where she was with the Elsie Inglis unit, which had just been transferred from Skoplje. Evelina Haverfield dropped in from her canteen work to discuss plans for setting up an orphanage on the borders of Bosnia: Olive Kelso King, now renowned in Serbia's devastated countryside because of her canteen, appeared with big plans for post-war relief in the provinces. Dr Katherine Macphail, Florence Maw and Jean Rankin had arrived in Belgrade from Corsica to see what they could do to continue helping the Serbs; and Dr McIlroy was there from Salonika to discuss the proposal of the SWH Committee to amalgamate all three SWH units—the Girton and Newnham, the Elsie Inglis and the America units—and eventually present the entire hospital, complete with equipment, the beds, operating theatres, surgical instruments, orthopaedic department, X-ray units etc, to the Serbs to form the nucleus of the future Elsie Inglis Memorial Hospital in Belgrade. There were excited reunions, but any modest satisfaction at what they had achieved was greatly tempered by the sober awareness of the magnitude of the relief work that lay ahead.

During the war, in recognition of their gallant service, many women had been decorated by grateful governments—France, Belgium, Russia and Serbia. In 1916 Dr Inglis became the first woman to be invested with Serbia's highest Order, the Order of the White Eagle. Later both Mrs Haverfield and Dr Emslie also had this Order conferred upon them. Many unit members who served in Serbia received the Order of St Sava; an exclusive few like Dorothy Brindley and Olive Kelso King earned the Serbian medal for valour under fire; some, especially those in the America unit, received the Serbian Red Cross Medal for their work in front-line hospitals; and others the Serbian Samaritan Cross. One of the most treasured of all decorations was that known as the 'Albanian Medal', awarded to all who participated in the retreat through Albania. Many members of the Girton and Newnham unit received the French *Médaille des Épidémies*, and the *Croix de Guerre avec Palme* was awarded to, among others, Dr Louise McIlroy and Dr Isabel Emslie. And now, before they were to be demobilised by the Serbs, Kathleen Dillon's column was summoned to the palace for a royal speech of thanks and an investiture. The drivers were awarded the Gold Medal for Meritorious Service and Kathleen the Order of St Sava, by the crown prince himself who 'dashed rapidly along our line, followed by an ADC with the medals in a blue paper bag'.

Deep winter dragged on into 1919, and Belgrade was now something of an anti-climax after the intensive months of the

207

offensive. A reaction set in and the unit members began to long for their demobilisation, to return to their families, to resume their private lives, so grossly interrupted by years of active service in Serbia and elsewhere. A few were committed to staying on to finish the work they had begun, for example Dr Emslie and her team in Vranje. Some, like Evelina Haverfield and Dr Macphail, would elect to remain in Serbia to do even more for this country they had grown to love; but others were becoming restless—it was time to go home. Kathleen Dillon sums up the spirit of their impending departure in a succinct diary entry towards the end of her active service:

'And so we finished our trek of 740 kilometres from one end of Serbia to the other. Our army gave us very flattering mention in dispatches; and the Prince Regent reviewed us and presented medals; and now we are waiting in a little town in Hungary till the right time comes to be demobilised.'

EPILOGUE

In a luncheon speech at Edinburgh Dr Louise McIlroy 'remarked that the position of women doctors had been firmly established by their work during the war; the attitude of officials of all countries had entirely changed from doubt and some amusement to trust and respect'.

Scotsman, 29 October 1917

Although the end of the war marks the end of this book, relief work in Serbia continued. Once the victory parades had faded away the grim realities of the war's aftermath—the devastation, disruption and chaos—had to be faced. Prisoners of war and refugees had to repatriated, agricultural areas were ruined, and transport services and communications had broken down. Again the spectre of a grim winter loomed ahead. In Serbia people were dying of neglect, starvation and disease, and in their weakened state the survivors were natural victims of the influenza epidemic that was sweeping through Europe.

Many of the unit women, especially doctors and nurses, plunged into post-war relief work in Serbia. They ran hospitals, canteens, roadside dispensaries and ambulance stations. Some units stayed on until 1920, and individuals remained far longer, some devoting their entire lives to work among the Serbs. Olive Kelso King, generously endowed by her wealthy father and the people of Sydney, kept up her canteen work in the provinces long after the war ended; Dr Katherine Macphail opened a hospital for tubercular children, first on the Dalmatian coast and later in Sremska Kamenica near Novi Sad north of Belgrade, which she administered until the beginning of World War II and for some years afterwards. Today a commemorative plaque to Dr Macphail dominates the entrance hall of this beautifully situated hospital on the hills above the Danube.

Sister Jean Rankin, formerly with Lady Paget in Skoplje, and Miss Florence Maw, who had been with Mrs Stobart and had taken part in the retreat, worked together in Corsica, then in

Serbia and, after the war, opened an orphanage in Niš. They ran it until 1941 when the Germans expelled the two women to eastern Serbia. After 1945 and some initial difficulties they were accorded the dignity and honour that were their due and given Yugoslavian state pensions that enabled them to live out their days in security in their tiny villa in Dubrovnik. Both died in 1953.

After the war Mrs Evelina Haverfield opened a hospital for tubercular and orphaned children at Bajina Bašta, a pretty spa on the Bosnian border. In March 1920 this wonderful woman, who had served the Serbs so generously since 1915, died, a victim of double-pneumonia brought on by overwork and undernourishment. (Not long ago, when in Bajina Bašta, at the small Serbo-Orthodox church I met a young priest who, on learning of my quest for the grave of an Englishwoman, responded immediately, '*Ah! naša Evelina*' (our Evelina), and led me to it.)

Dorothy Brindley met her future husband, Colonel Milić, when she was stationed at Sorović and married him soon after the war. They settled in Serbia until the German occupation in 1941 when both were transported to Germany, Mrs Milić to a women's internment camp at Liebenau, and her husband to the officers' prisoner-of-war camp at Osnabruck. Colonel Milić was repatriated at the end of the war to Yugoslavia, but two years later he died and Mrs Milić returned to England. Today she lives at the foot of the Malvern Hills and, despite her advanced years, is as lively, witty and game as ever.

Flora Sandes remained in the Serbian army for some years and became an officer, an event that required a special act of parliament for the commissioning of a woman. Later she married Yuri Yudenitch, a White Russian emigré and former army colonel, and they settled in Belgrade. Yuri, who had been ill, died in 1941, but Flora, fearless as ever, had managed to bully the Gestapo into not transporting her to Germany because of her age and her ailing husband. Mrs Milić, who of course knew Flora well, delights in telling how Flora, forced to report regularly to the Gestapo, one day towards the end of the war reported as usual, saying 'I've come to say good-bye.' 'And where do you think you're going?' snapped the irate Gestapo officer, 'You're not leaving Belgrade!' 'No', replied Flora sweetly, 'but you are.' In 1956, aged eighty, she died in Suffolk where relatives had given her a cottage on her return to England in 1945, and the present

Yugoslav government—after some characteristic pressure from Flora—granted her a full army pension for life.

Of the Berry unit, Dr (later Sir) James Berry returned to his consultant work as one of Britain's leading goitre surgeons and was knighted in 1925; his two artistic orderlies, Jan and Cora Gordon, led colourful lives, travelling and painting in many countries and writing articles and books about their adventures.

Dr Frances Wakefield, on reaching Cairo from Serbia in 1915, studied Arabic and took to vanishing for months on end into the remotest desert regions of the Middle East where she championed the cause of nomadic tribes. Later she went to Tamanrasset in the central Sahara to spend the remainder of her very long life, among other things studying the language of the Tuaregs. A mixture of missionary, physician, scholar and romantic, she never lost her essential Englishness or her enthusiasm for all learning.

Elsie Corbett and Kathleen Dillon returned to a country life in England, where the two friends shared Kathleen's fine home, Spelsbury House at Charlbury, hunting, taking part in local affairs and travelling abroad. In 1960 Elsie Corbett published *With the Red Cross in Serbia*, comprising her own memories of those far-off days in Serbia and excerpts from Kathleen's diaries.

Dr Louise McIlroy, created a DBE some time after the war, pursued her brilliant medical career as a consultant gynaecologist; Miss Edith Stoney's outstanding scientific work flourished as she went from one academic achievement to another; Dr Isabel Emslie, after remaining at the Vranje Hospital until 1919, enduring another typhus epidemic, became CMO of the Girton and Newnham unit when it was moved up to Belgrade and Dr McIlroy had resigned to take up another post. In 1921 Isabel Emslie married Major, later Lieutenant General, Sir Thomas Hutton, whom she had met as a young officer in Constantinople. Lady Hutton never abandoned her medical career; she wrote several medical works as well as two books on her wartime service in Serbia and Russia.

Dr Agnes Bennett recovered from malaria to lead a full and rewarding medical life in New Zealand and Australia, including work with the Flying Doctor Service in northern Queensland. Before she died in 1960 aged eighty-eight she founded the William and Agnes Bennett Laboratory at Sydney University in memory of her father.

Unfortunately it is not possible to summarise the subsequent lives of all the people mentioned in these pages, chiefly because reliable information is meagre, conflicting, or difficult to trace. Nevertheless, many certainly led lives as unique as those mentioned here. In attics and trunks in many houses in Britain there are surely letters, diaries and albums from mothers, aunts or grandmothers who served in these units. They should never be thrown away, but given to some museum; future researchers will be very grateful for them. Apart from any other considerations they are so often a joy to read.

Up on the hills of Belgrade's loveliest residential area, Dedinje, lies a huge hospital complex—the Železnička Bolnica or Railway Hospital. At its centre one of the older buildings has a simple tablet on the wall by the entrance: 'The Elsie Inglis Memorial Hospital for Women and Children'. After the war, with equipment from the three SWH units in Serbia, and later with funds collected in Britain and the United States of America, the Elsie Inglis Memorial Hospital was founded. Unfortunately, within a few years the hospital ran into financial difficulties and, despite valiant efforts in Britain and Serbia to save it, the State railways took it over as a sanatorium for their employees. But at least the Serbs never removed the name of Elsie Inglis or the imposing dedication plaque in the main hall.

These women were not Amazons—many were physically refined, even frail like Mrs St Clair Stobart or Miss Edith Stoney; most came from cultivated backgrounds and were accustomed to an elegant, or at least comfortable, way of life. Occasionally it was sarcastically implied that many women joined up only for the sake of adventure. Of course some did, and why not? Did no soldier ever join the army, or sailor the navy, out of a sense of adventure, 'to see the world'? Probably few would object to the concept that a feeling of duty combined with a sense of adventure are the best qualifications for a recruit in any enterprise.

Though they had wills of iron, nerves of steel, and remarkable self-discipline, most of the women were extremely gentle with others and acutely sensitive to the suffering around them. They had considerable inner resources and an unwavering faith in something larger than themselves—for some it was God, for others a future of peace, justice and humanity; some were quite simply patriotic. But all shared a strong feeling of duty towards their fellows.

Perhaps their impact is fading now in the wake of so much that has happened since 1918, but the women from the various medical units are still remembered in parts of Serbia where they served so valiantly, and where they more than vindicated their claims to be the professional equals of their male colleagues. Thus, it is perhaps not so remarkable that a young priest of today in a provincial Serbian town can still refer to one of them as '*naša Evelina*'.

ACKNOWLEDGEMENTS

Many years ago, when travelling in north Africa, I met Dr Frances ('Daisy') Wakefield in Tamanrasset, where she had lived for many years. During the days that followed I listened entranced as she related her experiences as a doctor, missionary and linguist among the nomadic peoples of the Middle East and the Tuaregs of the Hoggar mountains in the central Sahara. Then one day she spoke about her service as a young doctor with a Scottish Women's Hospital unit in Serbia during World War I. This was the first I had heard of such units and it was a revelation to learn of the extraordinary wartime medical service of so many women—surgeons, nurses, VADS and drivers—in front-line hospitals and field stations.

Later, during a year spent in Yugoslavia, I met Sister Jean Rankin and Miss Florence Maw, living out their retirement in Dubrovnik, and they continued the story Dr Wakefield had begun—Sister Rankin had been with a Serbian Relief Fund unit under Lady Paget in Skoplje, and Miss Maw was with Mrs St Clair Stobart's unit in Kragujevac; later she took part in the winter retreat through Albania. Thus, to these three women, Miss Maw, Sister Rankin and Dr Wakefield— all, I regret to say, now dead—I owe the foundations of this book.

Over the subsequent years, as I garnered more information through chance meetings with relatives and friends of various unit members who had been in Serbia, I resolved to write about them, and this book is the belated result. It is impossible to do justice to so many remarkable women, and I apologise for inevitable omissions and inadequacies, but at least I hope this book reveals something of the little-known but courageous and outstanding service of a large number of British women in hospitals and dressing stations in one of the most merciless campaigns of World War I.

For primary material I am greatly indebted to Lord Wakefield of Kendal for putting at my disposal letters and documents belonging to his aunt, Dr Wakefield; to Lord Abinger for corrresponding with me about his relative, the Hon. Mrs Evelina Haverfield; and to Lord Rowallan for his help concerning his sister, the Hon Elsie Corbett. Lieutenant-General Sir Thomas Hutton kindly lent me many books from the collection of his late wife, Lady Hutton; and Mr David St Clair Stobart and his brother, Mr Robin St Clair Stobart, helped me generously with information about their grandmother, Mrs Mabel St Clair Stobart, and gave me permission to have her decorations photographed. Also I wish to thank Mrs Ann Davidson for permission to use

214

material from Dr Katherine Macphail; and Miss Helen M. Lowe for her interest and kind assistance.

In Belgrade I learned more from the late Professor Dr Vladimir Stanojević of the Srpsko Lekarsko Društvo, a distinguished medical historian, who showed me a collection of memorabilia regarding the British medical women and their work in Serbia. He admired them boundlessly. Also I am grateful for the reminiscences of Mrs Sečerović and Mrs Naumović about their friend Leila, Lady Paget; and for the help given me by Mrs Smilja Kovačević in searching for photographs at the Vojni Muzej at Kalemegdan in Belgrade; and for the interest shown by Mr Vivien Rankin-Pithey, who kindly lent me the service decorations and some material from his mother's collection.

My deepest gratitude goes to my friends, Mrs Lilian Vidaković and Mrs Mary Stansfield-Popović, the former for giving me so much of her time and many reminiscences, letters and photographs of her two close friends, Miss Flora Sandes and Dr Katherine Macphail; and Mrs Stansfield-Popović, whose connections after many years as head of the English department at the University of Belgrade, opened doors at all levels. Her generous help and advice, and many introductions—including that to the Secretary of the branch of the Officers' Club in Belgrade for Serbian veterans of the Albanian retreat—helped me enormously.

Very special thanks go to Mrs Dorothy Milić, who as Miss Dorothy Brindley, features in this book. Mrs Milić gave me much of her time and lent me some rare and fascinating photographs, letters, press cuttings and supplements, which have proved invaluable.

For additional primary material I should like to thank the staff of the Department of Documents, the Library, and the Photographic Department of the Imperial War Museum, especially Miss Jean Liddiard, Miss Valerie France, Miss Celia Petty, Miss Janet Vitmayer, and Mr Michael Willis, for their help and patience; I am similarly indebted to Mrs Rita Pankhurst and Mrs Amanda Golby at the Fawcett Library. And I should like to acknowledge the help of a number of people who took such trouble to correspond at length in answer to many queries: Mr W. A. Thorburn of the Scottish United Services Museum; Mrs P. Woodgate, Archivist of the County Hall, Ipswich, Suffolk; Miss E. D. Yeo of the National Library of Scotland; and Mrs P. M. Eaves Walton of the Royal Infirmary of Edinburgh and Associated Hospitals. And I am extremely grateful to my friend, Mr Guy Hartcup, and to Mr Matthew Wier, for their research on my behalf at the Public Records Office.

Unless other credits are given, the photographs are the copyright of the Imperial War Museum. Those belonging to the Army Museum, Kalemegdan, Belgrade, are marked (AMB) and those taken by the author (MK). Author and publishers make grateful acknowledgements to the Army Museum, Belgrade and the Imperial War Museum, London, for their assistance and permission to use their photographs. Finally, I wish to thank Mr Rankin-Pithey for the photograph of Sister

ACKNOWLEDGEMENTS

Jean Rankin and I am indebted to the late Mrs Lilian Vidaković for the photograph of Flora Sandes in her later years. The typhus chart on page 50 is reproduced from the original document lent to me by Lord Wakefield.

Writing a book as a spare-time occupation when engaged in a full-time profession is not easy; other priorities take precedence and long interruptions are inevitable; hence the whole undertaking lasts a considerable time. Therefore, I wish to extend my warmest thanks to my friends for their encouragement, valuable comments and forbearance during the years I have been working on this book.

MONICA KRIPPNER
Vienna 1980

PRIMARY SOURCES
AND REFERENCES

The basic material in this book was culled from diaries, reports, letters, contemporary newspaper and journal articles etc. Among these the most important were: *Captain Finley's* diary; *Captain Gooden's* papers, diaries and reports from Corfu and Salonika 1916–17; *Lady Paget's* First and Second Serbian Relief Fund Reports entitled "With Our Serbian Allies"; *Sir Ralph Paget's* Report of the Retreat of the British Hospitals Units from Serbia; *Mrs St Clair Stobart's* diary of her column's part in the Serbian retreat; *Vice-Admiral Troubridge's* official diary; extensive files of reports, letters etc., from the *Scottish Women's Hospitals* and the *Serbian Relief Fund* units and personnel; and the letters of *Flora Scott, Dr Katherine Macphail* and *Kathleen Royds*. All this material came from the Imperial War Museum. From the Fawcett Library came many newspaper articles; the corrrespondence of *Dr Elsie Inglis*; and the letters of *Frances Elinor Rendel*. Valuable documents from the Public Records Office included the War Office files on Serbian army casualties up to 1919; the composition of the Serbian military forces; a long letter from *Captain E. F. Phillips*, the British Military Attache in Serbia, describing the chaos of the Serbian retreat; and the letter from *Mr Henry Dundas* complaining about the SWH unit in Corsica. Among journal and newspaper articles the most important were *Dr Čurčin's* "British women in Serbia and the war", *The Englishwoman*, September 1916; *Dr Mary Ivens*, "The part played by British medical women in the war", *BMJ*, 18 August 1917; *Professor Morrison's* "Experiences in Serbia, 1914–15", *Lancet*, 6 Nov. 1915; the *Times History and Encylopaedia of the War*: The Tragedy of Serbia, vol. 7, April 1916; and *Dr Robert Seton-Watson's* talk, "The spirit of the Serb", delivered at King's College, London, 10 March 1915.

Balfour, Lady Frances, *Dr Elsie Inglis* (Hodder & Stoughton, 1919)
Berry, James *et al*, *A Red Cross Unit in Serbia* (Churchill, 1916)
Carline, Richard, *Stanley Spencer at War* (Faber & Faber, 1978)
Collinson, Owen, H., *Salonika and After* (Hodder & Stoughton, 1919)
Corbett, Elsie, *With the Red Cross in Serbia* (Cheney, 1960)
Crankshaw, Edward, *The Fall of the House of Habsburg* (Longmans, 1964)
Dearmer, Mabel, *Letters from a Field Hospital* (Macmillan, 1916)
Emslie Hutton, Isabel MD, *With a Women's Unit in Serbia, Salonika and Sebastopol* (Williams & Norgate, 1927)
——, *Memories of a Doctor in War and Peace* (Heinemann, 1960)
Encylopaedia Britannica, 11th Edn (1910–11), vols 30–32, the New

Volumes, published after the war and containing detailed accounts of all the campaigns

Hutton, Lady, *see* Emslie

Jászi, O., *The Dissolution of the Habsburg Monarchy* (Phoenix Books, 1961)

Jones, Fortier, *With Serbia into Exile* (Century Co, New York, 1918)

Laffan, R. G. D., *The Serbs, Guardians of the Gate* (Oxford, 1919)

McLaren, Barbara, *Women of the War* (Hodder & Stoughton, 1917)

McLaren, Mrs Eva Shaw, *The History of the Scottish Women's Hospitals* (Hodder & Stoughton, 1919)

Miyatovitch, Cheddo (Mijatović, Čedo), *Serbia of the Serbians* (Pitman, 1915)

Pribichevich (Pribičević), S., *Living Space* (Heinemann, 1940)

Sandes, Flora, *Autobiography of a Woman Soldier* (Witherby, 1927)

——, *An English Woman-Sergeant in the Serbian Army* (Hodder & Stoughton, 1916)

Seton-Watson, R. W., *Sarajevo* (Hutchison, 1927)

——, *German, Slav and Magyar* (Williams & Norgate, 1916)

Stanley, Monica, *My Diary in Serbia* (London, 1916)

St Clair Stobart, Mrs Mabel, *The Flaming Sword in Serbia and Elsewhere* (Hodder & Stoughton, 1917)

——, *Miracles and Adventures* (Rider, 1936)

Steiner, Zara S., *Britain and the Origins of the First World War* (Macmillan Press, 1977)

Taylor, A. J. P., *From Sarajevo to Potsdam* (Thames & Hudson, 1966)

——, *The First World War* (Penguin Books, 1963)

Temperley, H. W., *History of Serbia* (G. Bell, 1917)

Thomson, David, *Europe since Napoleon* (Penguin Books, 1966)

Waring, L. F., *Serbia* (Home University Library, 1917)

Wickham Steed, H., *Through Thirty Years*, 2 vols (Heinemann, 1924)

Wilson, Francesca, *On the Margins of Chaos* (John Murray, 1944)

PLACE-NAMES

Many Macedonian, Italian or Turkish names in common usage during World War I, which often appear in the text, are today known by their modern Albanian, Greek or Yugoslav equivalents, which are given below. Regarding the spelling of Greek and Albanian place-names, *The Times Atlas of the World* (1974) has been taken as the reference.

Greek		Yugoslav	
1914–18	*Modern*	*1914–18*	*Modern*
Fort Rupel	near Neon Petritsi	Ipek	Peć
Gorničevo	Kellí	Mitrovica	Kosovska Mitrovica
Moglena Mts	Vóros Óros	Monastir	Bitola (Bitolj)
Ostrovo	Árnissa	Podgorica	Titograd

Greek			*Yugoslav*
1914–18	*Modern*	*1914–18*	*Modern*
Ostrovo, L.	Vegorrítis, L.	Uskub	Skopje (Skoplje)
Salonika	Thessaloniki		
Sorović	Amíndaion		
Verria	Véroia		
Vodena	Edessa (Edhessa)		

Albanian	
1914–18	*Modern*
Alessio	Lezhë
Durazzo	Durrës
Fieri	Fier
Kavaia	Kavaje
Čukes (Chukus)	Qukeš
Medua,	Medeš
Giovanni di	
Scutari	Shkodër
Scutari, L.	Shkodrës, Liqeni
Valona	Vlorë
Viosa, R.	Vjosë

PRONUNCIATION KEY

(Most examples given are place-names that appear in the text)

c   pronounced *ts* as in *bats* (Mladenovac)
č   pronounced *ch* as in *church* (Čačak)
ć   similar to č but softer (Peć)
dž pronounced as *j* in *jazz* (džez = jazz)
dj similar to dž but softer (djeneral = general)
j   pronounced *y* as in *yet* (Valjevo)
r   strongly trilled, (i) as a consonant, eg in Prizren; or (ii) as a partial vowel, eg Vrnjačka Banja
š   pronounced *sh* as in *ship* (Niš)
ž   pronounced as *s* in *pleasure* (Žiča)
a   pronounced as in *father* (Novi Sad)
e   pronounced as in *bed* (Peć)
i   pronounced as *e* in *we* (Niš)
o   ranges between *not* and *ought* (Podgorica)
u   pronounced as *oo* in *room* (Čuprija)

ABBREVIATIONS

CMO   Chief Medical Officer
DMS   Director of Medical Services
SRF   Serbian Relief Fund
SWH   Scottish Women's Hospitals
VAD   Voluntary Aid Detachment

INDEX

Serbia and the First World War form the background to this narrative; thus, to save space, they are not listed in this index. For other entries only the most important references are given.

220

223